FIFTY KEY THINKERS
IN PSYCHOLOGY

Fifty Key Thinkers in Psychology introduces the life, thought, work and impact of some of the most influential figures who have shaped and developed modern psychology. It features accessibly written and fully cross-referenced entries on such figures as:

- Sigmund Freud
- Noam Chomsky
- Carl Jung
- Ivan Pavlov
- Jean Piaget

- Anne Anastasi
- Konrad Lorenz
- Hans Eysenck
- William James
- Abraham Maslow

This fascinating and informative guide is an invaluable resource for those studying, working in, or who simply want to find out more about psychology.

Noel Sheehy is Professor of Psychology at Queen's University, Belfast.

ROUTLEDGE KEY GUIDES

Routledge Key Guides are accessible, informative and lucid handbooks, which define and discuss the central concepts, thinkers and debates in a broad range of academic disciplines. All are written by noted experts in their respective subjects. Clear, concise exposition of complex and stimulating issues and ideas makes *Routledge Key Guides* the ultimate reference resources for students, teachers, researchers and the interested lay person.

FIFTY KEY THINKERS IN PSYCHOLOGY

Noel Sheehy

Routledge
Taylor & Francis Group

LONDON AND NEW YORK

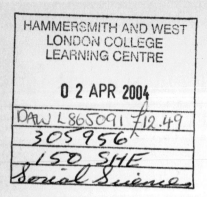
First published 2004
by Routledge
11 New Fetter Lane, London EC4P 4EE

Simultaneously published in the USA and Canada
by Routledge
29 West 35th Street, New York, NY 10001

Routledge is an imprint of the Taylor & Francis Group

© 2004 Noel Sheehy

Typeset in Bembo by Taylor & Francis Books Ltd
Printed and bound in Great Britain by
MPG Books Ltd, Bodmin

British Library Cataloguing in Publication Data
A catalogue record for this book is available from the British Library

Library of Congress Cataloging-in-Publication Data
A catalog record for this title has been requested

ISBN 0–415–16774–4 (hbk)
ISBN 0–415–16775–2 (pbk)

ALPHABETICAL LIST
OF CONTENTS

CHRONOLOGICAL LIST
OF CONTENTS

PREFACE

Modern psychology has its roots in the intellectual and cultural life of Germany during the 1840s and 1850s. Compared to the natural sciences, psychology is in its infancy and, like every infant, its growth in the early years has been extraordinary. A hundred and fifty years ago it would have been possible to list the names of all of the psychologists in Europe and North America on the back of an envelope. Today the number of people with degrees in psychology runs to many hundreds of thousands. This book considers how fifty people have influenced the shape and direction of this success.

Who are these fifty key thinkers? The foundations of psychology can be traced to the convergence of ideas and methods from philosophy, medicine and the natural sciences. To varying degrees the ideas and influence of the key thinkers considered here reflect those origins. Some, such as von Helmholtz, have backgrounds in medicine and physics; some are neurologists (e.g. Sperry) and others are mathematicians (e.g. Luce). Several, such as the linguist Noam Chomsky and the ethologist Konrad Lorenz, have never regarded themselves as psychologists and would decline that description. Nevertheless, their ideas and investigations are in areas closely related to psychology and have had a profound impact on the ways psychologists think about and explain behaviour.

European and American approaches to psychology have identified a number of facets of the human condition as crucially important. These include the brain, perception, motivation, learning, intelligence, language, thinking, personality, development and social relationships. The profiles included here reflect the thinking of key individuals in each of these areas. Choosing those for inclusion has been a marvellously difficult task.

The essays follow a common format. Psychologists are attracted to the idea that the kind of person one is as an adult can often be traced to one's childhood experiences, so biographical details are provided. Each profile also identifies some of the main intellectual influences in the development of each of the thinkers and gives a critical appreciation of the way their work was received. Each essay concludes with a list of major writings and suggestions for further reading. The fifty profiles are not entirely unconnected: conceptual, thematic and biographic interconnections are noted. However, the profiles have been written so as to encourage a reader to dip in and out of the book as they like. For those new to psychology, a glossary of terms has been provided; this should make it easier to access some of the language psychologists routinely use when they think and write.

The philosopher and historian George Santayana once remarked that those who do not know their history are doomed to repeat its mistakes. A perusal of some of the essays will reveal that this is not always true. In some cases psychologists have known about the mistakes of the past and sought to repeat them. But the recurrence can sometimes be fruitful: going round in circles can be a good thing, provided the circle is sufficiently large that when one returns to the task one sees it in a new light and the error brings new insights.

Noel Sheehy
Queen's University, Belfast
2003

FIFTY KEY THINKERS
IN PSYCHOLOGY

ALLPORT, GORDON WILLARD (1897–1967)

Allport pioneered an approach to the study of personality that emphasises the influence of social processes on personality development and stresses the importance of free will and personal responsibility.

Gordon Allport's father, John, was a country physician, and his mother, Nellie Wise, a former teacher. The family moved to Cleveland, Ohio, shortly after Gordon, the youngest of four brothers, was born in Montezuma, Indiana. Much of his adolescence was spent helping his father run his busy medical practice. In an autobiographical piece he recalled his home as 'marked by plain Protestant piety and hard work' (1967: 4). He was a shy, modest man and a devout Episcopalian. It has been suggested that, being imbued with values of cleanliness, piety and virtue, Allport was left with a particular sensitivity to certain aspects of personality that others, such as **Freud**, tended to overlook (Elms, 1972). Allport met with Freud on only one occasion. It was during a visit to Vienna, and he retold the story on many occasions: ' ... I told him about an episode on the tram car coming out. I had seen a little boy about four years old and the little boy obviously was developing a real dirt phobia. ... the little boy was saying: "I don't want to sit *there*! Don't let *him* sit near me, *he's* dirty". He kept this up all the time, and I thought it might interest Freud how early a phobia of dirt can set in. He listened, and fixed his therapeutic eye upon me and said: "Was that little boy you?" Honestly, it wasn't, but I felt guilty' (Elms, 1993: 39).

Allport's decision to study at Harvard University was partly influenced by his brother, Floyd, who was a graduate psychology student there and who went on to an eminent career as a founder of experimental social psychology. Gordon took a number of courses in psychology but majored in economics and philosophy. After graduating in 1919 he taught English and sociology at Robert College, Constantinople, Turkey, and in 1920 won a fellowship to study psychology at Harvard. There he completed his Ph.D. (on personality traits – the first such study conducted in the United States) under Herbert S. Langfeld, who strongly influenced his general approach to psychology. Langfeld had studied under Carl Stumpf at the University of Berlin and subscribed to a motor theory of consciousness – the idea that sensations, emotions and thoughts are all linked to motor processes. Later, Allport was to argue that personality similarly involves complex linkages between physiological processes and mental processes. After completing his doctorate in 1922 Allport was granted a Harvard travelling scholarship. This allowed him to spend time in England, where he was influenced by **Bartlett**'s ideas on the role of myth, legend and folklore as devices used by cultures as a kind of memory that allows information about social values and social order to be passed from generation to generation. He also travelled to Germany where he came into contact with the emerging Gestalt school of psychology which was being developed by Wolfgang Köhler, **Wertheimer** and others. In 1924, he returned to Harvard, this time to the Department of Social Ethics, and remained there for two years before accepting a position at Dartmouth College. While at Dartmouth his wife, Ada Lufkin Gould, also a psychologist, gave birth to their son. In 1928, the family returned again to Harvard where Allport took up a position vacated by William McDougall. During 1946, Allport and several of his Harvard colleagues broke away and formed the separate Department of Social Relations. This new department included social, developmental and clinical psychologists, as well as some social anthropologists and sociologists who felt a closer intellectual affinity with the psychologists than with colleagues in their native departments. **Bruner**, **Milgram** and **McClelland** were among the many distinguished psychologists to have passed through his department. That department retained an independent existence until 1964 – coincidentally, the year that Allport retired. The demise of the Social Relations department was largely due to the fact that, with the departure of Allport, the social anthropologists and sociologists considered their interests might be best served by returning to their respective departments (with which many of them had retained links). Allport was a heavy smoker and died from lung cancer three years after his retirement.

Allport and Henry Odbert's study of English language descriptions of personality laid some of the foundations on which the Five-Factor Model of personality was subsequently built. The model was developed during the 1980s through the convergence of the work of several theorists, including Raymond **Cattell**, Joy Guilford, Hans **Eysenck** and L. R. Goldberg. It suggests that human personality comprises fundamental dimensions: extraversion, agreeableness, neuroticism, conscientiousness and 'openness to experience' or intellect. The origins of the model can be traced to Allport and Odbert, who set about selecting terms relevant to personality from Webster's *New International Dictionary*. They identified 18,000 terms and, in order to impose some order on this list, four categories were devised: personality traits (e.g. social, aggressive), temporary states (e.g. moods), evaluative judgements (e.g. average, unworthy) and physical characteristics (e.g. talents). Although it was clear that four categories was too few in the sense that there was enormous variability among the words falling within each category, Allport always considered it better to err in the direction of over-inclusiveness and preferred to retain as many fine-grained distinctions as possible. For example, he considered that 200 words would be required to accommodate every possible description of politeness. He was aware that further abstraction and simplification could be possible by applying factor analysis, a statistical technique for examining the relationships between very large numbers of variables and reducing them to a small number of underlying factors or dimensions. However, he remained doubtful of the true merit of such analyses and left it for others, such as Cattell (who later eliminated 99 per cent of Allport's personality terms), to pursue that avenue of investigation. One of the major weaknesses of the analysis of words is that it shifts the focus of investigation away from an examination of similarities and differences between individuals towards an assessment of how the terms used to describe individuals are similar to and different from each other.

In his first book, *Personality: A Psychological Interpretation* (1937), Allport classified fifty different definitions of the concept 'personality' and concluded that they had in common a concern for determining 'what a man really is' (p. 48). Elsewhere he defined personality as 'the dynamic organization within the individual of those psychological systems that determine his characteristic behavior and thought' (1961: 28). No two people are completely alike, and Allport explained this using the concept of trait, which he regarded as a predisposition to act in the same way in a wide range of situations. He suggested that traits generalise to individuals and situations: there are traits that are specific to individuals and other traits that are shared by most individuals. In *Traits Revisited* (1966), he identified several criteria that can be used to determine the existence of a personality trait: a trait has more than nominal existence, is more generalised than a habit, and its existence can be established empirically. In addition, traits are only relatively independent of one another, they are different from moral or social judgements, they may be considered in the context of either the personality that contains them or their distribution in the general population, and behaviours that are inconsistent with a trait are not proof of the non-existence of the trait. In his early work, Allport distinguished between common/dimensional/nomothetic traits – characteristics shared by a number of people in a particular culture, and individual/ morphological traits – characteristics peculiar to individuals that do not allow comparisons among people. Later he considered that using the terms 'trait' in connection with both individual and common characteristics caused unnecessary confusion, and he called individual traits 'personal dispositions' and common traits simply 'traits'. He distinguished between three types of personal disposition: cardinal dispositions (so pervasive that almost everything a person does can be traced to their influence), central dispositions (the building blocks of personality) and secondary dispositions (less consistent and less generalised, such as food and fashion preferences).

For Allport the unifying core of the personality is the self (the proprium), which strives to realise its potentialities and life goals. Allport regarded the person as motivated more by social factors (e.g. groups and other people) than by physiological influences (e.g. temperament), and as constantly striving to become something new and different. The core of his personality theory, the self or proprium, he saw as a breathtaking enigma, but with characteristic tenacity he set about defining it. He suggested that the proprium consists of seven subjective aspects of the self that include the sense of bodily self, continuing self-identity, self-esteem, self-image, the extension of the self, the self as a rational coping agent and the sense of striving. This definition, together with a theory of motivation, enabled Allport to formulate a detailed theory of personality based on the ideas of his book *Becoming: Basic Considerations for a Psychology of Personality* (1955). Allport took the view that a person's basic convictions about what is and is not of real importance in life are founded on values, and he proceeded to identify and measure basic value dimensions. This led to the development of the widely used personality test *The Study of Values*. While not denying the importance of social influences on the development of the person, he took the view that 'the interest of psychology is not in the factors *shaping* personality, rather in personality *itself* as a developing structure' (1937: 8). Consequently his analysis of personality prizes individualism, integrity and unique-ness over a socially contextualised formulation that takes account of the role of social processes in shaping individual behaviour.

Allport's most influential work, *Personality: A Psychological Inter-pretation* (1937), offered a survey of what he called 'the most important fruits of psychological research', and is distinguished by its attempt to provide a theory embracing the results of this research. It appeared later in a much revised form as *Pattern and Growth in Personality* (1961), in which he once again demonstrated an undogmatic but relentless concern for precision and finesse in pursuit of the intricacies of human personality. Although historical texts often refer to Allport as 'the dean of American personality study', his theory of personality has attracted a modest degree of research interest. There are two reasons for this: first, the theory makes extensive use of somewhat loosely defined concepts (e.g. propriate striving, personal disposition); and second, the linkages between traits and the development of the proprium are not clearly specified. Nevertheless, Allport's ideas have had a profound impact in promoting methods for studying people that focused on the analysis of individuals rather than groups, and were highly influential in debates on what came to be known as the nomothetic and idiographic approaches to personality. The nomothetic was originally differentiated from the idiographic approach by the philosopher Wilhelm Windelband, and within psychology it surfaces in debates as to whether there are one or two kinds of prediction. Those who contend there are two types distinguish between actuarial forecasting, which uses statistics and probability theory and makes predictions about what people in general will do, and clinical prediction, which is concerned with predicting the behaviour of individuals. The psychiatrist and neurophysiologist Kurt Goldstein had been particularly influential in promoting the merits of the idiographic approach, a perspective that was often presented as directly opposed to nomothesis. Neither Goldstein nor Allport agreed with this characterisation of the two approaches, and Allport in particular argued for treating them as complementary. For example, a clinical psychologist uses an idiographic approach when conducting diagnostic investigations with individuals but relies on nomothetic information when deciding on the presence of specific psychological conditions. Thus, it is not *what* the problem is that is important but *how* one has it.

Perhaps of all Allport's publications, the most fascinating is his departure from abstractions about personality in general to an attempt to explain a single concrete life. This approach was taken up with considerable success by several of his students, including the historian of psychology Raymond Fancher, who used it to explore the relationship between the biography of a psychologist and the kind of psychological theory they develop. In *Letters from Jenny* (1965) Allport provided a unique teaching instrument for subsequent generations of students. This work represents the clearest exposition of his view that there are as many ways of growing up as there are individuals, and in each case the end product is unique. If general criteria are sought to distinguish a fully developed personality from one that is still unripe, then there are three differentiating characteristics that seem both universal and indispensable. He did not demonstrate the universality or indispensability of the three characteristics: self-extension (e.g. a variety of autonomous interest), self-objectification

7

(e.g. the development of self-insight, including a sense of humour) and a unifying philosophy of life (a theology or belief system that places a person in the scheme of things); however, the idea of *becoming*, as contrasted to being, is central to these three characteristics and this aligned him with humanistic psychology and an approach that came to be known as the 'third force': 'depth' psychologies such as psycho-analysis constituted the first force, behaviourism was the second force, and humanistic psychology constituted the third force. His thoughtful eclecticism allowed him to accept parts of both the psychoanalytic and behavioural viewpoints into his framework – this 'open system', as he called it. That framework is mapped out and refined in twelve books and 228 other publications, and was the basis of a psychology of the person as distinct from a psychology of behaviour.

Gordon Allport's major writings

'Personality traits: their classification and measurement', *Journal of Abnormal & Social Psychology*, 1921, 16, 6–40 (with F. H. Allport).
'Trait-names: a psycho-lexical study', *Psychological Monographs*, 1936, 47, 211 (with H. S. Odbert).
Personality: A Psychological Interpretation, Holt, 1937.
Becoming: Basic Considerations for a Psychology of Personality, Yale University Press, 1955.
Pattern and Growth in Personality, Holt, Rinehart and Winston, 1961.
Letters from Jenny, Harcourt, Brace and World, 1965.
'Traits Revisited', *American Psychologist*, 1966, 21, 1–10.

Further reading

Allport, G. W. (1967) *Autobiography*, in E. Boring and G. Lindzey (eds), *A History of Psychology in Autobiography*, Beacon.
Elms, A. C. (1972) 'Allport, Freud and the clean little boy', *Psychoanalytic Review*, 59, 627–32.
Elms, A. C. (1993) 'Allport's *Personality* and Allport's Personality', in K. H. Craik, R. Hogan and R. N. Wolfe (eds), *Fifty Years of Personality Psychology*, Plenum.
Holt, R. R. (1962) 'Individuality and generalization in the psychology of personality', *Journal of Personality*, 30, 377–404.
Nicholson, I. A. M. (2002) *Inventing personality: Gordon Allport and the Science of Selfhood*, American Psychological Association.

ANASTASI, ANNE (1908–2001)

Anne Anastasi influenced several generations of psychologists through her immensely popular textbooks on the construction and use of psychological tests.

Anne Anastasi's Sicilian father, Anthony, died when she was one year old. Soon afterwards, her maternal relatives became estranged from her father's family, and she never met any of them. She was supported by her mother, Theresa Gaudiosi Anastasi, who was the office manager for the Italian newspaper *Il Progresso*, and educated at home by her grandmother. She started attending public school at the age of nine and graduated at the top of her class. Anastasi was particularly drawn to mathematics, even to the point where she taught herself spherical trigonometry (the study of figures on the surface of a sphere) during her teens. She enrolled at New York's Barnard College (at the age of 15), intending to pursue a degree in mathematics. However, she was attracted to psychology partly through her reading of **Spearman**'s work on correlation coefficients – a statistical measure of the relationship between two variables. After graduating in 1928 she enrolled for a Ph.D. at Columbia University under the supervision of Henry E. Garrett. Garrett wrote extensively on race differences in intelligence and the need for an educational system that could take those into account, and was a staunch opponent of racial integration in the southern states of America. As will shortly become apparent, Anastasi took a rather different view.

While working on her doctorate, Anastasi met her future husband, John Porter Foley Jr., who was also completing a Ph.D. Jobs were hard to come by so, on completion of her doctorate in 1930, Anastasi took a position at Barnard College while Foley worked more than 200 miles away at George Washington University, Washington DC. They were married in 1933 and a year later she was diagnosed with cancer, the treatment for which left her unable to have children. In 1944 Foley secured a position with the Psychological Corporation in New York City. This meant that Foley and Anastasi were able to reside full-time at the home they had purchased shortly after their marriage.

It was through her husband that Anastasi became acquainted with the work and ideas of the anthropologist Franz Boas and the psychologist Jacob Kantor. Boas introduced her to his concepts of cultural relativism and historical particularism: the suggestion that differences between groups of people are the product of historical, social and geographic conditions and that each culture has a unique history and one cannot presume the existence of general laws about how cultures change. Kantor was a behaviourist who coined his approach 'interbehaviorism' because he considered both the organism and the stimulus of objects surrounding it to be equally important. The significance of interactions between an organism and its environment is a key feature of Anastasi's work. She was particularly interested in process accounts of human abilities: she wanted to understand *how* genetic and environmental factors influenced the development of human abilities, but she argued against attempts to quantify the relative contributions of each.

The name 'Anastasi' came to be synonymous with psychometrics (the design and use of psychological tests and the application of statistical and mathematical techniques to psychological testing) and with differential psychology (the quantitative investigation of individual differences in behaviour) for several generations of students and professional psychologists, because of the popularity of the numerous editions of her standard texts on the topics. Some of the earliest insights into the importance of individual differences can be found in Plato's writings. When Plato set out his vision of an ideal state he considered one of its most important principles to be the correct assignment of individuals to the tasks to which they are best suited. More than two thousand years later **Binet** and his student Victor Henri started publishing studies that constitute the first systematic examinations of the aims, scope and methods of differential psychology – the analysis of differences between individuals. Fifty years on, Anastasi published *Psychological Testing* (1954), a carefully crafted encyclopaedic introduction to psychological assessment that brought the reader through the fundamentals of test design, selection and interpretation. She continued to work on updates of *Psychological Testing* well into her eighties.

Anastasi's intellectual influence was also due to the lucidity of her writing on complex topics and to her forthright approach to politically sensitive debates on the role of genetic and environmental influences. Her textbooks grew out of courses she began to teach early in her career. In those texts, as in her teaching, one of her key objectives was to try to explain difficult statistical and psychological concepts in readily understandable ways. Her books and her research reflect a generalist orientation similar to that of the experimental psychologist Harry Hollingworth, in whose department at Barnard College she worked for nine years. In *Fields of Applied Psychology* (1964), for example, the reader is introduced to a wide range of applications, from engineering psychology to clinical psychology, and considerable attention is given to inter-relationships between disciplines and the importance of corroborating findings. Her interest in integrating research from diverse areas is also illustrated within the treatment of single topics, such as the formation of psychological traits, which draws from such varied data sources as animal experimentation, observations of infant behaviour, educational psychology and personality research.

In an autobiographical piece she identified 'chance encounters and locus of control' as a theme running through her career, and she illustrated these by use of anecdotes. For instance, her first full-time academic position arose from a chance encounter with Hollingworth – they met crossing 119th Street at Broadway. He asked what her plans were for the autumn of 1930 and, on hearing she had none, he offered her a position. The appointment was subsequently confirmed in a brief letter from Hollingworth. Another happy accident occurred in 1947 when she was elected president of the Eastern Psychological Association. She described her response as 'astonishment bordering on shock ... What caused my surprise was that I was only an assistant professor' (1988: 62). This discrepancy between the great esteem in which she was held by her peers – she was only the third woman President of the American Psychological Association – and her self-assessment of her own contributions, she attributed to her single-minded focus on completing the tasks that needed to be done. In 1987 US President Reagan conferred on her a National Medal of Science in recognition of her contribution to the development of differential psychology (B. F. **Skinner** was also honoured with a medal in the same year). Notwithstanding this and other laurels of recognition, Anastasi was not driven by a need to attain status and prestige, nor by winning the acceptance, admiration and approval of others. She was primarily motivated by a desire to pursue the tasks she had chosen for herself and to be immersed in that subject matter. Much of her work stemmed from a concern with prevalent misconceptions about psychological tests and common forms of misuse. Such misuse and misinterpretations became a problem in the 1920s and 1930s, following the development of group tests and the popularisation of fast, affordable testing. By the late 1960s she had come to the view that psychologists 'have been devoting more and more of their efforts to refining the techniques of test construction, while losing sight of the behavior they set out to measure ... [T]he isolation of psychometrics from other relevant areas of psychology is one of the conditions that have led to the prevalent public hostility towards testing' (Lindzey 1980: 297). During the 1970s, the notion gained popularity that a pure, culture-free measure of intelligence, aptitude or achievement could be devised, partly because such tests seemed to offer the potential of resolving some of the disputes on racial differences in these areas. However, Anastasi argued that attempts to devise such tests were inherently flawed because they could never avoid measuring some of the effects of gender socialisation, ethnic or racial influences. This was not a particularly popular message because it clearly implied that 'pure' measures of any aspect of human psychology – intelligence, personality, aptitude or whatever – are an impossibility.

In a reflective piece, written at the age of 83, she examined the role of advanced statistical techniques in the rapprochement between mainstream experimental psychology and the psychometric tradition. She concluded that the psychometric approach – the construction and use of psychological tests – had much to offer the experimental approach, which favoured laboratory-based studies of behaviour. Within the experimental approach there is a tendency to regard variability in the behaviour of research participants as something of a nuisance. Anastasi took a different view: 'When dealing with human behavior, in any form and from any angle, you will encounter variability – extensive and pervasive variability. If you ignore this variability, it will come back to haunt you in the form of incorrect conclusions in basic research and wrong decisions in applied research and practice' (1991: 71).

Questions about the role of genetic and environmental factors on the development of behaviour underlie much of Anastasi's writing. She was a forceful exponent of the cognitive differentiation hypothesis – the suggestion that the development of human intelligence involves a process of differentiation and specialisation of abilities as a function of age, education and other, less formal, learning experiences. This is illustrated in her analyses of the relationship between intelligence and family size; her research on creativity in children and adolescents; and a long-term project on drawings by hospitalised psychiatric patients which suggested that many alleged signs of pathology were more closely related to educational, occupational and other aspects of an individual's experiential history than to specific pathology. She also argued that questions of heredity and environment are involved in the nature and origins of psychological traits, and therefore in the interpretation of psychological test scores. Anastasi was concerned with understanding the underlying causes of ability long before models concerned with the processes of trait formation – how psychological characteristics are formed – were popular. Her books tell a convincing story of how properly constructed, well-validated and psychologically well-founded tests can prove valuable in both theoretical and applied fields, provided that the underlying socio-cultural, developmental and cognitive processes are properly understood.

Anne Anastasi's major writings

Differential Psychology, Macmillan, 1937.
Psychological Testing, Macmillan, 1954.
Fields of Applied Psychology, McGraw-Hill, 1964.
'Psychology, psychologists and psychological testing', *American Psychologist*, 1967, 22, 297–306.
'The gap between experimental and psychometric orientations', *Journal of the Washington Academy of Sciences*, 1991, 81, 61–73.

Further reading

Anne Anastasi. 'Autobiography', in A. N. O'Connell and N. F. Russo (eds), *Models of Achievement: Reflections of Eminent Women in Psychology*, Vol. 2, Erlbaum, 1988.
Lindzey, G. (ed.), *A History of Psychology in Autobiography*, Vol. 7, Freeman, 1980.

ANDERSON, JOHN ROBERT (1947–)

Anderson developed a computer-based system capable of simulating a wide variety of intelligent behaviour and used it to build a tutoring system for mathematics and computer programming.

Born in Vancouver, John Anderson grew up in a poor section of the city. During his childhood he pursued several 'dreams', and his parents were supportive of them all. One of those dreams was to become a writer and that was one of his aspirations when he enrolled to study psychology at the University of British Columbia. Although his high school performance was good, his progress as an undergraduate student was often characterised by poor preparation coupled with doubts about whether he was really cut out for a career in psychology. He pulled out all the stops in his final year, to graduate in 1968 at the head of his class and be awarded the Governor-General's Gold Medal. For his senior thesis he worked with Arthur S. Reber on the perception of clicks in linguistic and non-linguistic messages. Undergraduate programmes of the 1960s typically included courses on learning theory, the psychology of language, and cognitive psychology (the psychology of thinking and problem-solving), but connections between the three topics were few and far between. Anderson was particularly interested in the relationships between language and thought, and an opportunity to pursue investigations in this area arose when he was offered a doctoral position at Stanford University. That opportunity provided working relationships with Gordon Bower, who had published ground-breaking work on mathematical models of human learning; Richard Atkinson, who was working on computer-assisted instruction; Herbert Clark, who was running studies on the comprehension and use of language; and Edward Feigenbaum, who was working on knowledge-based systems. He had intended pursuing a doctorate in mathematical psychology but his work on the structure of memory recall, supervised by Bower, was the start of another dream – to develop a theory of human thought processes sufficiently well specified that it could be implemented in a computer simulation. The case for such a formally specified theory has been stated by **Baddeley**: 'While simple qualitative conceptual models have proved very useful, one eventually reaches a point at which some form of detailed and preferably quantitative model is necessary if the concepts are to develop' (1994: 363). His first attempts were implemented in the FRAN (Free Recall in an Associative Network) computer simulation of memory, and later in the HAM (Human Associative Memory) theory. HAM was a model of the structures and processes of human memory and dealt in detail with how human memory processes language.

After receiving his Ph.D. from Stanford in 1972, Anderson took up a position at Yale University as an assistant professor. He remained there for a year, teaching undergraduate and graduate courses on the psychology of thinking, during which time his interest in cognitive psychology broadened to include cognitive processes and structures. He moved to the University of Michigan where Lynne Reder was a graduate student. They married in 1973 and formed a close intellectual partnership. During his three-year stint at Michigan, his interests in language and learning developed, and he designed a computer simulation of language acquisition. His association with James G. Greeno, who was working on learning and reasoning, directed his interests to the application of cognitive psychology to education. Both of these developments were to become significant later in his career. During this period he developed the HAM theory and conducted experiments that were to lead to ACT (Adaptive Control of Thought) theory. ACT, like HAM, was a computer model of human memory, but with an important extension that dealt with the ways that cognitive procedures, such as problem-solving, interact with memory. His work with HAM was concentrated on developing a model of factual information or 'declarative knowledge' about the world. ACT built on this by employing an ordered set of rules called a production system. For example, if you were making a cake then the declarative knowledge would consist of the list of ingredients and the production system would be the rules dictating how they should be put together. If you are using an unfamiliar recipe, it is usually impossible to keep all of the ingredients and all of the production rules in memory at the one time. ACT attempts to simulate this in a computer model of working memory – a temporary memory store where different pieces of information and rules are brought together.

Anderson returned to Yale, where he continued to develop and test the ACT theory, focusing on how past knowledge interacts with and influences the acquisition of new knowledge. The Andersons moved to Carnegie Mellon University in the autumn of 1978, and, in the company of Herb **Simon** and Alan Newell, the emphasis in his work shifted to the computer simulation of problem-solving. Anderson uses the term 'cognitive architecture' to refer to the design and organisation of the mind, and in *The Architecture of Cognition* (1983) he gave an account of the fully evolved theory, ACT* (ACT star), which he described as a theory of the basic principles of operation built into cognitive systems. It examined high-level cognition, the elements that give direction to thought, such as planning and the way that production systems constrain adaptive processing choices in the human cognitive system. To give an example, consider the following analogy: the quantity of declarative or factual knowledge about the world stored in a computer might be increased enormously over several years, but the usefulness of that information will be limited by the rules determining how it can be combined and applied. In this sense, ACT* is a simulation of the kinds of processing limitations that constrain human problem-solving and learning.

In 1980 and then in 1985, the Andersons had two sons, Jay and Abe. Anderson's fascination with the development of their cognitive abilities is reflected in a simulation of his eldest son's language acquisition, published in *The Architecture of Cognition*. His earlier interest in the application of cognitive psychology to education was rekindled, and he became involved in the boys' education by tutoring them in mathematics. His attempts to develop a computer that could teach mathematics involved generating a cognitive model of the particular mathematical skill that was to be learned (e.g. subtraction) and emphasised the use of real-time cognitive modelling in instruction. He did this by trying to develop a set of production rules that solve a class of problems, such as subtraction problems, in the same way and at the same speed that students should solve the problems. In other words, Anderson's computer-based maths tutor tried to simulate the world as a learner would understand it. A good computer model of the learner's world should be able to diagnose the sources of any errors made by the learner and then provide appropriate assistance through carefully guided instruction.

ACT* was so titled because Anderson believed that ACT theory had gone just about as far as it could. Since then he has embarked on two major attempts to 'break' ACT theory. One of these involved the development of an intelligent computer-based tutor based on ACT theory. The basic idea was to build into the computer a model of how ACT would solve a very complex thinking task, such as generating proofs in geometry. The computer-based tutor used ACT's theory of skill acquisition to get the student to emulate the model stored in the computer. To Anderson's surprise, this approach to the development of computer-based tutors proved remarkably successful, and it is often cited as one of the most fruitful intelligent tutoring initiatives. His second attempt to do away with ACT theory began with a sabbatical, in 1987, spent at Flinders University, Australia. There he focused on how cognition might be adapted to the uncertainty that is an essential feature of any environment. He developed what he called 'rational analysis', based on the idea that to understand human thinking it is *not* necessary to develop a theory of its mechanisms. Rather, it is only necessary to understand the organisation of uncertainty – the probabilistic structure – of the problems facing the person trying to solve a problem. This led to successes in developing theories of human memory and categorisation, and to a computer program capable of accounting for a wide range of data collected in studies on humans solving different kinds of problems. Anderson went on to develop a new theory of procedural learning that incorporates rational analysis. This, the ACT-R theory, was published in *Rules of the Mind* (1993), with an accompanying ACT-R simulation on a computer disc. ACT-R emphasises the importance of practice in learning the components of any skill. Its basic assertion is that, in order to learn a complex skill, each component must be mastered individually. This position contrasts with the Gestalt claim (see **Wertheimer** for a fuller description) that learning includes moments of insight or transformations when whole knowledge structures become reorganised or learned – akin to 'eureka!' insights when, after minutes or hours of problem-solving, a solution suddenly becomes apparent.

In his more recent work Anderson has addressed the distinction between psychologists' preferences for conducting experiments on psychological effects spanning no more than tens of milliseconds and educationists' concern with the achievement of significant educational outcomes that may take hundreds of hours. His analysis recapitulates some of the issues that taxed **Wundt** and **Bartlett**, both of whom were concerned about the relationship between minuscule psychological events studied under laboratory conditions and gigantic phenomena such as language and culture. Anderson poses the question: 'Is there any reason to believe that learning can be improved by paying attention to events that are measured in tens of milliseconds?' (2002: 86). His answer employs Alan Newell's suggestion that there are 'four bands of cognition': biological, cognitive, rational and social. The millisecond level of analysis is situated within the biological band, whereas significant educational achievements lie within the social. Some have argued that trying to link biological processes to large-scale educational outcomes is a bridge too far, but Anderson argues for the plausibility of three smaller 'bridges' of consecutively longer spans: biological–cognitive, cognitive–rational and rational–social. He contends that learning that takes places over hundreds of hours can be meaningfully decomposed to learning events spanning tens of milliseconds, while he also recognises that further empirical work is required to underpin his arguments concerning the 'bridges' between the cognitive–rational and the rational–social bands. Using this approach, Anderson has shown how his own work on the computer simulation of the minutiae of human thought processes can be linked with much larger phenomena. The power in Anderson's approach lies in his demonstration of how a common architecture or structure might be used to perform a very wide range of cognitive tasks, from the simple to the relatively complex. The common architecture approach used in ACT contrasts with that taken by others who maintain that each mental function (e.g. memory, language, perception) has its own distinctive structure and must be studied on its own merits. Whatever the final outcome of this debate, there is general agreement that there are many other features of human memory, such as retrieval, that remain to be properly simulated. Notwithstanding this limitation, the prognosis for the future of ACT theory is not bad; the theory is certainly a long way from being broken.

John Anderson's major writings

'Recognition and retrieval processes in free recall', *Psychological Review*, 1972, 79, 97–123 (with G. H. Bower).

Human Associative Memory, Winston and Sons, 1973 (with G. H. Bower).

Language, Memory and Thought, Erlbaum, 1976.

'Acquisition of cognitive skill', *Psychological Review*, 1982, 89, 369–403.

The Architecture of Cognition, Harvard University Press, 1983.

Transfer of Cognitive Skill, Harvard University Press, 1989 (with M. K. Singley).

Rules of the Mind, Erlbaum, 1993.
Learning and Memory, Wiley, 1995
'Spanning seven orders of magnitude: a challenge for cognitive modeling', *Cognitive Science*, 2002, 26, 85–112.

Further reading

Baddeley, A. (1994). *Attention*, Oxford University Press.
Fodor, J. (1983) *The Modularity of Mind*, MIT Press.
Laird, J. E., Newell, A. and Rosenboom, P. S. (1987) 'SOAR: an architecture for general intelligence', *Artificial Intelligence*, 33, 1–64.
Simon, H. A. (1981) 'Information-processing models of cognition', *Journal of the American Society for Information Science*, 32, 364–77.
Kolodner, J. L. (1983) 'Reconstructive memory – a computer model', *Cognitive Science*, 7, 281–328.

ASCH, SOLOMON (1907–96)

Asch conducted experimental studies of persuasion, social pressure and conformity within the tradition of Gestalt psychology.

Asch was born in Warsaw, Poland, but the family emigrated to North America when he was 13. He grew up in New York City where he completed his high school education at Townsend Harris Hall, a school for academically gifted young men. As a graduate student at Columbia University, Asch was influenced by Ruth Benedict, the cultural anthropologist, Otto Klineberg, the first head of Columbia's social psychology department, and Robert S. Woodworth, whose work on motivation was important to the development of the school of thought referred to as functionalism. After graduating, Asch taught for a time at Brooklyn College and the New School for Social Research at Swarthmore College, but his principal faculty appointment was at Swarthmore College (1947–66) where he was part of a very influential group of Gestalt psychologists that included Wolfgang Köhler. This period included a two-year stint (1958–60) as a member of Princeton's Institute for Advanced Study, working with his research assistant Stanley **Milgram**. Asch was one of the founding members of the Institute for Cognitive Studies at Rutgers University, established in 1966. The Solomon Asch Center of the University of Pennsylvania was created in 1998 with the purpose of advancing training and research in the areas of ethnic group conflict and violence.

Much of Asch's distinctive contribution can be linked to the ideas of his most significant mentor, Max **Wertheimer**, whom he succeeded at the New School after Wertheimer's death. It was

Wertheimer who introduced Asch to the fundamentals of Gestalt psychology; and it was Asch, along with **Lewin**, who offered a Gestalt alternative to the then prevailing behavioural explanations of social phenomena. Like Lewin, he worked to develop a social psychology that would contribute to the solution of major social problems. In his classic work *Social Psychology* (1952) he set out his 'intention ... to produce, in contrast to the prevailing non-cognitive versions, a phenomenological psychology in which social facts and processes held central place' (p. ix). Central to his approach is the idea that social perception, like visual perception, is relational. In order to understand how this could be, it is useful to start with a description of a classic series of studies by Asch and his colleague Herman A. Witkin. These experiments examined visual perception of the upright with the purpose of resolving a contradiction between one set of studies that suggested our orientation in space is anchored mainly to postural factors (e.g. sense of balance and orientation), and work conducted by Wertheimer, within the Gestalt tradition, which indicated that visual field factors (what we are looking at) are more important. In one of the studies, participants viewed the laboratory in which they were located through a cardboard tube aimed at its reflection in a tilted mirror. In the room there was a rod that the participants were instructed to position so as to keep it in alignment with the true vertical. Unknown to the participants, Asch and Witkin manipulated the tilted mirror so that the perceived visual scene was up to 30° from true vertical alignment. The participants' alignment of the rod was found to be much closer to the information available to them from the visual scene than from postural information that might have signalled a discrepancy between the perceived and actual vertical. Their demonstration that a sparse visual stimulus can generate considerable orientation distortions is similar to **Gibson**'s demonstration of a tilt-induction effect, whereby observers report a vertical line as appearing to tilt in the direction opposite to surrounding context lines and so, when attempting to adjust a line to true vertical, the tendency is to err in the direction of the context lines. More recent studies have shown that changes in the perception of vertical and horizontal caused by local visual cues have the potential to account for many classical visual illusions (Prinzmetal and Beck, 2001). Ash and Witkin noted large individual variations in observers' susceptibility to the tilted-room effect, and Asch's description of the phenomenon implies that he initially placed a positive value on what he termed 'field relatedness'. However, in later years Witkin moved away from this position and formulated a theory of field dependence based on the extent to which a person is dependent or independent in their organisation of the surrounding perceptual field.

Asch's work on social perception used a conceptually analogous paradigm. For example, in one study he gave people lists of personality characteristics (e.g. tender, determined, sociable) and elicited further judgements of their impressions as to other characteristics of the person so described. These studies led to the identification of the 'primacy effect', whereby the traits one reads or hears first have an anchoring or biasing effect and carry more weight in an overall evaluation than traits that appear later in the list. Moreover, by giving different groups the same lists, except for one key item (e.g. tough, determined, sociable, as opposed to tender, determined, sociable) it was possible to estimate the effect of the target trait on the impression formed. Asch established that some traits are more central than others, in the sense that a change in the key trait had quite a marked effect on the participants' overall impression of the hypothetical person described. In so doing, he described the inferential structure to people's organisation of traits, and showed that impression formation is more than a summary of the individual pieces of information available to them about a person. Thus, any two traits that are understood to belong to someone are not interpreted and summed as isolated units but '[t]he two come into immediate dynamic interaction. The subject perceives not this and that quality, but the two entering into a particular relation' (1946: 284). Although there was considerable debate as to whether or not Asch's results could in fact be explained using more complex (e.g. multiplicative) elementist models, there is little disagreement about the importance of the line of research he initiated, and studies of impression formation are still being pursued within the general framework he originated. Asch showed that the same approach could be used to clarify 'prestige suggestion' in a series of studies in which he changed the attribution of quotations such as: 'I hold it that a little rebellion, now and then, is a good thing, and as necessary in the political world as storms are in the physical.' Americans agreed more with this quotation when they were told that it was taken from one of Thomas Jefferson's speeches than when they were told it was attributed to Lenin. The prevailing behavioural interpretation of this finding was premised on associationist principles – people were making linkages based on learning principles rather than any high-level, unobservable rational appraisal of the content – but Asch contended that the meaning of the quotations was influenced by participants' knowledge of the authors. Thus, when he asked people to paraphrase the quotations and found the summaries varied depending on the author, a finding that could not be explained using simple associations, Asch concluded that people interpret the meaning of stimulus information within a rational framework.

Asch is best known for his classic studies of persuasion, social pressure and conformity. In these he gathered a series of groups of seven or eight people who volunteered to participate in what they thought was a study of visual acuity. In fact only one of the participants was a real volunteer, the remainder being Asch's confederates. Each group was shown a series of sets of three straight lines. A fourth line was added and the group was asked whether the fourth one was the same length as the others. Every member in the group indicated their answer, the real volunteer being the last to answer in each case. After several trials, where everyone gave the correct answer to establish an atmosphere of normality, the confederates started to give answers that were obviously incorrect. Under these circumstances Asch found that fewer than 25 per cent of participants resisted conforming their reported perception to those of the group on at least some of the trials. However, there were differences: some individuals always conformed to the decisions of the group, whereas others would conform only some of the time. Asch's research on conformity to group pressure had a significant impact on the field of group dynamics and anticipated Milgram's and **Zimbardo**'s research on obedience. In this respect Milgram's work was a conscious continuation of the study of conformity pioneered by Asch.

Asch had planned his studies of conformity with the expectation of finding evidence similar to that reported by Muzafer Sherif, which showed that people would conform to a group judgement when viewing a visual illusion only when circumstances were ambiguous. This expectation was based on his approach to understanding how people could come to know one another's minds. Asch, like Gibson and others within the Gestalt tradition, argued that it was impossible for people to infer the presence of others' minds simply from experiencing other people, and that this capacity must be based on genetically influenced predispositions. This nativistic position, coupled with his concern to establish a phenomenological psychology in which social facts and processes are central, combined to find expression in his studies of cultural influences. This was an interest he shared with his wife, Florence, as reflected in the time they spent on a Hopi Indian reservation: ' ... we start with the assumption that individual men possess authentic properties distinctive of Homo Sapiens and that their actions in society alter them in authentically distinctive ways' (1952: 119). Unlike many eminent figures in psychology, Asch published little, and his major contributions are contained in just one book and thirty-five journal articles, which goes to show that one doesn't have to write a lot to make a big difference.

Solomon Asch's major writings

'Forming impressions of personality', *Journal of Abnormal Social Psychology*, 1946, 41, 258–90.
'Studies in space orientation: 1. Perception of the upright with displaced visual fields', *Journal of Experimental Psychology*, 1948, 38, 325–37 (with H. A. Witkin).
'Studies in space orientation: II. Perception of the upright with displaced visual fields and with body tilted', *Journal of Experimental Psychology*, 1948, 38, 455–77 (with H. A. Witkin).
'Studies in space orientation. III. Perception of the upright in the absence of a visual field', *Journal of Experimental Psychology*, 1948, 38, 603–14 (with H. A. Witkin).
'Studies in space orientation. IV. Further experiments on perception of the upright with displaced visual fields', *Journal of Experimental Psychology*, 1948, 38, 762–82 (with H. A. Witkin).
Social Psychology, Prentice Hall, 1952.
'Opinions and social pressure', *Scientific American*, 1955, 193, 31–5.

Further reading

Leyens, J. P. and Cornellie, O. (1999) 'Asch's social psychology: not as social as you think', *Personality and Social Psychology Review*, 3, 345–57.
Prinzmetal, W. and Beck, D. M. (2001) 'The tilt-constancy theory of visual illusions', *Journal of Experimental Psychology: Human Perception and Performance*, 27, 206–17.
Rock, I. (ed.) (1990) *The Legacy of Solomon Asch: Essays in Cognition and Social Psychology*, Erlbaum.

BADDELEY, ALAN D. (1934–)

Baddeley developed a sophisticated theory of memory that has been fruitfully applied in a wide range of settings.

The second son of Donald and Nellie Baddeley, Alan grew up in the working class district of Hunslet in Leeds. His father was a compositor, his mother a homemaker. His academic performance at Cockburn High School was even less than mediocre, and it was not until his mid-teens that he acquired a serious interest in academic pursuits and started to think about the possibility of going to university. His ambition to enter either Oxford or Cambridge was largely motivated by a desire to play rugby for one or the other, but this was thwarted by their lack of interest in enrolling him. Thoughts about taking a degree in philosophy were weighed against the poor employment prospects after graduation, but psychology offered an attractive compromise and he was offered a place at University College London. The American experimental psychobiologist Roger W. Russell had been appointed to the chair in 1950 and provided Baddeley with an introduction to both the North American and the British traditions. After graduating, he went on to complete an MA at Princeton, based on work on a cognitive approach to secondary reinforcement in rats – a perspective that favours the idea that animals are capable of creating crude but effective representations, such as memories, of things in their environment. He returned to England only to find jobs still as scarce as ever, and he spent some time as a hospital porter and then as a schoolteacher. Talk of an opportunity to study the beneficial effects of alcohol at the Burden Neurological Institute, Bristol – it was to be funded by Guinness, the brewers – appeared to offer many attractions, but the post never materialised. However, he secured a position at the Medical Research Council's Applied Psychology Unit (APU) at Cambridge, financed by the Post Office which was funding research on the design of postal codes. It was during this five-year stint at the APU that he married Hilary Anne White; they had three sons, one of whom, Roland, pursued a career in psychology and computational neuroscience. Time at the APU (at that time directed by **Broadbent**) was followed by a period as lecturer and Reader at Sussex University. He was joined at Sussex by Graham Hitch, his first post-doctoral fellow, and they commenced a career-long collaboration on memory. A sabbatical at the University of California offered opportunities to collaborate with George Mandler, who was working on structural and organisational factors in memory, and Donald Norman, who was working on memory and attention. On returning to the UK, Baddeley took up a Chair at Stirling University. This was a short appointment – just two years – because Baddeley took the post at a time when Stirling's plans for expansion were thwarted by the Government's policy of curtailing public expenditure in universities. When Broadbent retired from the APU, Baddeley returned to Cambridge where he served as Director between 1974 and 1995. He then moved to the position of Professor of Psychology at the University of Bristol. Although Baddeley's name is inexorably linked with the study of memory, both within the discipline of psychology and in the public mind (a feat attributable to his capacity to communicate complex ideas in a non-technical style that engages the lay reader), he has also made valuable contributions in the fields of language development and breakdown, developmental disorders and cognitive aspects of rehabilitation. Some of this work (e.g. on Alzheimer's disease) has included research collaboration with his wife Hilary.

Baddeley's first appointment at the APU sparked his interest in human memory and in the application of psychology outside laboratory settings. While a graduate student he became interested in diving. He was intrigued by the problems of measuring diver performance in the open sea, and continues to work in this area. An interest in short-term and working memory came from a project where he tried, unsuccessfully, to develop ways of evaluating the quality of telephone lines. In one study he used immediate memory for similar and dissimilar words, and was struck by the robustness of the phonological similarity effect. He discovered that similarity of meaning had a much less powerful effect than phonological similarity in immediate memory, while for long-term learning exactly the opposite occurred, with phonological similarity being unimportant and semantic similarity dominant. This finding led him to regard memory as having separate long-term memory (LTM) and short-term memory (STM) components. A similar conclusion came from collaborative work with Elizabeth Warrington on amnesic patients who showed normal performance on an STM task but grossly impaired functioning on a task requiring LTM.

Baddeley was publishing his theory of memory at a time when the simple dichotomous view of memory as comprising a system of interlocking but separate storages, short-term and long-term memory, had been superseded by Fergus Craik's account based on levels of processing. According to Craik, stimulus information is processed at multiple levels simultaneously, depending upon its characteristics. The 'deeper' something is processed the more it will be remembered. For instance, information that involves strong visual images or many associations with existing experience and knowledge will be processed at a deeper level. While regarding this approach as a useful re-conceptualisation of earlier findings on the role of coding in memory, Baddeley's approach was to accept the limitations of earlier unitary concepts of STM proposed by Broadbent and others, which he then elaborated into a multi-component model of working memory. Baddeley and Hitch (1974) proposed that STM comprised at least three components: a Central Executive and two subsidiary systems – the Articulatory Loop (later re-named the phonological loop) and the Visuo-Spatial Scratch-pad. The Central Executive is responsible for organising and planning cognitive activities and is intimately involved in processes to do with understanding, planning and the control of actions. Brain injury to the frontal lobes is reflected in damage to the

Central Executive, as indicated by evidence that people who suffer such injury endure particular difficulties structuring and controlling their actions. The Visuo-Spatial Scratch-pad is that part of the system responsible for visual mental imagery and is so called to accommodate evidence indicating that mental images appear to have both visual and spatial properties. The Phonological Loop allows speech-based information to be available to the Central Executive for extended periods of time but, rather like an old-fashioned looped tape recording, the quantity of information it can hold is quite limited. Evidence supporting the existence of neurological processes underpinning the Phonological Loop can be found in studies of people with brain damage who manifest specific deficits in memory span without total loss of short-term memory.

While the Central Executive is the most important component of the model, it has proved least tractable. Attempts to fractionate the attentional control mechanism have postulated a hypothetical split between the capacity to focus attention (switch focus) and to divide attention across two concurrent tasks. Studies of patients with Alzheimer's disease suggest that dual-task performance is markedly impaired in a manner consistent with Baddeley's predictions. Other evidence does not fit the model, such as that of a densely amnesic patient who retained a capacity to play bridge, even to the point of remembering the contract and the cards played earlier in the hand. Cases of this type point to the existence of some type of storage involving the temporary activation of long-term representations in order to create and maintain novel cognitive structures – something akin to long-term working memory (Baddeley and Hitch, 2000). In order to accommodate the growing corpus of evidence bearing on the operation of the Central Executive, Baddeley has postulated a fourth component of working memory – the Episodic Buffer. This is hypothesised to be a limited capacity system that provides temporary storage of information held in a multi-modal code. It is thought to be capable of binding information from the subsidiary systems, and from long-term memory, into a unitary episodic representation. Conscious effort is required to retrieve information from the buffer. This expansion of the model places greater emphasis on understanding processes of information integration rather than on the segregated analysis of the subsystems. In so doing, it provides a more robust theoretical base from which to fractionate the more complex aspects of executive control in working memory.

The Baddeley and Hitch model has proved both robust and fruitful, being applied to a range of situations from the analysis of adult reading to the breakdown of memory in aphasic patients, and from the development of memory in children to the memory deficit of patients suffering from senile dementia. The model works well because it allows continuous theoretical development based on empirical research, as illustrated by the addition of the Episodic Buffer, and offers a robust model that is applicable to a wide range of real-world problems. Ever concerned with the need to refine and elaborate the model, Baddeley concluded that: 'Postulating a new component after 25 years does not solve the deep and important problems underlying the issues tackled. It does however focus attention on the need for our working memory model to be able to account for the integration of information from multiple sources' (Baddeley and Hitch 2000: 135).

Alan Baddeley's major writings

'Working memory', in G. Bower (ed.), *Recent Advances in Learning and Motivation*, Volume VIII. Academic Press, 1974 (with G. J. Hitch).
The Psychology of Memory Basic Books, 1976.
'The trouble with levels: A re-examination of Craik and Lockhart's framework for memory research', *Psychological Review*, 1978, 85, 139–52.
Your Memory: A User's Guide, Sedgwick and Jackson, 1982.
Working Memory, Clarendon Press, 1986
Working Memory and Language, Erlbaum, 1993 (with S. E. Gathercole).
'Exploring the central executive', *Quarterly Journal of Experimental Psychology*, 1996, 49, 5–28.
'Development of working memory: should the Pascual–Leone and the Baddeley and Hitch models be merged?', *Journal of Experimental Child Psychology*, 2000, 77, 128–37 (with G. J. Hitch).
'The episodic buffer: a new component of working memory?', *Trends in Cognitive Sciences*, 2000, 4, 417–23.

Further reading

Collins, A. F., Gathercole, S. E., Conway, M. A. and Morris, P. E. (eds) (1995) *Theories of Memory I*, Psychology Press.
Conway, M. A., Gathercole, S. E. and Cornoldi, C. (eds) (1998) *Theories of Memory II*, Psychology Press.
Tulving, E. and Craik, F. M. (eds) (2000) *The Oxford Handbook of Memory*, Oxford University Press.

BANDURA, ALBERT (1925–)

Bandura pioneered the development of a theory of social learning that has been particularly influential in understanding aggression and how a wide range of human behaviour is motivated and regulated by self-evaluations.

Albert Bandura, the only son in a family of five older sisters, grew up in Mundare, northern Alberta, Canada. He spent his elementary and high school years in the village's one-and-only school. His career in psychology came about by chance. He commuted to the University of Iowa in a carpool of engineering and pre-med students whose day started early. A psychology course with an early morning start was available, so he took it and was soon hooked. At Iowa he studied with the learning theorist Kenneth Spence, an associate of **Hull**, and in 1952 he earned a doctorate in clinical psychology under the supervision of the clinical neuropsychologist Arthur L. Benton. While working on his doctorate he met Virginia Varns, an instructor in the nursing school. They married and later had two daughters. In 1952 he moved to Wichita, Kansas, to a one-year internship at the Wichita Guidance Center. He then moved to Stanford University.

At the start of his career, Bandura focused on learning. Most of the research at that time was concerned with learning from direct experience. At that time it was widely assumed that learning could only occur by responding to stimuli and experiencing their effects. Bandura felt that this line of theorising was at odds with informal evidence that virtually all learning resulting from direct experience occurs on a vicarious basis – by observing other people's behaviour and its consequences for them. Whereas behaviourism tended to emphasise the influence of the environment on behaviour, Bandura was interested in the influence of behaviour on the environment. In this respect his position is closer to that of Jacob Kantor, whose 'interbehaviourism' argues that the organism and stimulus objects surrounding it should be treated as equally important, a position that presaged the emergence of ecological psychology. Bandura referred to his concept of environment–behaviour interaction as 'reciprocal determinism' – the notion that the environment and a person's behaviour cause one other. He developed this idea to a point where he began to consider the interaction between environment, behaviour and the person's psychological processes. Once he started to consider a role for mental imagery, he ceased to be a strict behaviourist and became a cognitive psychologist. Indeed, he is often regarded as a 'founding father' of cognitive behaviourism. His theoretically ambitious *Social Learning Theory* (1977) set out to 'provide a unified theoretical framework for analyzing human thought and behaviour' (p. vi). While his introduction of cognitive concepts into behaviourism marked a clear departure from traditional behaviourism, it also marked a point where Bandura began to consider observational learning (modelling) and self-regulation. This interest led to a programme of research on the determinants and mechanisms of observational learning and modelling of rule-governed behaviour. He distinguished between three kinds of models: live (e.g. the behaviour of a friend); symbolic (e.g. the behaviour of an actor on TV); and verbal (e.g. the behaviour of someone described in a short story or novel). The enormous advances in communication technology through the last century (from radio to television and the internet) mean that the symbolic environment plays an increasingly powerful role in shaping values, ideas, attitudes and lifestyles, so Bandura's work is particularly relevant to contemporary developments in the growth of information and communication technology.

Bandura paid special attention to the role of symbolic modelling in the social diffusion of new ways of behaving, and is most closely associated with a classic investigation called the 'bobo' doll study, in which he examined whether young children could learn aggressive behaviours by watching adult models perform aggressive acts. Children between 3 and 6 years old watched either an aggressive model (an adult who hit a doll with a mallet), a non-aggressive model (an adult who played quietly with toys and ignored the doll), or no model (a control group who did not see any model). Children who had seen the aggressive model tended to imitate the violent behaviour they observed more often than children in the other two groups. Bandura's social cognitive theory has offered one of the most influential psychological explanations of how people may come to regard their injurious actions against others as trivial and even acceptable. Bandura and his colleagues identified a number of cognitive mechanisms that offenders may use to minimise their perceptions of the impact of their actions on others. These include moral justification (e.g. 'I lied to protect my family'), euphemistic labelling of severe assaults (e.g. 'I messed him up a bit'), and denial of consequences (e.g. 'I only steal from big chain-stores').

Another major line of interest for Bandura aims to clarify the different mechanisms of personal agency. This work is concerned with how people exercise control over their own motivation and behaviour and over their environment. One focus of this research is on how human behaviour is motivated and regulated by internal standards and anticipatory self-evaluative reactions – how I will feel if I do such and such. Bandura argues that, among the mechanisms of personal agency, none is more central or pervasive than people's perceived efficacy to exert control over different aspects of their lives. His studies of familial causes of aggression, with his first graduate student Richard Walters (who died at an early age in a motorcycle accident), promoted an increasing emphasis on the role of modelling in personality development. Like the personality theorist Walter Mischel, he developed a social cognitive theory that considers the person as an active agent using cognitive processes such as memory and problem-solving to reflect on experiences of the world and to make decisions and plan behaviour. This contrasts with views in which the person is regarded as a more or less passive respondent to environmental circumstances or as a victim of unconscious drives. In fact Bandura, like **Eysenck**, is highly critical of psychoanalysis for its reliance on concepts that cannot be clearly defined and for promoting the use of therapeutic methods that he contends have failed to demonstrate their effectiveness in achieving sustained changes in psychological functioning. He is also critical of its emphasis on the seemingly unavoidable consequences of early childhood experiences. In this regard he can be considered closer to the more optimistic and humanistic psychology of **Rogers**. Unlike Rogers, Bandura's approach reflects a significantly stronger commitment to empirically guided theory development and to the therapeutic importance of actual experiences rather than to the creation of a therapeutic climate conducive to change.

Bandura's emphasis on the study of processes that account for the acquisition, maintenance and change of behaviour contrasts with that of trait theorists, who place greater value on the import of innate dispositions. Social cognitive theory sees the adaptively functioning person as a well-tuned organism capable of adapting the environment and of changing parts of the environment to suit themselves. The self is considered not as a fixed structure but as a set of cognitive processes: the person does not have a psychological structure called the 'self' but self-processes that are part of the person. Bandura regards the self-efficacy belief system as the foundation of human motivation, well-being and personal accomplishments. In other words, unless people believe that they can bring about desired outcomes by their actions, they have little incentive to act or to persevere in the face of difficulties. There is a good deal of empirical evidence to support his argument that personal-efficacy beliefs shape just about every aspect of people's lives – whether they think pessimistically or optimistically, their vulnerability to stress and depression, and the life choices they make. However, critics contend that self-efficacy theory misses the point that it is outcome expectancies that actually guide behaviour: if people believe they can perform the tasks presented in a particular situation then it is the expectation of receiving a positive outcome that motivates their actions. Bandura has replied that well-designed empirical studies should resolve this type of dispute and he points to the corpus of evidence showing that empirical self-efficacy beliefs can predict behaviour more accurately than measures of outcome expectancy.

Self-efficacy theory has proved particularly effective in clinical interventions. For instance, self-efficacy analysis suggests that phobias, such as snake phobia, result from people losing their sense of self-efficacy – their sense of being able to respond effectively to the situation presented to them. Because people are most convinced that they can manage a situation by actually managing it, therapeutic interventions emphasise overt ability to perform specific behaviours, such as handling snakes. While Bandura concurs with Eysenck's position that therapies are effective because they reduce anxiety reactions, he does not agree that therapeutic interventions should focus on attenuating levels of emotional distress. Instead, the focus should be on developing a person's sense of belief that they can cope effectively. The therapist's role is to promote successful outcomes by bringing to bear various techniques that will engage the client with frightening tasks and help them perform those tasks proficiently. For example, people who develop anxieties and fears may do so because their planning abilities either switch off or diminish in effectiveness and the person focuses on planning to cope with their emotional distress rather than planning to address the reality of the situation as it is presented to them. Bandura suggests that a therapist's role may initially involve vicarious mastery: a client with a snake phobia would observe others handling snakes. As therapy progresses, the client and therapist work in closer collaboration in order to sustain a reciprocal interaction between increases in self-efficacy and greater performance successes. Although this type of protocol has enjoyed considerable success, critics point out that it does not address the source of a person's phobia, underplays the role of unconscious processes that may be implicated in the phobia, and often requires a fairly sophisticated, adult-like, development for the client to benefit from a therapeutic intervention.

Bandura's social learning theory has influenced a diverse range of applied work as illustrated in John Farquhar's classic 'Three-Community Study', in which matched farming communities received one of three interventions. One community received messages about the prevention of heart disease by mass media and direct mail; another received additional instruction for those considered at high risk; and a third acted as a control. The mass media were found to be as effective as direct instruction in reducing heart disease risk. More generally, Bandura's ideas have enjoyed considerable influence and respect across five decades. Their impact is due in no small part to his readiness to embrace empirically-founded ideas from a range of sub-disciplines within psychology. This willingness is indicated by the changes to the name given to his theoretical position from observational learning, which reflected a more traditional behavioural position, to social learning theory, which reflects a stronger emphasis on the ways in which social behaviours are learned by watching other people, and then to social cognitive theory, which emphasises the greater role given to cognitive processes in mediating social learning.

Albert Bandura's major writings

Adolescent Aggression, Ronald Press, 1959 (with R. H. Walters).
Social Learning and Personality Development, Holt, Rinehart and Winston, 1963 (with R. H. Walters).
Principles of Behavior Modification, Holt, Rinehart and Winston, 1969.
Social Learning Theory, Prentice-Hall, 1977.
'Self efficacy: toward a unifying theory of behavioral change', *Psychological Review,* 1977, 84, 91–215.
Social Foundations of Thought and Action: A Social Cognitive Theory, Prentice-Hall, 1986.
Self-Efficacy in Changing Societies, Cambridge University Press, 1995.

Further reading

Evans, R. I. (1989) *Albert Bandura, the Man and His Ideas: A Dialogue*, Greenwood.
Hall, C. S. and Lindzey, C. (1957) *Theories of Personality*, Wiley.
Mowrer, R. R. and Klein, S. B. (2000) *Handbook of Contemporary Learning Theories*, Erlbaum.

BARTLETT, FREDERICK CHARLES (1886–1969)

A theorist of human cognition, Bartlett popularised the concept of schema as a basic unit of thought.

Bartlett's childhood was spent in Stow-on-the-Wold, situated about thirty miles from Oxford and eighty-five from London, where his father ran a successful footwear outlet. The local grammar school was defunct, so it was his parents' intention that he and his older brother should go to boarding school. However, a near-fatal attack of pleurisy at the age of fourteen put an end to those plans and Bartlett was left to educate himself, supported by his father's encouragement and the library of a local minister. He enrolled as an external student at London University, taking courses in philosophy and logic offered by the University Correspondence College, based at Cambridge. His first-class degree prompted the Correspondence College to offer him a position as tutor. While filling that role he read for a University of London MA and gained distinctions in sociology and ethics. This was followed by a decision to make a fresh start as an undergraduate at Cambridge. He achieved a second first-class degree and, while it was his intention to continue with a career in anthropology, his tutor, the physiologist and psychologist William Rivers, encouraged him to take charge of the course in experimental psychology because it would broaden his career opportunities. The First World War shaped his career through the departure of the psychologists Charles Myers, William McDougall and William Brown to do military service. A combination of poor health and lack of medical training meant that Bartlett could not enlist. It fell to him to fill Myers's role, and he was appointed assistant director of the Psychology Laboratory. In 1924 he became Reader in experimental psychology and Director in the same year, when Myers left to found the National Institute of Industrial Psychology in London.

It was during the war years that he met his wife to be, Mary Smith. They collaborated on the perception of weak intensity sound, the work being of importance to the operation of hydrophone anti-submarine detection equipment. During this period he completed a thesis based on the studies. Several years later these studies formed the core of his classic text *Remembering* (1932). Notwithstanding the demands imposed by his new responsibilities, Bartlett found time to spend on his love for social anthropology. Travel to undertake fieldwork was out of the question, but he was able to apply his psychological expertise in a novel analysis of the social and cultural transmission of memory through devices such as myth and folklore, reported in *Psychology and Primitive Culture* (1923). This aspect of his work is reminiscent of **Wundt**'s Völkerpsychologie (social psychology).

Bartlett is best known for his investigations into memory and in particular for his book *Remembering*, which examined the influences of social factors on memory. His first account of the affects of those social influences was a product of his knowledge of anthropological accounts of the outcomes of cross-cultural contacts on conventions. He defined the process of 'conventionalisation' as one in which 'cultural materials coming into a group from outside are gradually worked into a pattern of a relatively stable kind distinctive of that group. The new material is assimilated to the persistent past of the group to which it comes' (1958: 280). He drew a connection between these ideas and his experimental data on memory which implied that, after repetitive recall, the participants' protocols reached a fairly stable form and that any changes in recall usually demonstrated the impact of old information on new. However, although he originally regarded his research to be 'an all out experimental attack upon conventionalizing' (1958: 143), he became disillusioned with this approach because conventionalisation seemed less like an explanatory concept and more like a tag for a similarity between phenomena in different disciplinary domains.

Bartlett's strongest influence is in his theory of schemata: a schema (singular for schemata) is constantly changing in the light of new experiences, but it provides a dynamic framework or model into which new experiences are interpreted and structured. Bartlett was not the first to use the term – **Piaget** also made considerable use of the concept in his theory of cognitive development. Bartlett's concept of schema was developed in part through discussion with the physiologist Sir Henry Head, who used 'postural schema' to explain how past information about the position of one's body informs current actions, and to account for disorders of body orientation. Bartlett's observations on making tennis strokes capture the core elements of his idea of movement schemata: 'When I make the stroke I do not, as a matter of fact, produce something absolutely new, and I never merely repeat something old. The stroke is literally manufactured out of the living visual and postural "schemata" of the movement and their interrelations' (1932: 202).

The concept of schema posed a fundamental challenge to the prevailing views on memory that were exemplified in the classic work of Hermann von Ebbinghaus. Ebbinghaus had argued that, in order to study memory in its purest form, it was necessary to establish experimental conditions that would remove potentially confounding variables. His experiments were designed to uncover rudimentary laws of memory by using nonsense syllables to create situations where the memory content was meaningless and therefore isolated from other memories and prior experience. He contended that more complex forms of memory could be explored once the simpler laws describing its structure and operation had been uncovered. However, Bartlett argued that, if a psychologist is concerned with understanding relatively high-level processes like recall and proceeds to try and isolate the response – the memory to be recalled – by making the stimulus extremely simple, she has performed a very different kind of procedure. This kind of experimental procedure does not lead to the identification of simpler laws because, when people learn nonsense syllables, they typically use a variety of strategies to *impose* meaning on the task, such as contriving associations between the meaningless stimulus and meaningful memories. In other words, human memory has emergent properties that are not captured in highly simplified memory tasks, and even the very simplest tasks can never fully exclude those properties because people invariably attempt to impose meanings on the material they are learning. Not only were Bartlett's ideas counter to those of Ebbinghaus, they were also hostile to the behaviourist school which, at the time Bartlett was publishing, was eschewing the study of any kind of covert mental entity. Thus, his concept of schema was relatively neglected until the emergence of cognitivism, an approach that focuses on the analysis of higher mental processes such as problem-solving and artificial intelligence. For example, **Broadbent** (1970) concluded that ' ... the term "schema" appears to have become completely disused ... the schema itself had no list of defining properties, but was simply a label for something whose operation was illustrated by experimental results ... Theoretical concepts of this kind, without public definitions, are almost bound to be self-defeating' (p. 4). Moreover, there is a good deal of argument and evidence that Bartlett presented two versions of schema theory: an official version in which he contends that memory is a constructive process, and an unofficial or private version (Ost and Costall, 2002). The latter has a place for the concept of the memory trace and acknowledges that, if memory is a process of construction and reconstruction, there must be some entity on which to base the construction. Notwithstanding these ambiguities, for a period of time the vagueness of the notion of schema provided a useful theoretical anchor for the nascent cognitive sciences, an interdisciplinary approach to the way the brain processes information.

With the outbreak of the Second World War Bartlett, a member of the Air Ministry's Flying Personnel Research Committee, was drawn into the analysis of psychological problems revealed by the expansion of the RAF. His close association with Kenneth Craik, who joined the Cambridge laboratory in 1936, was indispensable. Craik had the ingenuity and engineering talent required to fabricate the experimental simulations that were needed to study pilot behaviour and fatigue. Their work was supported with the establishment of the Medical Research Council's Applied Psychology Unit in 1944. Craik was its head, but he died in a road traffic accident just before the end of the war. This was a profound personal loss to Bartlett. Bartlett later adapted Craik's methods in his investigations of remembering and thinking. As a practical activity he considered thinking to involve the completion (by interpolation or extrapolation) of some previously incomplete state of affairs, and he devised experimental procedures to explore this idea systematically. His book *Thinking* (1958) is less remarkable than the earlier *Remembering*, although in many ways it reveals more of his personal attitudes and thoughts (e.g. his involvement with anthropology, sociology and philosophy) than any of his earlier published work.

Bartlett twice switched his interests from lively academic fields to ones where there were practical problems to be solved. The first was a switch from sociology and anthropology to the experimental psychology of perception and remembering. The second was from a purely academic psychology to the application of psychology in occupational settings. He holds a pre-eminent position in the development of psychology in Britain. Starting with just one laboratory assistant in 1922, he was guiding the efforts of more than seventy staff and researchers some thirty years later, and most of the important psychological appointments in Britain during the middle of the twentieth century were made from among those who had been trained under him.

Frederick Bartlett's major writings

'An experimental study of some problems of perceiving and imaging', *British Journal of Psychology*, 1916, 8, 222–66.
Psychology and Primitive Culture Cambridge University Press, 1923.
'Experimental method in psychology', *Nature*, 1929, 124, 341–5.
Remembering: A Study in Experimental and Social Psychology, Cambridge University Press, 1932.
The Problem of Noise, Cambridge University Press, 1934.
'Psychological methods and anthropological problems', *Africa*, 1937, 10, 401–20.
Thinking: An Experimental and Social Study, Allen and Unwin, 1958.

Further reading

Brewer, W. F. and Nakamura, G. V. (1984) 'The nature and functions of schemas', in R.S . Wyer, Jr. and T. K. Srull (eds), *Handbook of Social Cognition*, vol. 1, Erlbaum.
Broadbent, D. E. (1970) 'Frederick Charles Bartlett 1886–1969', *Biographical Memoirs of Fellows of the Royal Society*, 16, 1–11.
Ost, J. and Costall, A. (2002) 'Misremembering Bartlett: a study in serial reproduction', *British Journal of Psychology*, 93, 243–55.

BINET, ALFRED (1857–1911)

Binet invented the intelligence test and used it to quantify children's intelligence.

Born in Nice, Binet was the son of a wealthy physician and was raised by his mother Moïna Binet, an amateur artist, following the separation of his parents. His father regarded his young son as a bit of a wimp and, to toughen the boy up, he forced him to view and touch corpses. It didn't work, and to make matters worse he developed a lifelong fear of his estranged father. Alfred attended the prestigious Lycée Louis-le-Grand and later obtained a degree in law, but law was a profession he despised and he turned to medicine. Perhaps predictably, Binet's medical career was cut short by his squeamishness about cadavers. Starting late in 1887 or early in 1888, Binet attended courses at the embryological laboratory of Edouard-Gérard Balbiani, where he also became familiar with botany and zoology. There he developed his skills in experimental methods and acquired an appreciation of the importance and benefits of systematic observation. His thesis on the sub-intestinal nervous system of insects secured him a Doctorate in Natural Science in 1894. Binet married Laure Balbiani, daughter of E. G. Balbiani, and they had two daughters, Madeleine and Alice. Both were participants in Binet's research, where they appear under the pseudonyms Marguerite and Armande. The young Binets lived in Paris on the rue du Regard and rue Meidon, and later moved to the suburb of Meudon before settling in the avenue de Maine.

As a person of independent means Binet was able to pursue his own interests, and he read widely in the Bibliothèque Nationale in Paris, focusing on the available works in psychology. He developed an interest in the ideas of John Stewart Mill, and sought someone who could advance his understanding of an empirical associationist psychology. In 1892 he met Jean-Martin Charcot, the neurologist at the Salpêtrière Hospital, and worked under his guidance for the next eight years. The outcome of this work was seventeen publications on the topics of animal magnetism, hypnosis and hysteria. During this period he continued to develop his experimental skills and to publish his findings, producing two additional books and more than twenty research articles, most of which appeared in Théodule Ribot's *Revue Philosophique*, a journal devoted to fostering scientific and philosophical debates on a broad range of questions of contemporary importance. The first French psychological laboratory, inaugurated by Ribot, was established in January 1889 as part of the division of natural sciences within L'École Pratique des Hautes Études in the Sorbonne. Henri Beaunis, a physician and physiologist, originally attempted to fashion it on Wundt's model, but he gave Binet a free hand to try out novel alternatives as he saw fit. Binet was appointed associate director in 1892 and succeeded Beaunis on the latter's retirement in 1894. In that year Binet founded and became the first editor of *L'Année Psychologique*, the first journal in France to be devoted to the discipline of psychology. By this time Binet's wide-ranging interests had also resulted in many publications on the following topics: fetishism, hallucinations, animal magnetism, hypnotism, hysteria, suggestion, perception, visual imagery, extraordinary memories, blindfold chess-players, music, theatre, fear, religion, the physical correlates of normality versus abnormality, dementia, manic depression, mental fatigue, handwriting and deaf mutes.

During the summer of 1895 Binet lectured at the University of Bucharest as a visiting professor, but declined the offer of a permanent chair. In collaboration with Victor Henri, who had studied under Külpe at Würzburg, he commenced a series of studies on school-children in Paris. The intention was to develop a library of tests that would allow him systematically to examine individual differences in detail. Tests associated with the work of **Galton** and **Cattell** were already in circulation, but many intellectual faculties remained unexplored. The Paris schools provided Binet and Henri with children (usually boys) that were not available to their psychological laboratory. In particular, Binet began to appreciate the significance of studying samples of children beyond the average range of abilities, and schools in some of the poorest regions of Paris provided many children of below-average ability. Binet became both an advocate and a promoter of what he termed 'Psychologie Individuelle' and methods of measuring individual differences.

In about 1899 Binet made the acquaintance of Théodore Simon, a physician who was to be an important collaborator over the next eleven years. Binet became a member of the Société Libre pour l'Étude Psychologique de l'Enfant, and set about trying to convince its members of the importance of observation and experimental method in pedagogy. In 1901 Ribot resigned his chair of experimental psychology at the Collège de France, and Binet tried, unsuccessfully, to secure the position. Pierre Janet was appointed, vacating a position at the Sorbonne to which Binet applied but was once again turned down, in favour of Georges Dumas. His disappointment was compounded by the death of his close friend Léon Marillier at about this time. Notwithstanding these professional setbacks and personal losses, by the end of 1904 Binet was heading a Ministerial Commission to track 'abnormal' children in the schools of Paris. For the French government the problem was to objectively identify children who would probably not benefit from the standard education that the state provided. Binet and Simon considered that this commission required a psychological and experimental method. By May 1905 they had produced sufficient test items that, in hierarchical order of difficulty, constituted what was immediately recognised to be the first workable measure of intelligence. The easiest task required a child to follow a light with his/her eyes, something most very young children could do, but that some children with developmental delay or learning disability could not. The difficulty of each task was gradually increased through sentence completion problems that could be solved only by precocious eleven-year-olds. Having developed a test to meet the needs of the Commission, Binet found himself on a path that would lead to the formulation of an assessment instrument that would allow him to state, with some precision, whether a particular child was performing at the level of an average child of that age. In November 1905 he announced that he and his colleagues had established the first Laboratory of Experimental Pedagogy in a Parisian school located at 36 rue Grange-aux-Belles à Belleville, where his friend V. Vaney was principal (a commemorative plaque in honour of Binet was placed on the building on the 5th of June 1971). Binet and Simon used the pupils at this school to develop their scale of intelligence and in 1908 they published a major revision of an earlier scale. Binet, still not satisfied, made a further revision in 1911. Vaney was co-author of several influential papers on measurement issues that appeared in the *Bulletin de la Société Alfred Binet*.

The popularisation of the Simon–Binet tests in North America was largely due to two people: Henry H. Goddard, who translated them from French, and Lewis M. Terman, who administered Goddard's translation to North American children. Goddard was a pioneer of the American eugenics movement, and his interests in the inheritability of intelligence secured him a position with the Vineland Training School to work on the genetic basis of 'feeble-mindedness'. Terman's interests were in understanding the genetic basis of genius and in promoting the development and application of technologies for measuring intelligence. Goddard's and Terman's modifications took account of the fact that some items on the Simon–Binet test were too easy and others too difficult. The title of Terman's 1916 revision, the *Stanford–Binet* test, indicates that the work was done at Stanford University, which Terman joined in 1910 as Assistant Professor in the School of Education. Further substantial revisions were made to the test during the 1920s, by which time Terman had moved to Stanford's psychology department and was collaborating with child clinical psychologist Maud Merrill.

In 1912 Binet's work enjoyed great public esteem in France. His personal circumstances were rather different: his wife was in poor health and, at fifty-four years of age, Binet was growing increasingly macabre. Circumstantial evidence for this is revealed in his theatrical interests: he penned nine plays in total, most of which were performed at the Grand-Guignol and Sarah-Bernhardt theatres. He produced four plays between 1905 and his death: 'L'Obsession', 'L'Expériment horrible' and 'L'Homme mystérieux' were co-authored with the director and actor André de Lorde (also known as 'The Prince of Terror'). 'Les Invisibles' was performed in 1912, after Binet's death, following a stroke. In 1923 de Lorde produced 'A Crime in the House of the Insane', of which Binet was cited as co-author. These explore morose themes in which psychopathological problems are explored in plots based on horror and suspense. For example, in one plot a physician releases a patient with paranoid schizophrenia, only to find that the patient goes on to kill the doctor's brother.

It may be more than coincidence that the early childhood experiences of de Lorde and Binet are somewhat similar: de Lorde was the son of a poor French count who practised as a doctor, and as a toddler he regularly accompanied his father to the deathbed of his patients. When he was five his father died, and his mother, who married the classical actor Jean Mounet-Sully, raised him in an artistic environment populated with thespians.

Binet did not formulate a systematic theory of intelligence, but considered that comprehension, judgement, common sense and to some extent memory, manifested themselves in many ways. Unlike Galton he was convinced that individual differences in intelligence lay in the higher mental processes rather than in sensory acuity. He resisted theoretical speculations about the nature of intelligence – what it is and how it should be defined – and adopted the view that it was relatively unimportant what the tests were as long as they were numerous and well designed. It could be said that, for Binet, intelligence is that which is measured by his tests. However, he did not consider that poor test performance imposed a life sentence of intellectual deficit and he ardently believed that teachers should be disabused of any belief that intellectual performance is wholly innately determined. He was a good deal more pragmatic and optimistic about the malleability of intellectual potential than some interpretations of his ideas would imply. Although he considered that genetic factors would set an upper limit on intellectual potential, special education could dramatically enhance low test scores in much the same way that everyone can grow intellectually if given the appropriate stimulation and support. Thus, while Binet's Scales of Intelligence are generally considered to represent a breakthrough in intelligence testing and are his principal contribution to psychology, he saw their principal value as being valid and reliable devices for identifying children who would benefit most from different modes of education.

Binet's work was a progenitor of later contributions by **Anastasi** and many others, and is widely recognised as such. However, much of his other work has been neglected or forgotten. For example, early work on imageless thought and a method of systematic introspection was equal to the ideas that have come to be linked with the Würzburg school. Binet's *L'Études de psychologie expérimentale* (1891) antedates Külpe's 1895 publication on imageless thought, and Külpe's failure to acknowledge Binet's claim that he first encountered the 'imageless thought' hypotheses in Külpe's treatment, 'L'intensité des images mentales', was something Binet protested on several occasions. Külpe's position was that it was he who formulated the concept first while supervising unpublished studies by two of his students, Karl Marbe and Narziss Ach. Binet's work on the psychology of suggestibility and eyewitness testimony, *La Suggestibilité* (1900), was equal to that of Hugo Münsterberg's classic studies and presaged the more widely acclaimed contribution of William Stern, who knew of Binet's work but did not cite it. In many respects Binet's intellectual influence was limited by the fact that he never held a professorship, the boundary indexed by the dearth of biographical and historical enquiries into his intellectual and professional contributions.

Alfred Binet's major writings

'Perceptions d'enfants', *Revue Philosophique*, 1890, 30, 582–611.
L'Études de psychologie expérimentale, Doin, 1891.
Les Altérations de la personnalité, Alcan, 1892.
La Fatigue intellectuelle, Schleicher Frères, 1898 (with V. Henri).
'La mesure en psychologie individuelle', *Revue Philosophique*, 1898, 46, 113–23.
La Suggestibilité, Schleicher Frères, 1900.
L'Étude expérimentale de l'intelligence, Schleicher Frères, 1903.
'Sur la nécessité d'établir un diagnostic scientifique des états inférieurs de l'intelligence', *L'Année Psychologique*, 1905, 11, 163–90 (with Th. Simon).
'Le développement de l'intelligence chez les enfants', *L'Année Psychologique*, 1908, 14, 1–94.

Further reading

Fancher, R. E. (1985) *The Intelligence Men*, W. W. Norton.
Wolf, T. (1973) *Alfred Binet*, W. W. Norton.

BOWLBY, EDWARD JOHN MOSTYN (1907–90)

A child psychiatrist, Bowlby's name is synonymous with attachment theory.

Bowlby was born to Mary ('May') Bridget Mostyn and Anthony Alfred Bowlby. His father was a celebrated surgeon who was first introduced to May at a party in 1897. They married the following year: he was 43, she was 31. When May moved into 24 Manchester Square (off Oxford Street and Baker Street), London, Anthony's sister, Fanny, was obliged to find accommodation elsewhere. Fanny had kept house for Anthony and was not best pleased at being so displaced. May, on the other hand, found herself living in a house she felt to be permeated by Fanny's over-bearing religious influence. To make matters worse the newly-weds were soon separated by the outbreak of the Boer War in 1899. After several stress-filled years Anthony and May moved next door – to 25 Manchester Square – and things greatly improved. They had six children who were referred to by their parents as 'the girls' (Winifred and Marion), 'the boys' (Tony and John), and 'the babies' (James and Evelyn). It seems very likely that 'the babies' were unplanned and that they had thought John would be their fourth and last child. Like any conventional upper-middle-class professional family of the time, much of the day-to-day childrearing was the responsibility of the nanny and nursemaid. It is tempting to regard such a family milieu as being particularly conducive to the production of adults who would spend much of their time thinking and writing about attachment and separation. However, the Bowlbys were typical of most well-to-do Edwardian families, few of which produce John Bowlby clones.

John's education began at home under the direction of a governess. This was followed by attendance at Edge's day school. The outbreak of the First World War meant that John's father was required to serve at the front line in France for about four years, punctuated by brief respites at the London home. In early 1918 John and his brother Tony were sent to Lindisfarne boarding school in Worcester (later renamed Abberley Hall). In 1921, at the age of fourteen, John left Lindisfarne and enrolled at the Royal Naval College, Dartmouth. It was undoubtedly during this period that he acquired the distinctive military countenance emblematic of the single-mindedness of his mission to understand the effects of childhood separation. In 1924 he commenced training as a midshipman on HMS Royal Oak, but found the work mostly dull and undemanding. However, extricating himself from the navy was not straightforward – his training costs of £440 had to be reimbursed to the Admiralty. John's father agreed to the outlay and encouraged his son to pursue a career in medicine because of the wealth of opportunities it afforded. This he did, first by taking at University College London the subjects required to gain admission to Cambridge University. At Cambridge he took several courses in the natural sciences that would lead to a career in medicine, but after two years he switched to moral sciences. This consisted of courses in philosophy and psychology that included lectures in biological psychology from **Bartlett**, who was at that time Cambridge's champion of psychology. During his final year Bowlby was reading Freud's *Introductory Lectures on Psychoanalysis* and William H. R. Rivers's classic *Instinct and the Unconscious.*

During the 1930s he almost became formally engaged to Lady Prudence Pelham, but that never materialised because he had an affair with her sister. This was followed by another tempestuous relationship, this time with Rose Elton, a close friend of his brother Tony. It was Rose who introduced him to Ursula Longstaff. Following a romantic holiday in Ireland they were married in 1938, on precisely the same day that Ursula's parents were divorced. Again, the making and breaking of attachments is potentially significant given the nature of Bowlby's contributions to psychology.

His therapeutic training included analysis sessions with Joan Riviere. These were sometimes problematic, and he attempted to change to a different analyst but was advised against it. Riviere's view was that Bowlby was suffering an extended depressive episode and she appealed to him to remain in therapy with her. Others were of the same view, and reluctantly he continued. It is perhaps not surprising that when he applied, in 1936, to the Psychoanalytic Training Committee to be granted a certificate of qualification, he was declined on the grounds that his request was overly-urgent and premature. Further analysis led to a qualification in 1937, though even then Riviere was doubtful that sufficient progress had been made.

It is sometimes speculated that, if Bowlby's interest in attachment processes was not a product of his childhood environment, then it must have grown from his observations and experiences of parent–child separation caused by homelessness and evacuation during the Second World War. However, such a view is contradicted by the fact that Bowlby was publishing work on attachment and separation in 1938. His first empirical study, based on forty-four case notes from the London Child Guidance Clinic, demonstrated the importance of links between clients' symptoms and their histories of maternal deprivation and separation. The Second World War interrupted Bowlby's career as a practising child psychiatrist, but work on officer selection procedures afforded him an opportunity to develop a degree of methodological and statistical expertise that was then unusual for a psychiatrist and psychoanalyst. Just after the war he was appointed head of the Children's Department at the Tavistock Clinic, which he renamed the Department for Children and Parents. Much of the Department's clinical work was Kleinian in orientation and did not fit particularly well with Bowlby's own interests in the analysis of actual family interaction patterns. As a result he established a research unit focused on mother–child separation, and in 1948 he recruited James Robertson to assist him with his studies of hospitalised and institutionalised children. As a conscientious objector, Robertson had worked as a boilerman in Anna Freud's residential nursery for homeless children. Anna Freud required that all members of the staff, including Robertson, keep records of the children's behaviour, and these were used to inform weekly group discussions. Robertson was the kind of person who could undertake the level of systematic observation that Bowlby required.

The original formulation of attachment theory is the joint work of Bowlby and Mary Ainsworth. Bowlby formulated the basic principles of the theory, and in so doing he revolutionised psychological thinking about the mother–child bond and the consequences of its disruption through separation, bereavement and deprivation. Ainsworth's contributions are associated with the development of a novel approach to testing some of Bowlby's ideas and thereby expanding and modifying attachment theory. Mary Ainsworth (née Salter) completed her graduate studies at the University of Toronto just before the Second World War and, like Bowlby, her professional career was shaped in part by a period of war service – in her case with the Canadian Women's Army Corps. She accompanied her husband Leonard to London, by which time James Robertson had amassed two years of data at Bowlby's clinic. She was offered a position involving the analysis of Robertson's data.

Bowlby considered that neither the psychoanalytic theories of the time, nor the claims of social learning that mother–child dependency is based on secondary reinforcement, could adequately explain why children needed a close and continuous care-giving relationship in order to thrive. The new field of ethology appeared to provide a framework that captured the observational data collected by Robertson. Robert Hinde provided him with the opportunity to master ethological principles, while Bowlby provided Hinde with new ideas to pursue his studies of individual differences in the separation and reunion behaviours of rhesus monkey mother–infant pairs. Harry Harlow's work on the development of affectional systems in rhesus monkeys was another strong influence, chiefly his claim that infantile attachment is not due to a learned drive, as had been suggested by both **Freud** and **Hull**. Bowlby was particularly interested in cybernetics, the science of communication and control in animals and machines. He replaced Freud's concept of *trieb* (which roughly means 'drive') with that of cybernetically controlled behavioural systems – the idea that complex behaviour is organised as a hierarchy of plans for performing simple behaviours. Attachment behaviours regulated by such systems need not be rigidly innate but can adapt, to varying degrees, to changes in environmental circumstances. Bowlby's first formal statements on attachment theory appear in three classic papers: 'The nature of the child's tie to his mother' (1958), 'Grief and mourning in infancy and early childhood' (1960) and 'Separation anxiety' (1960). The latter challenged Anna Freud's suggestion that bereaved infants cannot mourn because they are not sufficiently ego-developed. His claim that grief and mourning processes appear (in children and adults) whenever attachment behaviours are activated but the attachment figure continues to be unavailable attracted the attention of the psychiatrist Colin Parkes, who was well known for work on adult bereavement. Parkes joined Bowlby's unit at the Tavistock Institute, and his interviews with widows led to a joint paper with Bowlby in which the phases of separation response delineated by James Robertson for young children were elaborated into four phases of grief during adult life: numbness, yearning and protest, disorganisation and despair, and finally reorganisation.

Ainsworth, although an advocate of ethological methods, considered some of its theoretical positions on parent–child relationships to miss a key point, namely that a baby loves its mother because she satisfies its needs. Ainsworth is credited with developing a somewhat controversial research procedure, the Strange Situation, originally designed to examine attachment and exploratory behaviours in one-year-olds. The procedure is structured as eight episodes in which the mother and her baby are first introduced to a playroom. After some time they are joined by a stranger. The stranger plays with the infant and, during this episode, the mother leaves for a brief period. A second separation ensues during which mother and stranger leave – the baby is alone. After a short time they both return. The controversy with this seemingly innocuous procedure related to the level of distress exhibited by some children.

Ainsworth's early contributions to collaborative work with Bowlby centred on the development of a system for classifying three basic relationship patterns in school-age children who had been reunited with their parents after prolonged separation: those with strong positive feelings towards their mothers, those who showed ambivalent feelings and those who manifested either indifferent or hostile feelings.

Bowlby's attachment theory is based on an integration of concepts drawn from ethology, sociobiology, psychobiology, the cybernetic theory of control systems and a structural approach to cognitive development. He considered that complex behavioural systems of the kind he proposed can be used with prescience in animals capable of constructing internal representations of the environment and of their own actions within it. The basic explanatory principle of attachment theory is that humans are biologically predisposed to forming and maintaining attachment relationships with their primary caregivers. For Bowlby, attachment is any form of behaviour that results in a person achieving proximity to some other preferred individual. Attachment behaviour is distinct from other categories of behaviour such as feeding and sexual behaviour, but of equal importance to these. Attachment behaviour leads to the development of affectional bonds, first between child and parent and later between adult and adult. Mothering is a two-way process based on love, responsiveness and continuity. Fathering he considered usually to play a supporting role to mothering, and the family context enables the child–mother relationship to thrive. Attachments between mother and child are formed more readily within a developmentally sensitive period that commences around the third month after birth and lasts into the third year: 'No variables have more far-reaching effects on personality development than a child's experiences within the family. Starting during his first months in his relation to both parents, he builds up working models of how attachment figures are likely to behave towards him in any of a variety of situations, and on all those models are based all his expectations, and therefore all his plans, for the rest of his life' (1973: 369).

The formation, maintenance and disruption of attachment relationships are sources of intense emotional experience. Attachment behaviour contributes to the individual's survival by keeping the child close to his/her caretakers. Behaviour complementary to attachment behaviour and serving in a complementary function is care-giving (mothering). Attachment behaviour is potentially active throughout life. Disturbed patterns of attachment behaviour can be present at any age; and one of the commonest disturbance is anxious attachment. The principal determinants of a person's attachment behaviour are the experiences with attachment figures during childhood and adolescence. An adult's attachment behaviour affects the kinds of affectional bonds desired with other adults. Thus, social cycles may preserve styles of attachment between generations.

Bowlby's belief in the importance of mothering has led to nearly fifty years of controversial debate. Feminists, for example, have sometimes argued that his ideas constitute a subtle form of anti-feminism. A related contention is that, by placing such an enormous emphasis on early mother–child relationships, mothers can all too easily become cultural scapegoats for a range of political, social and economic failings. It has also been argued that some of the claims of attachment theory are too simple because they fail to take proper account of the full complexity of each child's life. Notwithstanding these criticisms, the scale of attachment theory is such that many of its predictions have yet to be adequately tested. More recent work on different kinds of attachment behaviour, for example on fathering, sibling attachments and grandparenting, has led to elaborations and refinements to attachment theory, rather than to its rejection.

John Bowlby's major writings

Forty-four Juvenile Thieves, Balliere, Tindall and Cox, 1946.
Child Care and the Growth of Love, Penguin, 1953.
'The nature of the child's tie to his mother', International Journal of Psychoanalysis, 1958, 39, 350–73.
'Grief and mourning in infancy and early childhood', The Psychoanalytic Study of the Child, 1960, 15, 3–39.
'Separation anxiety', International Journal of Psychoanalysis, 1960, 41, 89–113.
Attachment and Loss, Volume 1: Attachment, Basic Books, 1969.
The Making and Breaking of Affectional Bonds, Methuen, 1970.
Attachment and Loss, Volume 2: Separation, Basic Books, 1973.
Attachment and Loss, Volume 3: Loss, Sadness and Depression, Basic Books, 1980.

Further reading

Belsky, J. and Newworski, T. (1988) Clinical Applications of Attachment, Erlbaum.
Bretherton, I. (1992) 'The origins of attachment theory: John Bowlby and Mary Ainsworth', Developmental Psychology, 28, 759–75.
Hinde, R. A. (1991) 'Relationships, attachment and culture: a tribute to John Bowlby', Infant Mental Health Journal, 12, 154–63.
Rycroft, C. (1985) Psychoanalysis and Beyond, Chatto and Windus.

BROADBENT, DONALD ERIC (1926–93)

Broadbent used experimental methods to understand and enhance human behaviour in a wide range of settings, particularly through his work on selective attention.

Donald E. Broadbent was born in Birmingham, the son of an executive in a British-based multinational company who left both the company and his family at the start of the Second World War. For the early part of the war Donald lived with his mother in the small Welsh village of Llandyman and later they moved to Mould. His mother supported them with income as a clerical assistant in local business offices. He was educated at Winchester College, the fees being paid from his father's pension fund, an 'exhibition' and a school bursary. He enlisted for military service in 1944 and his RAF training was undertaken in North America, where he first encountered the subject of psychology – then largely unheard of by most young people in England. He was drawn to considering the problems that can arise when people are required to work with complex technologies and this motivated a switch from engineering to psychology. Thus he was originally attracted to psychology by the need to design technological environments suitable for human use. Throughout his career he remained committed to the idea that psychologists should develop sound theories capable of delivering applications that could be used in the public interest, and he provided numerous powerful demonstrations of how attempts to solve practical problems can motivate and inform theoretical innovation. The Cambridge Department of Psychology, headed by **Bartlett**, was a particularly appropriate place for someone with such interests. The admissions committee at Pembroke College was sure that he should study for a degree in chemistry but, after much persuasion, relented.

Wartime work on developing applications of cognitive psychology for resolving user-technology problems had led in 1944 to the foundation of the Medical Research Council's Applied Psychology Unit at Cambridge. On graduation, Broadbent joined the Unit and commenced work on topics relating to the influence of environmental stressors on human cognitive performance, a constant theme of his career. In 1958 he became its director, and over the next sixteen years he shaped the Unit, creating an enduring blend of pure and applied research.

Broadbent married Margaret E. Wright in 1949, and they had two daughters before the marriage was dissolved in 1972. He married Margaret Gregory (who had been married to Richard **Gregory**) in the same year. A couple of years later Broadbent moved to Oxford to pursue his own work without the administrative responsibilities of the Unit. Much of this work was conducted in collaboration with his second wife. The death of his daughter Liz, following a road accident in 1979, had an enduring impact on his life and almost certainly contributed in part to his renunciation of his previously strong Christian faith (Weiskrantz, 1994).

Broadbent was trained in Cambridge at a time when the influences of Alan Turing, an intellectual pioneer of artificial intelligence, and the gifted experimentalist Kenneth Craik, created an atmosphere sympathetic to his interests in designing technological environments suitable for human use and to the idea of explaining human behaviour in terms of the computational processes that must be undertaken by any system that behaves as people do. Although Craik had died in a road accident just before Broadbent arrived, the influence of his thinking on cybernetic and hierarchical control systems was well established. During the 1950s Broadbent worked on a variety of applied problems, first on the effects of noise on cognitive performance and then on the difficulties of handling a large number of speech messages simultaneously. These problems were readily handled in terms of the conceptual frameworks due to Craik, Turing, Bartlett and other influences on the Cambridge group; but they were problematic to handle in the terminology current in psychology laboratories at that time. Consequently he encountered some difficulty in publishing early work in the mainstream academic journals. His work on auditory selective attention (the perception of some stimuli in the environment relative to other stimuli of less immediate priority) was seminal for two reasons. First, it provided a methodology for investigating the psychology of attention at a time when behaviourism had rejected attempts to investigate such phenomena. Second, it exploited new information-processing concepts being developed in mathematics and engineering to develop a model of human cognition that would prove both theoretically sound and useful in practical matters.

Perception and Communication (1958) summarised many of the results obtained in his own laboratory and in a variety of others. Broadbent adopted an information processing framework and argued for its advantages over statements about the connections between stimuli and responses. The publication of the book proved timely and it became widely quoted by psychologists who were turning to a cybernetic, information processing, or cognitive approach to explaining human behaviour. The book set the agenda for what subsequently became known as cognitive psychology, and it is probably the contribution for which he is best known. It is often not fully recognised that the perspective proposed in the book was a by-product of research undertaken for applied reasons. This reflects an important feature of the individuality of his contribution: he demonstrated that psychological theory is best when grounded in the empirical analysis of practical problems.

A central theme of *Perception and Communication* is that a person undertaking several tasks might experience interference between the central processes involved in each of them, that it could be reduced by practise, and that in some cases certain tasks are selected rather than others by a 'filtering' mechanism. The conception was however determinate and, like many psychologists at that time, Broadbent thought of one internal event as succeeding another in a straightforward causal fashion. During the 1960s he and others produced a great deal of evidence to indicate that the central processes are not like that; on the contrary, each momentary event 'inside' a person is only statistically related to the things that have happened before; so that stable and efficient behaviour depends on the averaging of many separate processes. From this perspective, errors become very important as a way of sorting out the details of the process; it is also in principle impossible ever to eliminate human error totally. These arguments altered quite considerably conceptualisations of attention and workload and a number of questions were raised about the role of probability and motivation in perception. The revised views were presented in *Decision and Stress* (1971) but this had less impact than *Perception and Communication*. Broadbent attributed this to a failure of presentation and communication on his part and not to problems with the underlying arguments and evidence. In subsequent work, he continued to be concerned to argue against psychological theories that assume determinate and separate mechanisms of cognition. He argued that it was hopeless to attempt to find 'the' mechanism by which any particular psychological task is performed. Different people perform the same task differently, and the same person may perform it differently on different occasions. This led to his arguing for two lines of attack in psychology: first, the need to study the implications of one strategy of cognition rather than another; which ways of thinking show which kinds of advantages and disadvantages? Second, one should look at the external circumstances that cause one strategy to be adopted rather than another.

This change of emphasis coincided with a change in the practical needs of society; away from quick-fix cures for problems created by particular technological devices that have been badly made, to a demand for a more planned approach to the design of devices that might not be constructed for a long time ahead. Thus his move from the Applied Psychology Unit to Oxford afforded opportunities to demonstrate that the gradual accumulation of evidence from laboratory experiments on different styles of attention and memory could be linked to lengthy life experiences of the individual in the world outside. These efforts took him through the 1970s and into the 1980s and produced a number of important detailed findings, including evidence that people in certain kinds of jobs develop certain psychiatric symptoms. The kinds of symptoms that develop depend on the particular characteristics of the job, and the process is linked to particular individual patterns of selective attention that the person can be shown to display in the laboratory. Thus, in later years he addressed the effects of powerful, pervasive social stressors in the working environment. As part of this work he developed the Cognitive Failures Questionnaire, a widely used measure of absent-mindedness. His broad research interests – attention and memory, perception, stress, individual differences in temperament, occupational health and copying styles – address problems and applications which are related through an underlying theoretical fabric. In lighter moments, he would suggest that he was trying to contribute to establishing a new topic which he called 'Dyccop': Dynamic Cognitive Clinical Occupational Psychology.

Broadbent was firmly convinced that the test of the intellectual excellence of a psychological theory, as well as its moral justification, lies in its application to practical considerations. Moreover, psychology could clarify many of its major questions by considering the resemblances between all adaptive systems – whether mechanical, electronic or social. He applied this view in his assessment of his own contribution to psychology: ' ... at the end of a career, it is worth realising that the advance of knowledge is actually a network, not a single module, the interaction between individuals reduces the damage done by the errors of any one and the continual review of past outputs makes the final symbolic formulation increasingly accurate' (1973: 59–60).

Donald Broadbent's major writings

'A mechanical model for human attention and immediate memory', *Psychological Review*, 1957, 64, 205–15.
Perception and Communication, Pergamon, 1958.
Behaviour, Eyre & Spottiswood, 1961.
Decision and Stress, Academic Press, 1971.
In Defence of Empirical Psychology, Methuen, 1973.
'The Maltese Cross: A new simplistic model for memory', *Brain and Behavioral Sciences*, 1984, 7, 55–94.
'Implicit and explicit knowledge in the control of complex systems', *British Journal of Psychology*, 1986, 77, 33–50 (with P. Fitzgerald and M. H. P. Broadbent).

Further reading

Baddeley, A. and Weiskrantz, L. (eds) (1993) *Attention: Selection, awareness, and control: A tribute to Donald Broadbent*, Clarendon Press/Oxford University Press.
Weiskrantz, L. (1994) 'Donald Eric Broadbent', *Biographical Memoirs of Fellows of the Royal Society*, 40, 33–42.

BRUNER, JEROME SEYMOUR (1915–)

Bruner developed and applied a theory of cognition that focuses on the role of cultural, environmental and experiential factors in shaping the way people perceive and think about themselves in the context of the world in which they live.

Born the son of a New York watch manufacturer, Bruner was little more than a toddler when he underwent a series of cataract operations to repair his vision. After his father Herman died, when Bruner was twelve, his mother, Rose, moved the family from place to place and, despite the fact that his education was punctuated by several changes of school, he passed sufficient grades to enrol for a degree at Duke University, where he took William McDougall's courses in social psychology. After graduating, he worked on propaganda and popular attitudes for US Army intelligence with the social psychologist Rensis Likert, an associate of **Lewin**, and with the sociologist Hadley Cantril, noted for his work in public opinion and his study of people's reactions to Orson Welles's infamous 1938 'War of The Worlds' broadcast. For a time he was stationed at General Dwight D. Eisenhower's headquarters in France. While working on his doctorate he married Katherine Frost, and they had a son and daughter before the marriage was dissolved in 1956. After completing his Ph.D. at Harvard, where he was supervised by **Allport**, he became a member of the Harvard faculty. In 1960 he married Blanche Marshall McLane (the marriage was dissolved in 1984), and he co-founded, with George Miller, and directed the Center for Cognitive Studies. He left Harvard in 1972 to teach at Oxford University, returning as a Harvard visiting professor in 1979. Two years later he joined the faculty of the new School for Social Research in New York City, where he stayed until 1987, in which year he married Carol Fleisher Feldman, before moving to New York University.

During the 1940s Bruner and Leo Postman worked on the ways in which 'mental sets' (needs, motivations and expectations) affect perception. Their 'New Look' approach, as it was sometimes labelled, contrasted a functional perspective on perception and problem-solving with the prevailing view that treated perception as a stand-alone process that could be examined separately from the world around it. For example, in one of their studies they showed children toys and blocks of equal height, and demonstrated that the children, expecting toys to be larger than blocks, thought the toys were taller. In further studies of mental sets they used a tachistoscope to show adults brief views of playing cards. Some of these were contrived, such as a red ace of spades. Provided participants were not alerted to their presence, they reported seeing what they expected to see – in this case a black ace of spades.

Bruner's work in cognitive psychology led to an interest in the cognitive development and related issues of education, and during the 1960s he developed a theory that focuses on the role of cultural, environmental and experiential factors influencing each individual's specific development pattern. His contributions to the development of thinking are anchored around the notion that the major activity of human beings involves extracting meanings from their encounters with the world. Modes of representation are crucial here – they are the tools through which the child learns meaning. The ordered development of three modes of representation (enactive, iconic and symbolic) is central to his theory of cognitive development. While later modes depend on earlier ones, they do not comprise developmental stages. As we grow older we do not lose or out-grow earlier representational forms for making and interpreting meaning; we retain them and can use all three in different situations. Bruner's is an active view of mind that contrasts with nativist positions (knowledge matures and is triggered by events and experiences) and information processing theories (knowledge is acquired as developmental constraints are lifted and as memory and language expand).

Knowledge is active and functional, and it requires a social or cultural context.

In *Beyond the Information Given* (1973), Bruner offers the first systematic analysis of the idea that concept formation is based on the generation of hypotheses about the attributes of the concept in question. Concepts are important because they simplify environmental variability and make it easier to know how to act and to predict the consequences of action. Concept formation involves learning that there are classes of things, and the process of forming concepts is predominant in human development until early adolescence; thereafter, concept attainment becomes more important. Certain cognitive strategies are used to ensure concepts are acquired quickly. In order to explore concept formation in detail, Bruner developed a task based on eighty-one cards with printed geometric shapes in which participants were given feedback as they attempted to identify a pattern of cards that was hidden from view. This allowed the study of artificial concepts, because the cards had four dimensions, each with three values. Using this task he identified four selection strategies for the attainment of conjunctive concepts: simultaneous scanning, successive scanning, conservative focusing and focus gambling. It was generally thought that the interpretation of the findings was relatively straightforward: acquiring the artificial hypotheses is based on a hypothesis-testing approach in which people choose among a range of alternative strategies, and by choosing a particular strategy they engage in cognitive operations that would not otherwise have been active. However, by the mid-1980s there was a growing body of evidence that suggested that the use of different strategies did not influence the nature of the cognitive operations taking place, only the amount of information that had to be retained. Other studies suggested that people acquire artificial concepts, not by making a random choice among the available strategies, but by creating a mental representation of the problem and testing a hypothesis against observed events. In addition, alternative approaches that focused on natural categories suggested that many concepts do not have defining features. (A defining feature is an aspect of a concept that is a necessary or sufficient feature to admit specific instances into the concept.) For example, the concept 'car' cannot include as defining features tyres, a steering wheel and an internal combustion engine, because lorries and buses also have these features. Moreover, in many real-world situations the absence of defining features makes it very difficult to determine which instances should be included in concepts and which excluded. For example, in some circumstances distinguishing between people who are 'alive' and those who are 'dead' can pose considerable difficulties for the medical profession.

Bruner has been at the forefront of the cultural psychology movement, a thesis that has its philosophical origins in the work of the German romantic philosopher Johann Gottfried von Herder. Herder was particularly influential in developing a philosophy concerning the relationships between language and thought, and in formulating modern hermeneutics − otherwise known as interpretation theory. Bruner developed Herder's thesis: that to be in a cultural group implies thinking and acting in a certain way, and so culture is crucially important in shaping language and cognition. For Bruner, culture provides amplification systems for each mode of representation: enactive, iconic and symbolic. Thus he talks about amplifiers of action (e.g. hammers, levers and wheels), amplifiers of senses, ways of looking (e.g. pictures, diagrams), and amplifiers of thinking (e.g. language, logic and mathematics). Culture and cognitive development are closely linked, and a theory of development must include a theory of instruction that can relate the ordering of cultural amplifiers to the developmental sequence of the three representational modes. In exploring the social and cultural origins of the self Bruner developed an interpretive perspective on folk psychology in which he argues that each culture generates narratives about how people are, how and why they act, and how they deal with trouble. These narratives typically depict a canonical state of things and a deviation from that state, and are useful in making these deviations comprehensible.

Although the worlds we live in are symbolic constructions, and there are many possible worlds, Bruner regards the constructive activities themselves as reflecting universal properties of mind. This position sets him apart from traditional cognitive psychologists who, he argues, have failed to address the concept of the self adequately; he maintains that self-concept is inseparable from an elaboration of human meaning. Cultural context, the symbolic world of shared meaning, is composed of the vocabulary and linguistic peculiarities of the self-in-context. Some commentators (e.g. Greenfield, 1990) have pointed out that intentionality is another theme running throughout much of his work. Intentionality refers to the property of 'aboutness', such as beliefs, knowledge of hopes about someone or something. For example, in his analysis of the developmental psychology of poverty, Bruner suggests that children living in poverty lack the confidence to make means−end relations that are characteristic of purposive, goal-oriented or intentional behaviour. His views on language acquisition include the idea that the intentionality characteristic of speech antedates the development of speech itself. This means, for example, that infants know a great deal about communication, such as how to get the attention of someone, before they can speak. Thus, for Bruner, a child's mastery of language is founded on the development of an understanding that interactions between themselves and others are intentional. A great deal of the communication between children and their caregivers has the quality of intentionality that one would expect to see in any meaningful interaction between a learner and his/her tutor.

Bruner was often critical of psychology's approach to culture as reflected in its preference to understand the causal principles of human biology and human evolution by studying memory, thinking, perception and so on in a 'pure' form. He considered that the next chapter in psychology should pay greater attention to the subtle interplay of biology and culture.

Jerome Bruner's major writings

A Study of Thinking, Wiley, 1956 (with J. Goodnow and G. Austin).
The Process of Education, Harvard University Press, 1960.
On Knowing: Essays for the Left Hand, Belknap, 1962.
Toward a Theory of Instruction, Belknap, 1966
Processes of Cognitive Growth, Clark University Press, 1968.
Poverty and Childhood, Merrill-Palmer Institute, 1970.
Beyond the Information Given: Studies in the Psychology of Knowing, Norton, 1973 (co-edited with J. M. Anglin).
Child's Talk, Norton, 1983.
Actual Minds, Possible Worlds, Harvard University Press, 1986.
Acts of Meaning, Harvard University Press, 1990.

Further reading

Fiske, S. T. (1992) 'Thinking is for doing: portraits of social cognition from daguerreotype to laserphoto', *Journal of Personality and Social Psychology*, 63, 877–89.
Gopnik, A. (1990) 'Knowing, doing, and talking: the Oxford years', *Human Development*, 33, 334–8.
Greenfield, P. (1990) 'Jerome Bruner: the Harvard years', *Human Development*, 33, 327–33.
Olson, D. R. (1990) 'Possible minds: reflections on Bruner's recent writings on mind and self', *Human Development*, 33, 339–43.

CANNON, WALTER BRADFORD (1871–1945)

Cannon formulated a theory of emotions that was central to one of the great debates of twentieth-century psychology.

The province of Ulster was settled by large numbers of Scottish and English Protestants during the seventeenth century, but harsh economic conditions prompted many to migrate to North America. So it was for the family of Samuel Carnahan, a Scottish farmer living in the valley of the River Bann, who set out in 1718 to pursue a better life in Blanford, Massachusetts. The Scots–Ulster vernacular pronunciation of 'Carnahan' is phonetically similar to 'cannon'; thus the family name was transformed. One of Samuel's grandsons, Stephen, moved the family to land acquired in Aurora, Ohio. Stephen's fifth child, Lucius, was a storekeeper in Madison, Wisconsin, and later in Milwaukee. One of Lucius's sons, Colbert, was a newsboy and later a manager of newsboys on the Chicago, Milwaukee and St. Paul railroad. Walter Bradford was born in Prairie du Chein a year after Colbert's marriage to Wilma Denio, followed by three sisters, Bernice May, Ida Maude and Jane Laura. Wilma died of pneumonia on New Year's Eve, 1881, soon after giving birth to a fourth daughter who died some weeks later. Colbert was shattered.

Bouts of depression dating from a head injury Colbert sustained in 1871 made the Cannon household a fairly gloomy place. Marriage to Caroline Mower, eighteen months after Wilma's death, was motivated by Colbert's desire to secure a housekeeper and stepmother for his children. With Caroline taking care of his children Colbert found more time to pursue his dream – to be a physician. Without a shred of medical training, save for what he could glean from such medical texts as he could find, he established a practice from home from where experimental treatments were offered free of charge to friends and neighbours and inflicted on his own family. Determined that his children should be self-sufficient, he concocted all manner of makeshift scheme, including a do-it-yourself chick-rearing enterprise, intended to encourage them to learn to be independent. Paradoxically, he stopped Walter's formal education on his fourteenth birthday and sent him to work in a railroad office. After two years, Walter persuaded his father that he should return to school, and in 1888 he entered St. Paul High School where he completed a four-year course in three years. However, his time at the railroad office left its mark, for thereafter he was a stickler for punctuality.

Cannon enrolled at Harvard to pursue studies in arts and social science, and it was as an undergraduate that he first encountered William **James**, who at that time was head of Harvard's philosophy department. He considered changing to a career in philosophy and physiology, but James advised against this and Cannon entered the Medical School in 1896. Working in Henry Bowditch's laboratory, he began a series of innovative investigations in which he used the newly discovered 'X-rays' to non-invasively study the mechanism of swallowing and the motility of the stomach, and devised the use of radiopaque chemical (barium sulphate, an inert inorganic salt) for investigation of the gastrointestinal system. He was appointed to Harvard's Department of Physiology in 1900, promoted to assistant professor in 1902 and, when Bowditch retired in 1906, succeeded him as Higginson Professor, a position he retained until 1942. By the mid-1930s, Cannon had conspicuous X-ray burns to the skin of his face, hands, arms and thighs, and he died from leukaemia, in Franklin, New Hampshire. He suspected that his terminal illness was linked to his exposure to X-rays and requested that an autopsy be performed and the evidence be published so that others might benefit from the findings.

Cannon's impact on psychology commenced in May 1909, shortly after James's letter to the Vivisection Reform Society of New York, in which he criticised the values, standards and practices involving animal experimentation, appeared in the *New York Post*, and later the *Boston Evening Transcript*. Cannon and James were in sharp disagreement, not only on the issue of animal experimentation but also on the nature of emotion. Cannon's early work on the physiological effects of emotions included studies of the effects of trauma to the nervous system caused by haemorrhaging. This led him to suggest that the action of the adrenal glands on the sympathetic nervous system (which regulates pulse, sweating and related functions) is responsible for an animal's 'fight or flight' response. The context for this hypothesis was James's theory of emotion and that of the Danish physiologist Carl Lange, who published a similar theory, both theories coming to be referred to as the James–Lange theory of emotion. It is normally thought that a stimulus, such as news that you have won a prize, produces an emotion, such as delight, and the emotion triggers a complex physiological response, such as increased heart rate. The James–Lange theory reverses this and suggests that the stimulus triggers a response and that awareness of the physiological changes constitutes the emotion. Thus, affective reactions to stimuli are often more rapid and basic than cognitive evaluations. The James–Lange theory partly reflects Charles Darwin's view that emotions are evolved phenomena that have significant survival functions and are somewhat pre-programmed. However, whereas Darwin's focus was on the survival implications of emotions, James and Lange were mostly concerned with the relationship between physiological changes and feelings. Cannon challenged the James–Lange thesis on a number of substantive points. First, he argued that the empirical evidence from work with animals showed that the separation of the viscera from the central nervous system does not alter emotional behaviour. However, James had never claimed that all emotional feelings depend on visceral feedback and took the view that muscular feedback would be important. Thus, he countered that Cannon's physiological evidence was based on studies that did not abolish feedback from the muscles. Later studies on people with spinal injuries found a relationship between level of injury and intensity of feeling, which is consistent with the James–Lange theory. Second, Cannon showed that the experimental induction (e.g. by injections of adrenalin) of visceral changes characteristic of strong emotions does not produce those emotions.

Cannon and his student Philip Bard offered the Cannon–Bard theory of emotion as an alternative. In this view, two parts of the brain, the thalamus and the amygdala, play an essential role in interpreting an emotion-provoking situation. They simultaneously send signals to the autonomic nervous system, which is responsible for regulating respiratory, digestive and other involuntary bodily functions, and to the cerebral cortex, which is responsible for the interpretation of the particular situation. This formulation was partly influenced by Cannon's close intellectual ties with **Pavlov**, and incorporated a role for his concept of the conditional reflex. Pavlov's inclusion of sub-cortical functions, corresponding to Cannon's 'basic' emotions, into his model of higher central nervous system activity reflects a reciprocated influence. The intellectual linkages between Cannon and Pavlov extended to close personal ties: Pavlov usually stayed with the Cannons when he visited Harvard. The essential error of the Cannon–Bard theory was to posit the existence of a brain centre – supposedly located in the thalamus – for emotions. By 1937 the neuroanatomist James Papez had shown that emotion is not a function of a specific brain centre but a brain circuit involving four basic structures: the hypothalamus, the anterior thalamic nucleus, the cingulate gyrus and the hippocampus. In addition, studies by Stanley Schachter and Jerome Singer demonstrated that how a stimulus causes arousal and emotional feelings depends on how it is interpreted: identical physiological changes could be interpreted positively (e.g. as euphoria) or negatively (e.g. as fear). They showed that the meaning attributed to emotional arousal is more arbitrary than Cannon supposed, and is determined in part by chance situational factors.

Cannon's critique of the James–Lange theory of emotions sparked one of the great debates of twentieth-century psychology, and some of the contested issues were taken up by **Simon** in his work on the motivational and emotional controls of cognition. Although Cannon always felt secure when arguing with physiological evidence, he was less confident dealing with psychological concepts. For example, his 1913 presentation to the American Psychological Association attracted criticism for its brief treatment of psychological issues, although it also included an important acknowledgement of the influence of William McDougall on his thinking. McDougall developed what he called 'hormic psychology' to refer to a position that emphasised the purposive nature of behaviour, as reflected in the importance of instincts and the adaptive significance of emotions. Troubled by this criticism, Cannon made a conscious effort to spend more time discussing his ideas with the Harvard psychologists, but was disappointed with what he perceived to be little more than polite expressions of interest and encouragement. Eager to secure more thorough critical analysis he solicited detailed, and generally supportive, responses from Hugo Münsterberg and James McKeen Cattell.

Cannon's formulation of stress and homeostasis, described in *The Wisdom of the Body* (1932), is another enduring contribution. Homeostasis, from the Greek words for 'same' and 'steady', refers to any process that organisms use to actively maintain stable conditions necessary for survival. Cannon introduced it as a description for a dynamic process, such as how the human body maintains steady levels of temperature and other vital conditions, that had been discovered some seventy years earlier by the French physician Claude Bernard. Homeostatic reactions are the involuntary actions of a normally functioning system. A steady state or homeostasis may be maintained by many systems operating together. For example, blushing is an automatic response to heating: the skin reddens because its small blood vessels automatically expand to bring more heated blood close to the surface where it can cool. Negative feedback is a central homeostatic concept and refers to a situation where an organism automatically opposes any change imposed upon it. If a person's temperature rises to about 107 degrees Fahrenheit, for example, negative feedback systems stop operating. Processes designed to cool the body, such as sweating, cease to function and this leads to further temperature increases. The total system, being out of control, may cease to function, resulting in death. The concept of homeostasis has been taken up more generally throughout the behavioural and social sciences.

Cannon also published pioneering work on chemical neurotransmission; his 'sympathins 1 and 2' are now known as adrenaline and noradrenaline. Studies conducted during the 1920s and 1930s had shown that injected adrenaline caused the heart to beat faster (tachycardia) as well as an increase in blood pressure. The 'anti-adrenaline' drugs of the day reversed the rise in blood pressure, but did not affect the tachycardia. Cannon's sympathin theory attempted to explain these findings by proposing that certain unidentified molecules, sympathins E and I, combined with the adrenergic transmitters to produce an active substance in the cells: sympathin E was thought to cause excitatory actions, and sympathin I was supposed to cause inhibitory ones. Although there was no empirical evidence to support the existence of sympathins E and I, sympathin theory was generally well regarded into the 1940s.

Cannon's work on digestion led to a 1920 nomination for a Nobel Prize, but this was ruled out as coming too late. He was judged prize-worthy by the Nobel panel in 1934, 1935 and 1936, though he did not receive a prize.

Walter Cannon's major writings

'The influence of emotional states on the functions of the alimentary canal', *American Journal of the Medical Sciences*, 1909, 137, 480–7.
'The interrelations of emotions as suggested by recent physiological researches', *American Journal of Psychology*, 1914, 15, 256–82.
'Studies on the conditions of activity in endocrine glands: V. The isolated heart as an indicator of adrenal secretion induced by pain, asphyxia and excitement', *American Journal of Physiology*, 1919, 50, 399–432.
'The James–Lange theory of emotions: a critical examination and an alternative', *American Journal of Psychology*, 1927, 39, 106–24.
Bodily Changes in Pain, Hunger, Fear and Rage, Branford, 1929.
The Wisdom of the Body, Norton, 1932 (revised and enlarged, 1960).
'Stress and strains of homeostasis', *American Journal of the Medical Sciences*, 1939, 189, 1–14.
Autonomic Neuro-effector Systems, Macmillan, 1935 (with A. Rosenbleuth).

Further reading

Benison, S., Barger, A. C. and Wolfe, E. L. (1987) *Walter B. Cannon: The Life and Times of a Young Scientist*, Harvard University Press.
Schachter, S. and Singer, J. E. (1962) 'Cognitive, social and physiological determinants of emotional states', *Psychological Review*, 69, 379–99.
Wolfe, E. L., Barger, A. C. and Benison, S. (2000) *Walter B. Cannon: Science and Society*, Harvard University Press.

CATTELL, RAYMOND BERNARD (1905–98)

Cattell applied advanced statistical techniques to make fundamental contributions to the measurement and understanding of the structure of personality and ability.

Raymond B. Cattell was the second of three sons. His father (a mechanical engineer) and grandfather were owner-managers of several manufacturing plants. Born near Birmingham, the Cattell family moved to a seaside Devonshire town when Raymond was six, a lifestyle change that was to give him a lifelong love of the sea. He won a scholarship to attend Torquay Boys' Grammar School and, at the age of fifteen, he passed the university entrance examination. By nineteen he had gained a degree in chemistry from the University of London. Later he heard of the work of Sir Cyril Burt and of **Galton**, and this partly influenced his decision to study psychology. He registered for a doctorate, with Francis Aveling as his supervisor, and worked on the Subjective Character of Cognition and the Pre-sensational Development of Perception. On completion of his Ph.D. he secured a three-year position as lecturer at Exeter, during which time he married a childhood friend, Monica Rogers, and they had one son before the marriage was dissolved at about the time Cattell was appointed Director of the City Polytechnic Clinic in Leicester. During his time at Exeter, Cattell completed an MA in education from London. His dissertation, *Temperament Tests and Perseveration*, was his first attempt systematically to articulate his ideas on the structure of personality. He produced his first test of temperament the following year.

Thorndike offered him a research position at Columbia Universtity, and the following year, 1938, he was offered the G. Stanley Hall professorship at Clark University. Although the records of Barnard College, a constituent institution of Columbia University, indicate that he taught a course in experimental psychology there, Harry Hollingworth, founder of Barnard's psychology department, recalled that it was an assistant who actually designed and delivered the course. In 1941 Cattell moved to a lectureship at Harvard, and this brought him into contact with **Allport**, Henry Murray, co-developer of the thematic apperception test, and other personality theorists. It also afforded contact with the mathematical psychology of S. S. Stevens, who was establishing Harvard's Psycho-Acoustic Laboratory, a facility that did a good deal of military research on noise reduction and communications in combat vehicles and aircraft, and which trained many eminent scientists including George Miller and J. C. R. Licklider, an intellectual pioneer of the Internet. Three years later, Cattell accepted a research professorship at the University of Illinois, where he remained until his retirement in 1973. Soon after joining the Illinois faculty he married Karen Schuettler, a mathematician who later assisted him with mathematical and statistical aspects of his work. They had three daughters and a son. After his retirement from Illinois he spent five years conducting research at Colorado, and then took an unpaid professorial and advisory position at the University of Hawaii. The latter was partly motivated by a worsening heart condition that necessitated moving to a low-altitude residence. Karen remained in Illinois, directing the commercially successful Institute for Personality and Ability Testing. After settling in Hawaii, Cattell married Heather Birkett, a clinical psychologist, and continued to publish on a regular basis.

Cattell made fundamental contributions to our understanding of ability and the structure of personality. He defined personality as that which predicts what a person will do in a given situation. The implication in this definition is that we cannot define personality more fully until we define the concepts we plan to use in our investigations. He distinguished three methods for studying personality: bivariate (the analysis of two variables at a time); multivariate (the analysis of multiple variables simultaneously); and clinical. Cattell was critical of the bivariate approach because he considered that it could not adequately address the complexity of relationships among the many factors that make up personality. The clinical approach he regarded as useful because it permits observation of important behaviours as they occur. In combination, the multivariate and clinical approaches can describe and help us understand complex patterns of behaviour. In his investigations of personality he developed four research techniques. In P-technique, a person's scores on a number of measures are compared across different situations and over time. This was developed partly as a response to Allport's criticism that Cattell relied too much on statistical analysis of capacious data sets and neglected the analysis of individuals. Q-technique permits people to be correlated on a large number of different measures. With R-technique a large number of people are compared in terms of their scores or performance on a large number of specific measures. Differential-R technique involves taking measures of people on different occasions and examining the changes and similarities.

Traits (or 'predispositions') are fundamental to Cattell's theory of personality. Like Allport, Cattell focused on the systematic description and structural analysis of traits and was less concerned with theorising upon their origins. How many traits are there? Allport identified about 18,000 different trait terms in the English lexicon, clearly too many to conceptualise individual differences in personality. During the 1940s Cattell initiated a search for a more parsimonious universal structure, mostly using factor analysis and related statistical techniques. (Factor analysis examines the associations between a large number of variables with the aim of reducing them to a smaller number of underlying dimensions or factors.) He distinguished between two kinds of traits. The first is composed of ability traits, temperament traits and dynamic traits, and the second of surface traits and source traits. Ability traits relate to skills and abilities, and this group includes intelligence. Temperament traits relate to the emotional life of a person, while dynamic traits relate to a person's motivational life. Surface traits refer to behaviours that appear to co-vary at a superficial level but which do not necessarily have a common cause. Source traits refer to behaviours that co-vary and form a unitary, independent dimension of personality. Surface traits can be identified by clinical investigation and by asking people which characteristics they think go together, but source traits can only be discovered using multivariate statistical techniques.

Cattell began by applying his experience of factor analysis to the problems of personality structure, using three kinds of data-ratings, questionnaires and objective behavioural measures. This work resulted in the 16PF questionnaire series (16PF, HSPQ, CPQ, ESXO) and in the OA (Objective Analytic) personality battery. In support of his structural account of personality Cattell cited several sources of evidence: factor analysis of different kinds of data; replication across cultures; similarity of findings across age groups; usefulness in predicting behaviour; and evidence for a genetic contribution to many traits. In order to explicate the contributions of genetic and environmental factors to personality, he developed multiple abstract variance analysis which was a significant advance on traditional techniques of the time. He was a strong critic of racial bias in tests, and was acutely aware of the impact of cultural forces on psychological assessment instruments.

According to Cattell, abilities are organised hierarchically. At the top of the hierarchy is 'g', or general ability. Below 'g' are successive levels of gradually narrowing abilities, terminating with **Spearman**'s specific abilities. Cattell argued, with supporting empirical evidence, that there are twenty primary abilities and six secondaries. In addition, he drew a distinction between fluid and crystallised ability. Fluid intelligence reflects an individual's ability to solve novel problems, whereas crystallised intelligence reflects the acquisition and use of culturally valued knowledge. In collaboration with J. L. Horn (1966), he argued that crystallised ability increases over the whole lifespan, whereas fluid ability increases in childhood and adolescence but decreases in later years. Along with the majority of psychometricians of the time, Cattell based his approach on the ideas that: traits are coherently structured, with specific behaviours lying at lower levels of a hierarchy; within each level of the hierarchical structure traits are stable over time; traits can be observed consistently across a wide variety of different situations and cultures; and understanding of traits at any level in the hierarchical structure makes it possible to make predictions about traits at other levels.

Critics of Cattell's theory suggest that portions of his vast theoretical structure are supported by weak empirical evidence – some of the source traits he identified have not been replicated by other researchers. It has been suggested that the reanalysis of some of his original data using more sophisticated computer hardware and more advanced statistical packages indicates that his sixteen personality factors (16PF) can be reduced to just five. In addition, the 1960s were associated with an emerging dissatisfaction with trait theories of personality that cast doubt on the validity of his four main assumptions and witnessed the popularisation of a new perspective based on cognitive social learning theory. For example, it became clear that it was often quite difficult to predict the expression of specific behaviours from measures of generalised traits. Walter Mischel dubbed the term 'personality coefficient' to characterise, or even caricature, the weak associations between questionnaire measures of a trait and the occurrence of trait-specific behaviours in particular situations. Mischel's criticisms, which were partly over-stated for polemic effect, provoked vigorous replies that have continued to the present day. Although Cattell's work and theories have been received with enthusiasm, the derivation of so much from what seem to be complex factor-analytic and advanced mathematical models has sometimes stood as a barrier to acceptance and discussion by some practitioners.

In 1997, Cattell was selected to receive the American Psychological Foundation Gold Medal Award for Lifetime Achievement in Psychological Science. This provoked a large number of widely publicised objections from critics who accused Cattell of promoting racist principles. Many of the criticisms appear to have been in response to a combination of his orthodox Darwinian views on evolution, his idiosyncratic religious beliefs – 'Beyondism', a science-based religion that embraces many concepts from sociobiology and the principle that evolution is good – and a certain English aloofness that could be mistaken for patrician arrogance. The Foundation delayed the award and established a committee to investigate the allegations. In December 1997, Cattell wrote an open letter to the APA to correct what he considered to be a multitude of misconceptions and to put an end to the personal attacks against him: 'I believe in equal opportunity for all individuals, and I abhor racism and discrimination based on race. Any other belief would be antithetical to my life's work.' At that time he was in poor health, and he died a couple of months later.

Raymond Cattell's major writings

'The main personality factors in questionnaire material', *Journal of Social Psychology*, 1950, 31, 3–38.
'P-technique: a new method for analysing personal motivation', *Transactions of the New York Academy of Sciences*, 1951, 14, 29–34.
'Refinement and test of the theory of fluid and crystallized intelligence', *Journal of Educational Psychology*, 1966, 57, 253–70 (with J. L. Horn).
Abilities: Their Structure, Growth and Action, Houghton Mifflin, 1971.
Personality and Mood by Questionnaire, Jossey Bass, 1973.
Personality and Learning Theory, Springer, 1979.
The Inheritance of Personality and Ability, Academic Press, 1982.
Beyondism: Religion from Science, Praeger, 1987.
Intelligence: Its Structure, Growth and Action, North-Holland, 1987.

Further reading

Cattell, R. B. (1974) 'Travels in psychological hyperspace', in T. S. Krawiec (ed.), *The Psychologists*, vol. 2, Oxford University Press.
Goldberg, L. R. (1990) 'An alternative "description of personality": The Big-Five factor structure', *Journal of Personality and Social Psychology*, 59, 1216–29.
Schultz, D. P. and Schultz, S. E. (1994) *Theories of Personality*, 5th edn, Brooks Cole.

CHOMSKY, AVRAM NOAM (1928–)

The most significant figure in the science of linguistics, Chomsky's ideas on the way language is structured fundamentally affected the way psychologists thought about how language is acquired and used.

Noam Chomsky's father, William (Zev), fled from Russia to the United States in 1913 in order to avoid being drafted into the Czarist army. Zev worked in sweatshops in Baltimore but managed to support himself through study at Johns Hopkins University by teaching in Baltimore Hebrew elementary schools. After moving to Philadelphia he and his wife, Elsie Simonofsky, began teaching at the religious school of the Mikveh Israel congregation, and he later became its principal. He was also appointed to the faculty of Gratz College and became its president, a position he held for thirty-seven years. Noam and his younger brother David had a remarkably varied and rich home life. The Chomsky family was actively involved in Jewish cultural activities and issues, such as the revival of the Hebrew language. His father was regarded as a leading Hebrew grammarian, and it is difficult to avoid the inference that this had a strong impact on the development of Noam's interest in linguistics. Noam was born in Philadelphia and, just before his second birthday, he was sent to Oak Lane Country Day School, an experimental unit run by Temple University, where he remained until the age of twelve. The school was strongly influenced by the ideas of the philosopher John Dewey, who favoured the development of skills that would support independent enquiry, and considered learning-by-doing to be vastly superior to the prevailing preference for formal education based on rote learning and drill. At the age of twelve, Chomsky moved to Central High School, Philadelphia. This was something of a shock: he was astonished by the importance attached to the slavish achievement of grades, and over time he came to the view that society favours institutions such as Central High because they sustain the needs of the prosperous ruling class. Later, at the University of Pennsylvania, he studied mathematics, philosophy and linguistics, and was particularly influenced by the Russian linguist Zelig Harris. Harris was one of a coterie of linguists who achieved considerable success in specifying mathematical rules for describing grammatically correct utterances. It was Harris who introduced Chomsky to psychology, principally through the works of the psychoanalysts Harry Stack-Sullivan and Karen Horney. Chomsky's B.A. thesis, 'Morphophonemics of modern Hebrew', formed the basis of much of his later work. That thesis is generally regarded as the first example of a modern generative grammar – a grammar that can predict or generate every possible grammatically correct utterance. Although Harris was familiar with Chomsky's thesis he chose not to tell him about an earlier attempt to describe a generative grammar; titled 'Menomini Morphophonemics', it was published in 1939 by the American linguist Leonard Bloomfield. Chomsky was always puzzled why neither Harris nor Henry Hoenigswald, another linguist at Pennsylvania, brought it to his attention – perhaps it was because Bloomfield's ideas were much less developed than Chomsky's.

Although Chomsky completed his B.A. thesis in 1949, it wasn't published until 1979. It was during 1949 that he married Carol Schatz – they grew up in the same Philadelphia neighbourhood. She shared many of Noam's interests in Jewish culture and history and was also a linguist who went on to a successful career which focused on the child's acquisition of language. They had three children: Diane, Avi and Harry. After graduating, Chomsky went on to complete a Ph.D. in linguistics at Pennsylvania, although most of the work was conducted at Harvard between 1951 and 1955. His doctorate, 'Transformational analysis', was a 175-page segment of an unpublished tome called *The Logical Structure of Linguistic Theory*. It was largely written for himself, although he and Carol ran off a couple of dozen copies on a hectograph and gave them to interested colleagues. The thesis was not properly published until 1975.

For Chomsky, linguistics is the study of the structure of language – all language – and a theory of language should aim to be a theory of a speaker's knowledge of a language. This is important because a speaker of a language may actually know more about their language than is revealed in what they actually speak. For example, if one recorded the day-to-day utterances of a group of people, one might conclude that they use a number of grammatical rules over and over again. However, they may be capable of understanding sentences that are constructed using quite different rules, and they may be capable of using those rules in their own speech but for one reason or another choose not to. So, for Chomsky, a theory of language must account for what people know and are capable of understanding, not just what they are observed to utter and hear. This set him on a course that would lead him to demonstrate how a limited set of grammatical rules defines the knowledge or 'competence' of a language speaker. This knowledge or 'competence' is different from what is actually spoken – Chomsky called the latter 'performance', because it refers to the grammatical structure of sentences actually spoken or 'performed' by a language user. In so doing he offered a way of thinking about language that re-vitalised ideas first espoused by the German philologist Wilhelm von Humboldt. At this point it is important to introduce a caveat. The distinction between competence and performance may seem sensible, but the suggestion that one can absolutely discriminate one from another is in fact highly contentious. Nevertheless, the influence of the competence–performance distinction is strong, and is reflected in the fact that linguistics is primarily about the analysis of competence whereas the psychology of language – 'psycholinguistics' – is about understanding processes involved in performance, such as producing and understanding speech.

Chomsky's *Syntactic Structures* (1957) introduced what has become the most influential of all modern linguistic theories: transformational generative grammar. As the name implies, there are two parts to the theory: a transformational part and a generative part. The two parts are not logically interdependent, but it was Chomsky's formulation of the interaction between the two that offered such a powerful account of language. Prior to transformational generative grammar, most theories of grammar were concerned with the analysis of sentences that involved dividing or parsing a sentence into parts (e.g. phrases) and identifying the functions of the various parts and the connections between them. The advantage of such analysis is that structured comparisons can be made between different sentences. For example, 'Ted saw Gretta' is very similar to the sentence 'Gretta saw Ted'. Phrase structure grammars are reasonably good at describing the relationship between sentences. However, phrase structure grammars run into difficulties when dealing with sentences such as: 'Ted saw Gretta', 'Gretta was seen by Ted'. These kinds of sentences suggest a need for a transformational system that can take a sentence and rearrange its parts while retaining the same meaning.

The second feature of Chomsky's grammar is that it is 'generative'. This implies two things. First, a grammar must be so designed that it is capable of predicting or specifying all possible sentences of a language. Such a grammar must be capable of specifying or predicting sentences such as 'Dan supports Liverpool' and 'Sheila saw John' as legitimate, but not 'Sheila ice-cream John' or 'supports Sheila Dan'. A generative grammar is not concerned with accounting for any sentence that has been spoken, but with any possible sentences that might ever be spoken within a particular language. This may seem like a relatively minor point, but, when Chomsky published his theory, it amounted to a serious attack on a well-established empiricist tradition that valued the sampling of spoken language – the creation of a linguistic corpus – and the systematic application of analytic procedures to that language set. Why would Chomsky see a need for such a grammar? Because it allows for recursion – the same linguistic device can be applied over and over again. Think of a very, very long sentence. When you come to the end of it, add the word 'maybe'. This is analogous to thinking of the greatest number you can possibly imagine and then adding 1. A grammar must be able to account for the reality of recursion, the fact that grammatical rules can be applied one on another to generate ever-more-complex sentences.

The second implication of a generative grammar is that it should be comprehensively explicit about all the possible sentences allowable. The generative rules of Chomsky's transformational grammar are re-write rules. This means that they re-write one symbol (or sentence) as another until eventually the complete set of symbols (or sentences) that can possibly be generated by a language are specified. The requirement to specify all the rules up-front may seem like an obvious one, but in the prevailing intellectual context of the time – one that prized the creation of rich language corpora, the systematic application of analytic procedures and the extrapolation of grammatical rules – Chomsky's approach made it patently obvious that linguists were at the mercy of whatever had been spoken somewhere by someone. They would forever produce historical grammars based on their retrospective analyses of sentences spoken or written.

Chomsky's transformational generative grammar is a system of rules that recursively define and give rise to sentence transformations. 'A generative grammar may be said to generate a set of structural descriptions, each of which, ideally, incorporates a deep structure, a surface structure, a semantic interpretation (of the deep structure) and a phonetic interpretation (of the surface structure)' (1972: 126). Transformational grammar is equivalent to Chomsky's concept of 'deep structure'. The sentence 'Katy hugged Wendy' has the same meaning as 'Wendy was hugged by Katy'. In Chomsky's distinction between 'surface structure' and 'deep structure', the former refers to the actual order of the words in a sentence whereas the latter refers to the grammatical relationships from which a sentence is generated. He used the concept of transformation rules to map the relationships between deep and surface structures in order to explain why different sequences of words could have the same meaning. He suggested that rules governing the structure of phrases generate deep structures, and the application of further transformational rules yields the final surface structures in the spoken form of a sentence.

Chomsky takes the view that language competence – what a language user knows – cannot be explained inductively, by observing language as it is used and trying to infer the underlying laws that govern its use. Thus he was highly critical of the efforts of empiricists to proceed along this line of investigation: 'anyone who sets himself the problem of analysing the causes of behaviour will in the absence of independent neurophysiological evidence concern himself with the only data available, namely the record of inputs to the organism, and will try to describe the function specifying the response in terms of the history of inputs. This is nothing more than the definition of the problem' (1959: 26). Chomsky's alternative is to argue for the existence of an innate, uniquely human, language capacity as a way of explaining the nature of human language. He suggests that human beings have a language acquisition device (LAD) and he uses this to explain, for example, why children throughout the world develop language at the same pace and according to a similar developmental sequence – even though the language learned is different from region to region. The philosophical roots of his position can be traced to the philosopher Immanuel Kant. Kant's philosophy of mind is based on the view that we come to know reality through categories of thinking. He considered some of these categories, for example 'quantity', 'cause' and 'effect', to be *a priori*, or innate. Chomsky's LAD makes a similar claim for language, namely that humans are born with a model about what language will sound like. Thus children can discriminate language sounds from the multitude of other noises that bombard them. Chomsky's ideas on LAD have been developed and challenged by many, notably the psychologist Steven Pinker who, while arguing for an innate neural system for language acquisition, gives greater emphasis to the role of evolution – language is an adaptation promoted by processes of selection.

Although Chomsky was not a psychologist, his review of **Skinner**'s *Verbal Behavior* (1959) is regarded as a classic within psychology. Chomsky did not intend for that review to be a criticism of Skinner's position on language *per se*, but rather a more general critique of empiricistic approaches to the analysis of any complex behaviour. The effect of Chomsky's review was to popularise a rationalist, or in Chomsky's terms a 'Cartesian', alternative to the study of language and language acquisition. Chomsky describes his position as 'rationalist' and 'Cartesian' because he wants his approach to refer back to the ideas of Kant and to the philosophy of René Descartes, who had particularly strong views on the native or innate characteristics of the mind. Chomsky claims that, if he is correct and that human beings do in fact have an LAD, then by using a process of systematic reasoning it is possible to work out or deduce what the fundamental principle or laws underpinning the structure of language – every language – must be. One can then check whether the fundamental principles or laws so deduced are correct by using them to generate new utterances. If the utterances so constructed are nonsense, then the law is wrong. If the utterances are sensible, then the law is correct.

From one perspective his review of Skinner's *Verbal Behavior* could be considered little more than a critique by a Cartesian structuralist of the ideas of a pragmatic functionalist, but this view somewhat trivialises the magnitude of the impact of the debate on the way psychologists thought about language. Although the neurologist Karl Lashley had previously observed that there seemed to be more to language than could be encapsulated within the position of the behaviourists, Chomsky went much further. He argued that language is too complex to be explained by learning principles alone, and that each child is born with brain structures that make it relatively easy for him/her to acquire the rules of language. Children could not learn these rules if they had to rely solely on reinforcement and principles of association. Language development, for Chomsky, has less to do with learning than it does with inherent structures in the brain, pre-programmed for language acquisition. The language spoken to children is too poor a stimulus – a view known as the 'poverty of stimulus argument' – and reinforcement of correct grammar is too haphazard to be adequately captured within a learning-theory account of language acquisition on a global scale.

Prior to Chomsky, the interplay between psychology and linguistics had been largely limited to the analysis of words and word-pairs rather than sentence structures. Roger Brown and George Miller were among the first psychologists to recognise the significance of Chomsky's analysis of language for psychology. Brown's interest in children's attainment of their first language attracted him to Chomsky's account of language acquisition. Miller's doctorate was on the intelligibility of speech embedded in noise, and he used statistical techniques, specifically Markov models, to describe the dependency of each word in a sentence on the previous word. Chomsky's *Syntactic Structures* (1957) included a formal analysis of the limitations of Markov as a system for representing anything as complex as language. Miller recognised the psychological implications and embarked on a line of investigation that elucidated the psychological relevance of Chomsky's theory. Miller's efforts to provide intellectual leadership in the emergence of cognitive psychology (a branch of psychology specifically concerned with attention, thinking, problem-solving and related processes) were partly supported by a text, *The Logical Structure of Linguistic Theory*, written by Chomsky in the early 1950s. It was originally rejected by his publishers and didn't see the light of day until 1975. However, Chomsky gave Miller a copy – one of the copies he and Carol had run off on their hectograph, and one which was almost lost in a fire at Harvard's Memorial Hall in 1956.

Chomsky did not expect his theory of language structure to be treated as a psychological theory of language acquisition and production. He did not contend that when people prepare to speak they actually go through the procedures of using phrase structure and transformational grammars, but psychologists were drawn to the possibility that they might. Do phrase structure rules generate deep structures and does the application of further transformational rules yield the final surface structures in the spoken form of a sentence? The first attempts to answer these questions, for example in studies of how long it takes a speaker to change from active to passive tense, were at the forefront of the emergence of psycholinguistics, the psychology of language, as a sub-discipline. The weight of evidence suggests that speaking and understanding language does not rely on a precise application of Chomskyan rules and that contextual factors – the circumstances in which words are spoken – and the factual plausibility of an utterance are also critically important. Although the findings pointed to the naivety of his earliest formulations, they also provided directions for later revisions. Those revisions had two effects: first, they created an impression that Chomsky's theory might be inherently unstable; second, they led researchers to differentiate and refine their questions and thereby promoted growth in the fields of speech comprehension, speech production and child language acquisition at the expense of some lack of integration.

Chomsky's theory of language has been criticised in four major respects. First, there is a problem with the notion of an idealised or theoretically perfect language speaker. The problem is not that competence is defined as virtual but that this competence is identified with a non-linguistic component – the speaker – rather than the language itself. This criticism is usually made by linguists rather than psycholinguists, who have fewer problems with the idea that language is an individual mental capacity. Second, there is a problem with the emphasis placed on the competence of the speaker as the model speaker of a language. It could be argued that the native speaker is not necessarily the ideal language speaker. The ideal language speaker should, in principle, be able to acquire competence in several languages rather than one. It could also be argued that an essential feature of any language is that it should be possible to translate it. This aspect is overlooked in Chomsky's emphasis on the competence of the native speaker. Third, Chomsky's rationalist stance could be regarded as something of an over-reaction to the behavioural and empirical traditions. Many psychologists, Bruner among them, argue that language is not suddenly 'switched on' in the way implied in Chomsky's nativistic account, and there is a large body of evidence to show that learning is also crucial.

While Chomsky's contributions stand as one of the intellectual achievements of the twentieth century, it is also worth citing his influence as a dissenter, which included a stretch in prison (with the novelist Norman Mailer) for his part in a march on the Pentagon in 1967. Chomsky has made at least three fundamental and enduring contributions: he moved the emphasis in linguistics away from the descriptive, inductive level to an explanatory level; he stimulated psychologists to reconsider their ideas on language learning; his distinction between competence and performance, while not without its critics, has proved a powerful metaphor for structural investigations and explanations throughout psychology. The psychologist Steven Pinker has pointed out that Chomsky's theory of language is now a minority position, but the clarity and completeness of his theory is unrivalled – it remains the one to beat.

Noam Chomsky's major writings

Syntactic Structures, Mouton, 1957.
'Review of Skinner, "Verbal Behavior" ', *Language*, 1959, 35, 26–58.
Cartesian Linguistics: A Chapter in the History of Rationalist Thought, Harper & Row, 1966.
Language and Mind, Harcourt, Brace, Jovanovitch, 1968.
The Sound Pattern of English Harper & Row, 1968 (with M. Halle).
Studies of Semantics in Generative Grammar, Mouton, 1972.
The Logical Structure of Linguistic Theory, Plenum, 1975.
Rules and Representations, Basil Blackwell, 1980.
Language and Problems of Knowledge: The Managua Lectures, MIT Press, 1988.

Further reading

Alexander, G. (ed.) (1990) *Reflections on Chomsky*, Basil Blackwell.
Barsky, R. F. (1997) *Noam Chomsky: A Life of Dissent*, MIT Press.
Blumenthal, A. L. (1970) *Language and Psychology: Historical Aspects of Psycholinguistics*, Wiley.
Cogswell, D. (1995) *Chomsky for Beginners*, Writers and Readers.

ERIKSON, ERIK HOMBURGER (1902–94)

Erikson extended and modified Freud's ideas regarding the structure of human development across the lifespan and laid particular emphasis on the importance of interpersonal relationships and the creative qualities of the person.

Erikson's Danish parents separated before his birth and he was brought up in Karlsruhe in Baden, Germany, by his mother and a German paediatrician whom she married when Erik was a few years old. He kept his stepfather's name as his middle name. As a schoolboy his interests lay in art, language and history. As a teenager he considered himself to be morbidly sensitive. After leaving school he hitchhiked across Europe, studied art in Munich and settled for a time in Florence, before moving on to Vienna where a friend had invited him to help run a small school, developing and applying innovative teaching methods. Anna Freud had her professional practice there, and several of the children in analysis with her were attending the school at which Erikson was teaching. Erikson underwent training analysis with Anna Freud and routinely participated in the intensive seminars held by the Viennese Psychoanalytic Society. He was in close contact with the group around **Freud** and occasionally met with him, usually at Freud's house where Erikson went for his analytic sessions, and occasionally at social events. Erikson remained in Vienna for six years, studying Maria Montessori's methods of education, as well as teaching at the school and continuing to paint. In 1929 he married a Canadian (Joan Serson) whom he had met some years earlier while she was studying European schools of dancing. The early 1930s was a disturbing time – the Nazis had begun to burn Freud's books in Berlin and were threatening Austria. With their two young sons Kai and Jon (Susan, their third child, was born in America), the Eriksons joined the exodus of professional people, including many of their analyst friends. In 1933 they moved to Copenhagen where he tried, without success, to revert to his Danish nationality. Later, in autobiographical writing, he recalled that much of his theoretical work was influenced by early feelings of confusion and alienation, a theme that emerges in his work on identity crisis. After a short stay in Copenhagen the Eriksons moved to Boston in the USA, where he set up practice as one of the first child analysts. Three years later he took up a full-time academic appointment at Yale University's Institute of Human Relations.

In 1939 the Eriksons moved to the University of California at Berkeley, where he was engaged in a longitudinal study of child development. They remained on the West Coast for ten years, during which time he took up a permanent teaching post at the University of California. That was to prove a brief appointment. He felt forced to resign his position when, with several other staff at the University, he refused to sign a mandatory oath of loyalty dissociating himself from groups and individuals associated with the Communist Party. This was a point of principle for Erikson; he had no links with, nor allegiance to, communist politics. His first book, *Childhood and Society* (1950), was published towards the end of his period on the West Coast. He returned to Massachusetts to take up an appointment at the Austen Riggs Center, a clinic specialising in psychoanalytic training and research. Although he did not have a primary degree, he was appointed Professor of Human Development and Lecturer in Psychiatry at Harvard. There he came into contact with numerous academics, including Gregory Bateson, who worked on the science of communication and control in animals and machines (cybernetics) of social life, the personality theorist Henry Murray, and the Gestalt social psychologist Kurt **Lewin**, who shaped his attempts to integrate psychoanalysis with psychology and anthropology with particular reference to lifespan development. He focused much of his teaching and research on his notions of the cycle of psychological development across the lifespan.

Erikson is associated with the psychoanalytic tradition of ego psychology. One of the major innovations of ego psychology was the inclusion within psychoanalytic theory of the influences of the external environment. The ego is considered to develop and function through a combination of internal processes and external events. Thus Erikson built on the work of Sigmund and Anna Freud, and much of his work is a direct descendent of Freudian theory. He did not attempt a fundamental restatement of psychoanalytic propositions but rather sought to elaborate, clarify and extend some of them by introducing new considerations concerning the creative qualities of the ego and placing greater emphasis on interpersonal influences rather than intrapersonal or intrapsychic forces.

Erikson developed a theory of ego development using concepts from embryology, especially the principle of epigenesis. The principle states that a new living organism develops from an undifferentiated entity that is programmed to develop all of the organism's parts in sequence. The ego is thought to develop in a planned sequence of stages. Each stage consists of a unique developmental task that confronts individuals in the form of a crisis or challenge that must be faced. For Erikson, this crisis is not a catastrophe but a turning point of increased vulnerability and enhanced potential. The more an individual resolves these crises successfully the healthier their development will be.

Erikson defines eight developmental stages. Trust versus mistrust is Erikson's first psychosocial stage. It is experienced in the first year of life. A sense of trust requires a feeling of physical comfort and a minimal amount of fear and apprehension about the future. Trust in infancy sets the stage for a lifelong expectation that the world will be a good and pleasant place to live. Autonomy versus shame and doubt is the second stage of development. It occurs in late infancy (at 1–3 years). After developing a sense of trust in their caregivers, infants begin to discover the impact of their behaviour on others. They start to assert their sense of independence and autonomy. Erikson's theory suggests that, if infants are restrained too much or punished too harshly for expressing this newfound freedom, they are likely to develop a sense of shame and doubt.

Initiative versus guilt is the third stage of development, and it occurs during the child's pre-school years. As pre-school children encounter a widening social world, they are challenged more than when they were infants. Active, purposeful behaviour is needed to cope with the challenges. As they mature, children are encouraged to assume responsibility for their bodies, their behaviour, their toys and their pets. Developing a sense of responsibility increases initiative. Uncomfortable guilt feelings may arise, though, if the child is irresponsible and is made to feel too anxious. Erikson suggests that most guilt is quickly compensated for by a sense of accomplishment. Industry versus inferiority is the fourth developmental stage, occurring approximately in the early primary school years. Children's initiative brings them in contact with a wealth of new experiences. As they move into middle and late childhood, they direct their energy towards mastering cognitive skills. Thus at no other time is the child more enthusiastic about learning than at this stage. One danger in the primary school years resides in the potential for developing a sense of inferiority – of feeling relatively incompetent.

Identity versus identity confusion is the fifth developmental stage, encountered during adolescence. At this time, individuals are faced with finding out who they are and where they are going in life. Adolescents are confronted with many new adult roles. If these are explored in a healthy manner the adolescent arrives at a positive path to follow in life, and a positive identity will be achieved. If an identity is forced on the adolescent by parents or peers, if the adolescent does not adequately explore many roles, and if a positive future path is not defined, then identity confusion is likely to result. Intimacy versus isolation is the sixth development stage. It characterises development during the early adult years. At this time, individuals face the developmental task of forming intimate relationships with others. If the young adult forms healthy friendships and an intimate close relationship with another individual, intimacy will be achieved; if not, isolation will result.

Generativity versus stagnation is the seventh developmental stage, which individuals experience during middle adulthood. A chief concern for this stage of development is to assist the younger generation in developing and leading useful lives – this is what Erikson means by 'generativity'. The feeling of having done nothing to help the next generation is referred to as stagnation. Integrity versus despair is the final developmental stage, which individuals experience during late adulthood. In the later years of life, we look back and evaluate what we have done with our lives. Through many different routes, the older person may have developed a positive outlook in most or all of the previous stages of development. If so, the retrospective glances will reveal a picture of a life well spent, and the person will feel a sense of satisfaction. A sense of completeness may be achieved. If the older adult resolved many of the earlier stages negatively, the retrospective glances will likely yield doubt or gloom, and may be experienced as a sense of incompleteness and despair. It is important to bear in mind that, while Erikson's stages are presented chronologically, he never suggested that, once a stage has been completed, it is forever in the past. Rather, the developmental challenges associated with each stage are always present in all of our lives; it is just that the relative emphasis tends to vary across the lifespan.

Four criticisms have been directed against Erikson's theory. First, whereas Freud could be considered to be over-pessimistic of the human condition, Erikson is often considered to be over-optimistic. Erikson has countered that this is not true and that, for each psychosocial stage, there is a crisis and a specific negative ego quality (e.g. shame, mistrust) that may potentially lead to continued anxiety. Second, it has been argued that Erikson has exaggerated the role of the ego at the expense of the id and the unconscious. This is probably true, but it does not seriously impact on the integrity of his position. Third, it is sometimes argued that Erikson's theory places too great an emphasis on the need for the individual to adjust to the norms and expectations of society. However, Erikson's argument is that our sense of identity develops within the possibilities offered by society, and these may include stability or change. For example, in *Gandhi's Truth* (1969) he demonstrates a profound interest in people who create and sustain a healthy sense of identity through radical social upheaval. Finally, Erikson has been criticised for the nature of his research designs, which (except for some studies of children's play) are primarily based on personal observation rather than controlled experimentation. Thus, while Erikson offers a considerable corpus of empirical evidence in support of his theory, much of the evidence has been collected in ways that favour support for his position. Despite these criticisms, Erikson's contributions are significant: he emphasised the psychosocial as well as the instinctual basis for behaviour and development; his account of development embraces the whole lifecycle; and his theoretical position explicitly acknowledges that individuals often look as much to their future as they do to their past.

Erik Erikson's major writings

Childhood and Society, Norton, 1950.
Insight and Responsibility, Norton, 1964.
Identity, Youth and Crisis, Norton, 1968.
Gandhi's Truth, Norton, 1969.
Dimensions of a New Identity, Norton, 1974.
Life History and the Historical Moment, Norton, 1975.
The Life Cycle Completed: A Review, Norton, 1982.

Further reading

Coles, R. (1970) *Erik H. Erikson: The Growth of His Work*, Little, Brown.
Erikson, K. T. (1975) *In Search of Common Ground: Conversations with Erik H. Erikson and Huey P. Newton*, Norton.
Stevens, R. (1983) *Erik Erikson*, Open University Press.

EYSENCK, HANS JURGEN (1916–97)

Eysenck's emphasis on the biological basis of behaviour led to the development of biological measures of intelligence and personality, while his trenchant criticism of psychoanalysis led to the marginalisation of its influence within mainstream psychology.

Hans Eysenck's parents (Eduord and Ruth) were actors, but were divorced when he was two. Born in Berlin, he was raised by his Catholic grandmother, Frau Werner, who had been a budding opera singer and actress but had been disabled by a medical accident. She died in a Nazi concentration camp midway through the Second World War. After attending the Bismarck Gymnasium and Friedrich Wilhelm Real-Gymnasium, Eysenck decided to pursue a degree in theoretical physics at the University of London. Lacking the appropriate qualifications for admission, he elected to take an alternative degree – in psychology. At that time the teaching faculty was small, and included Sir Cyril Burt and the psychoanalyst J. C. Flugel. After graduating, he went on to complete a Ph.D. in experimental aesthetics under Burt's supervision. Although Eysenck became a British citizen in 1947, he was treated with suspicion during the war and, like others of German origin, excluded from military service. After the war, Philip Vernon, who was using the statistical technique known as factor analysis to examine the structure of personality and intelligence, recommended him for a position at Mill Hill Hospital. His knowledge of abnormal and clinical psychology was at that time very limited, and mostly derived from the German psychiatrist Alexander Herzberg.

Thus Mill Hill provided his formal introduction to abnormal psychology. Sir Aubrey Lewis, director at the Maudsley Hospital, put him in charge of clinical psychology, and he developed the first clinical training programme in Britain. He was later invited to organise a Department of Psychology at the Institute of Psychiatry (located at the Maudsley), and was appointed to its first chair, a position he held until his retirement. Michael was the son of his first marriage, to Margaret Davies – they were married on the day Eysenck graduated with his first degree. After their divorce, Eysenck married the psychologist Sybil Bianca Guiletta (daughter of the violinist Max Rostal), and they had four children.

Eysenck's ideas and work were strongly influenced by those of Sir Cyril Burt, **Galton**, **Spearman**, Louis Thurstone and **Hull**. His first published study reported a factor analysis of scores on a range of mental ability tests: a replication of Thurstone's seven primary mental abilities and support for Spearman's concept of general intelligence, 'g'. (Factor analysis examines the correlations between a large number of tests and reduces them to a smaller number of underlying dimensions or factors – analogous to the idea that all of the colours of the visible spectrum can be reduced to just three primary colours.) Eysenck also made extensive use of factor analysis, which he applied to derive a small number of dimensions or factors on which all personality traits are organised. His first attempt led to the identification of the two principal factors of Extraversion–Introversion and Neuroticism–Stability. Extraversion–Introversion is associated with sociability/assertiveness and aloofness/passivity. Neuroticism–Stability is related to moodiness/insecurity and emotional stability. A third factor, Psychoticism (associated with aggressive, cold, antisocial behaviour), was added a few years later but failed to attract widespread acceptance. Unlike **Jung**'s typology, Eysenck's approach sought to anchor personality traits in empirical meanings. His two primary factors were replicated in **Cattell**'s investigations of the structure of personality and also feature in what is commonly referred to as the 'Big Five' model of personality: extraversion, neuroticism, agreeableness, conscientiousness and intellect (also called openness to experience). Eysenck postulated an underlying biological basis for the two major traits of extraversion and neuroticism. His early thinking was informed by **Pavlov**'s notions of cortical inhibition–excitation. Pavlov suggested that two processes in the brain cortex are particularly important for learning: *excitation*, which leads to an organism acquiring conditioned responses; and *inhibition*, which suppresses them. Eysenck was also influenced by Clark Hull's concept of drive strength – the strength of a drive such as hunger or sex. He developed and modified his position, and later came to think of extraversion as modulated by lowered arousal levels in a part of the brain called the cortical–reticular activating system. This lowered arousal was thought to provoke a person to engage in stimulation seeking and other extraverted behaviours. Neuroticism is thought to be determined by instability in the brain's limbic system, and manifested in over-reactivity and fear.

His view of personality as being biologically-based identified him as a nativist, and he published several studies of personality in twins and families. Some of his students and colleagues pursued selective-breeding experiments to produce different strains (reactive–non-reactive) of rats. One of the larger implications of his work in behaviour genetics is the manner in which it raised an awareness of the importance of attending to individual differences and of understanding why each individual is more or less different from everyone else. Unlike **Allport**, he felt that this did not imply a significant role for an idiographic mode of enquiry, although his strength of opposition to the idiographic method was tempered through his career.

Eysenck's original studies of personality were based on, and intended to refer to, the normal adult population. However, he soon developed the thesis that personality is closely linked to behaviour change and to abnormal psychological phenomena, and in so doing he updated the **Watson**–Mowrer theory of phobia conditioning and avoidance behaviour. His theory predicts that certain personality types will be more prone to certain kinds of psychopathologies, and he found supporting evidence that neurotic introverts will tend to become depressed whereas neurotic extraverts will tend to develop pathologies of hysteria. According to his theory, extraverts are underaroused relative to introverts and tend to seek stimulation, whereas neurotics are liable to acquire fears more quickly than are stable personalities. Extending these ideas to the explanation of criminal behaviour, his theory predicts that people with a criminal record and others expressing strong antisocial tendencies are less easily conditioned and tend to have higher scores on neuroticism, extraversion and psychoticism. The suggestion that criminal behaviour may have a genetic basis associates Eysenck's position with a biological perspective that includes the constitutional theories of criminality proffered by Cesare Lombroso, Ernst Kretschmer and W. H. Sheldon. Could it be that antisocial behaviour is learned within a group setting? Selective socialisation or recruitment into an antisocial lifestyle may provide role models and rationales for continued and escalating criminal behaviour. Thus, personality measures of people with a criminal history may be tapping the consequences of socialisation processes rather than genetically determined biological factors. Evidence supporting Eysenck's position is mixed, partly because there are few well-controlled longitudinal studies that discriminate biological from social factors. Moreover, the evidence that those with a criminal history score high on a measure of E (extraversion) is somewhat inconsistent. This may be due in part to the possibility that E is measuring two things, impulsivity and sociability, which have different prevalence rates in different criminal populations (e.g. those who are in prison, as distinct from those who commit crimes but remain in society under the supervision of a probation service). Eysenck's strong commitment to a genetic and biological explanation for personality, and the emergence of psychopathology, did not lead him to a pessimistic prognosis, because he regarded maladaptive behaviour as learned and therefore something that could be unlearned. Genetic and biological predispositions merely increase the probability that a person would learn one type of maladaptive behaviour rather than another. Thus his views on therapy were strongly influenced by learning theory, and also by the ideas of Alexander Herzberg. Although Herzberg regarded himself as a Freudian psychoanalyst, many of his concepts presaged the influence of learning theories, as illustrated by his argument that the tasks set for patients should be graduated according to their difficulty.

Eysenck was a staunch critic of psychoanalysis and must take a large share of the credit (or the blame, depending on one's perspective) for spearheading the marginalisation of its influence within mainstream psychology. The major tenets of his critique are that: psychoanalytic theory is not falsifiable and therefore cannot be viewed as scientific; abnormal behaviour is due to learned maladaptive responses rather than unconscious drives; and empirical evidence indicates that neurotic and psychotic disorders are distinct and not, as psychoanalysis claims, points on a continuum of regression. He showed that the successes reported for psychoanalytic therapies were often based on faulty research designs and defective outcome measures, and attributed any success to therapists' unintended and unnoticed applications of learning principles.

Eysenck's unwavering allegiance to open-minded scientific enquiry is reflected in his criticism of scientific orthodoxy that dismisses enquiries into parapsychology and astrology as inherently worthless. He argued that those who take such a view are committing the same error as those who declare that anomalous findings *de facto* imply the existence of paranormal forces. His work on astrology, for example, was based on Michel Gauquelin's research pointing to the existence of carefully gathered data, indicating that there is an effect to be explained – without a commitment to non-materialistic, non-mechanistic explanations favoured by J. B. Rhine and other founders of the parapsychology movement. Eysenck was persuaded by Gauquelin's arguments that astrology makes testable assertions about the relationships, positions and personality.

Eysenck was a prolific writer, with seventy-nine authored or edited books to his name and over 1,000 articles or chapters. His major contribution was in formulating a theory of personality that: (a) used core concepts that could be operationally defined and investigated using both correlational and experimental techniques; (b) is linked to theory of central nervous system function and learning; and (c) is explicitly associated with a theory of psychopathology and behaviour change. Much of the controversy surrounding his strongly articulated views – he never baulked at the prospect of a good argument – focused on his dogmatic insistence on the inheritability of personality traits. The ferocity of some of the attacks against his position was partly an indication of the degree to which they ran counter to a zeitgeist favouring the primacy of environmental influences on behaviour. He was perceived by some as a racist and, incongruously, by a minority as a Nazi sympathiser. Although Eysenck's ideas and methods have had a profound influence on psychology, some have argued that there remains a deficit between the sheer volume of his published work and the scope and extent of its impact. This may be due in part to a tendency on Eysenck's part to over-emphasise the importance of studies consistent with his position. For example, he was almost alone among factor analytic theorists in arguing that personality could be explained using just two or three dimensions when the accumulating corpus of evidence was pointing to a larger number.

Hans Eysenck's major writings

Dimensions of Personality, Routledge and Kegan Paul, 1947.
'The effects of psychotherapy: an evaluation', *Journal of Consulting Psychology*, 1952, 16, 319–24.
Crime and Personality, Routledge & Kegan Paul, 1964.
The Biological Basis of Personality, C. C. Thomas, 1967.
Sex and Personality, Open Books, 1976.
The Structure and Measurement of Intelligence, Springer-Verlag, 1979.
'The conditioning model of neurosis', *Brain and Behavioral Sciences*, 1979, 2, 155–99.
The Causes and Effects of Smoking, Temple Smith, 1980 (with L. J. Eaves).
The Great Intelligence Debate, Lifecycle Publications, 1980 (with L. J. Kamin).
Genes, Culture, and Personality: An Empirical Approach, Academic Press, 1989 (with L. J. Eaves and N. G. Martin).

Further reading

Gibson, H. B. (1981) *Hans Eysenck: The Man and His Work*, Peter Owen.
Gray, J. A. (1981) 'A critique of Eysenck's theory of personality', in H. J. Eysenck (ed.), *A Model for Personality*, Springer-Verlag, pp. 246–77.
Modgil, S. and Modgil, C. (eds) (1986) *Hans Eysenck: Consensus and Controversy*, Taylor & Francis.

FREUD, SIGMUND (1856–1939)

The founder of psychoanalysis, Freud emphasised in his approach the importance of unconscious factors in guiding human behaviour and the value of interpreting dreams as an indirect route to the unconscious.

Sigmund Freud was born in Freiberg, Moravia (now Pribor in the Czech Republic) a year after the marriage of his parents, Jacob and Amalie Nathansohn. Amalie was Jacob's third wife, and Sigmund was his mother's eldest child of eight. His father, a wool merchant, had two adult sons, Emanuel and Philipp, from a previous marriage. Emanuel's children, John and Pauline, were Freud's early playmates in Freiberg. In 1859 the families of his half-brothers emigrated to Manchester, England. His mother taught him to read and write and he entered formal education at the Leopoldstaedter Realgymnasium in 1865. In 1873 he entered Vienna University to study medicine. This included training in physiology under Ernst von Brücke and philosophy under Franz Brentano. Aspects of von Brücke's dynamic physiology, an approach in which organisms are treated as part of a system of forces that keep it alive but ultimately lead to its demise, and Brentano's act psychology, whereby consciousness is regarded as essentially intentional (e.g., the act of seeing contains within it what is seen), later found expression in Freud's theory. Other influences came from the philosopher Schopenhauer, whose concept of 'the will' shaped Freud's ideas concerning the unconscious. As a medical student, he earned some money translating a volume of essays by John Stuart Mill. In 1881 he qualified as a doctor of medicine and became engaged to Martha Bernays. They married four years later. His first medical position was at the Vienna General Hospital, and this was followed by work at Theodor Meynert's laboratory of brain anatomy. This provided his introduction to psychiatry. In 1885 he became a Privat Docent at the University of Vienna, where he taught a course on disorder of the nervous system and in the same year won a scholarship that allowed him to study under Jean-Martin Charcot at the

Salpêtrière in Paris. Charcot had originally formed the view that hysteria was a physiological rather than a mental disorder, but his revised position emphasised its psychological origin. Charcot greatly influenced Freud both intellectually, for example in training him to use hypnosis to treat hysteria, and personally – Freud named his first son, Jean-Martin, after him. On returning from Paris, Freud opened a private practice specialising in nervous diseases and was appointed director of the neurological section of the Max Kassowitz Institute for Children's Diseases. In order to make some additional money, he translated a book by the physician Hyppolite Bernheim and spent some time with Bernheim at Nancy in order to improve his own hypnotic method, during which he became aware of its limitations as a therapeutic device. He turned his attention to a method introduced to him by the Viennese physician Josef Breuer. Breuer had treated a number of patients diagnosed with hysteria and found that, when he encouraged them to talk freely about the earliest occurrence of their symptoms, they often declined. Freud developed this idea by suggesting that many neuroses, such as phobias and hysterical paralyses, had their origins in very traumatic, long-forgotten experiences. By bringing these experiences back to conscious awareness and confronting them in a comprehensive manner, the underlying causes would be removed and the distressing symptoms would disappear. Breuer's and Freud's ideas and methods were published in a much-celebrated text, *Studies in Hysteria*, which first appeared in English in 1936. However, soon after its publication Breuer and Freud parted company because Breuer considered Freud's emphasis on the sexual origin and content of many neuroses to be both excessive and unjustifiable.

In 1891 the Freuds moved to an apartment at the newly-erected Berggasse 19, and in the following year Freud and a small circle of friends including Alfred Adler, Wilhelm Stekel, Max Kahane and Rudolf Reitler founded the Wednesday Psychological Society. It rapidly developed and organisational considerations demanded that it be disbanded in 1908 and re-established as the Vienna Psychoanalytic Society. In the following year Freud, Sándor Ferenczi and **Jung** took up an invitation from Stanley Hall to lecture at Clark University. The visit alerted them to the pervasive interest in psychoanalytic ideas among North American psychiatrists and psychologists.

Adler, who was elected chairman of the Vienna Psychoanalytic Society in 1910, decided to leave the following year because of theoretical differences with Freud. Adler founded his own Society for Psychoanalytic Research, later called the Society for Individual

Psychology. Following yet another disagreement, this time with Wilhelm Stekel about the editorial committee of the *Zentralblatt für Psychoanalyse*, Hans Sachs, Otto Rank and Freud founded a psycho-analytical journal devoted to the interdisciplinary research of mental life. Stekel responded by resigning from the Vienna Psychoanalytic Society. Freud's relationship with Jung, which had commenced on favourable terms in 1906, was also in jeopardy. Freud's *Totem and Taboo* appeared in 1913, partly as a riposte to Jung's interest in mythology. Jung had been developing his own psychology based on a new conception of libido, quite different from Freud's in many respects because of the diminished emphasis on sexual drives. In the following year Jung resigned from the presidency of the International Psycho-analytical Association. In the face of these resignations and with the emergence of several splinter movements, Ernst Jones initiated the 'Secret Committee' comprising himself, Freud, Karl Abraham, A. Brill, Sándor Ferenczi, Otto Rank and Hans Sachs. This was quickly followed by Freud's *On the History of the Psychoanalytic Movement* (1915). It was mostly a polemical response to the earlier schisms.

By 1918 Freud's entire fortune, which he had invested in Austrian State Bonds, had been lost. The First World War had also reduced his clients to a trickle, and he struggled to make a living. A saviour appeared in the form of a Budapest manufacturer, Anton von Freund, who gave a large sum of money to Freud. The money was rapidly consumed by inflationary pressures, but not before the establishment of The International Psychoanalytical Press, with Otto Rank, Freud's closest colleague, as its first director. Freud developed oral cancer, the first signs of which were detected in 1923, and the following year saw the outbreak of another internecine war, this time with Rank over the importance to be attached to birth trauma. Freud did not agree with Rank's claim, that the shock of birth creates a kind of psychic basin of anxiety and that this reservoir accounts for the emergences of neuroses, such as phobias, in later life.

Freud's ideas, the findings from his analysis of dreams and the application of psychoanalytic method in patients who were required to free-associate to the analyst – essentially, to talk about whatever memories, thoughts or feelings came to mind – were initially greeted with derision, scepticism and antagonism. These reactions were largely a product of the European Victorian zeitgeist that was far from ready to embrace notions of childhood sexuality, that sexual drives were the important dynamics of human behaviour, and that human beings are ruled not by reason but by unconscious drives. Freud interpreted the outrage as clear evidence for the painful truth of his ideas. By the

1920s and 1930s the psychoanalytic method was commonly referred to as the 'talking therapy', and was seen as a powerful mode of treatment for a range of psychological disorders. Freud's fame was so great that the Nazis were reluctant to destroy his practice, and allowed him to migrate to England even after he had mockingly recommended their ideals and values – an irony that – fortunately for Freud – eluded the political leaders of the time.

Freud's method of enquiry proceeds from the recording of observable phenomena to the formulation of general laws, and, as such, reflects the influence of the empiricist philosophers such as Francis Bacon and John Stuart Mill. For Freud, this involved devising huge, far-reaching hypotheses and testing them against evidence collected in clinical settings. Psychoanalytic theory embraces every aspect of the human mind and seeks to explain every aspect of human behaviour. For example, humour and wit are explained as the expression of unconscious, forbidden wishes. Joke-work is akin to dream-work in allowing the socially sanctioned expression of aggressive and sexual statements that would otherwise be impossible. Similarly, there is no such thing as an 'error' because errors of every kind, or 'parapraxes', as Freud called them, were expressions of repressed desires. Every fragment of human behaviour, no matter how trivial, has a meaning. Early on, Freud developed a theory of dreaming which was central to psychoanalysis and was the focus of much of what was discussed in therapy. Dreams were the road to the unconscious because the actual dream, the manifest content, was regarded as a disguised version of the latent content which always expressed a repressed wish. This disguise, the dream work, exemplifies the workings of the unconscious, primary psychical processes that are normally hidden. Thus the analysis of dreams reveals the unconscious motives, fantasies and desires of the patient. The fact that Freudian theory appeared to offer an explanation for so many aspects of the human condition accounts for both its popularity and the fact that it has been banished from many areas of psychology. For example, most students of psychology learn about Freud in the first year of their university course and are told that it is probably the last they will hear of his ideas for the remainder of their study. Groans of dismay usually ensue.

Freud's output was enormous, and all of it was structured around the tenet that unconscious drives and wishes have a considerable influence on our lives, and that, unless these are understood, real change is impossible. The practice of psychoanalysis, Freud argued, provides a particularly powerful approach to achieving real change.

Thus, psychoanalysis is both a set of ideas and a therapeutic method based upon them. The 'id' is the Freudian structure of personality that consists of drives, which are an individual's reservoir of psychic energy. The id is unconscious; it has no contact with reality and works according to the pleasure principle, always seeking pleasure and avoiding pain. As children experience the demands and constraints of reality, a new structure of personality is formed – the 'ego'. The ego is considered to be the executive branch of personality because it makes rational decisions. The ego abides by the reality principle; it tries to bring an individual's pleasures within the boundaries of reality. The id and the ego have no sense of morality. The superego takes into account whether something is right or wrong.[1]

How does the ego resolve the conflict between its demands for reality, the wishes of the id, and the constraints of the superego? It does so through defence mechanisms: unconscious methods used by the ego to distort reality, thereby protecting the person from anxiety. In Freud's view, the conflicting demands of the personality structures produce anxiety. The anxiety alerts the ego to resolve the conflict by means of defence mechanisms. Repression is the most powerful and pervasive defence mechanism. It works to push unacceptable id impulses out of awareness and back into the unconscious mind. Repression is the foundation from which all other defence mechanisms work. Other important defence mechanisms are: displacement – the defence mechanism that occurs when an individual shifts unacceptable feelings from one object to another, more acceptable object; projection – the defence mechanism used to attribute our own shortcomings, problems and faults to others; and sublimation – the defence mechanism that occurs when an individual replaces a socially distasteful course of action with a socially useful one.

Freud's theory suggests that development of the person is associated with an orderly progression through five psychosexual or libidinal stages: oral, anal, phallic, latent and genital. These are referred to as psychosexual or libidinal stages because of the primacy of the different erogenous zones (mouth, anus and genitals) during the development of the child. The adult personality is thought to be determined by the way conflicts between the early sources of pleasure – the mouth, the anus, and then the genitals – and the demands of reality are resolved. When these conflicts are not resolved, the individual may become fixated at a particular stage of development. Fixation is a defence mechanism that occurs when an individual remains locked into an earlier developmental stage because needs are either under- or over-gratified. For example, the Oedipus complex is a hypothetical construct which proposes that the young child develops an intense desire to replace the parent of the same sex and enjoy the affections of the opposite-sex parent. How is the Oedipus complex resolved? At about five to six years of age, children recognise that their same-sex parent might punish them for their incestuous desires. To reduce this conflict, the child identifies with the same-sex parent. If the conflict is not resolved, the theory predicts that the individual may become fixated at the phallic stage, as illustrated by an adult whose personality is characterised by self-assured recklessness, vanity and exhibitionism.

The healthy person is characterised by a dynamic balance between the forces of the ego, concerned with reality, and largely conscious; the superego, dealing with morality; and the id, the storehouse of drives and unacceptable repressed wishes, and entirely unconscious. Neurotic individuals are thought to be ruled by their superegos. Psychotic individuals have had their ego defences penetrated and are ruled by their id. Thus, in the case of psychotics, the aim of therapy is to replace id activity with that of the ego.

At the time of his death, Freud was regarded as one of the major scientific thinkers of his age, one whose intellectual stature was equal to that of Darwin and Einstein. (Although Freud never explicitly compared himself with Darwin and Einstein, his first diary note for 1929 is 'Passed over for the Nobel Prize'.) There is no doubt that Freudian theory was one of the most influential scientific theories in any field in the twentieth century. Many psychologists would concur with **Eysenck**, one of its most vociferous critics, that it has been a baleful influence on the progress of psychological science, not least because many concepts cannot be defined in ways that allow them to be measured. In fact some, particularly those relating to the unconscious, are so formulated that they can never be measured. Moreover, the theory makes very few accurate predictions about how someone will behave, but it always claims to provide a satisfactory explanation for everything a person has done in the past. The claim that women are driven by penis envy and are inferior to men is now widely regarded as offensive, and feminist critiques have indicated that the content and growth of psycho-analysis as envisaged by Freud are the reflections and products of a patriarchal society. Nevertheless the theory continues to be developed throughout the world, particularly in Europe and America. Its continuing popularity may be due in part to the fact that its core ideas appear to be widely perceived to concur with everyday human experience and to offer the promise of a coherent explanation that cannot be matched by more mainstream psychological frameworks. For example, much of the language of psychoanalysis has become the dominant idiom in which most of us explain why we think, feel and behave as we do. However, Freud never believed that psychoanalysis was the last word in psychological explanation, and he assessed its shelf-life to be limited by the rate of progress in biochemistry, which, he considered, would provide a level of explanation of human behaviour to which psychoanalysis could hardly begin to aspire.

Sigmund Freud's major writings

The Standard Edition of the Complete Psychological Works of Sigmund Freud, Hogarth Press and the Institute of Psychoanalysis, 1966.

Further reading

Appignanesi, L. and Forrester, J. (2000) *Freud's Women*, Penguin.
Ellenberger, H. F. (1981) *The Discovery of the Unconscious: The History and Evolution of Dynamic Psychiatry*, Basic Books.
Grünbaum, A. (1984) *The Foundations of Psychoanalysis: A Philosophical Critique*, University of California Press.
Hall, C. S. (1999) *A Primer of Freudian Psychology*, New American Library.

GALTON, FRANCIS (1822–1911)

Galton pioneered the study of differences between individuals and developed a theory that explained individual differences with reference to their genetic origins.

Erasmus Darwin (physician, philosopher and evolutionary theorist) was the grandfather of both Charles Darwin and Francis Galton. Galton was born to a Quaker family living in Birmingham, whose fortune was founded on gun manufacturing and was subsequently extended as a result of success in the banking sector. His mother was a half-sister of Charles Darwin's father. The youngest of seven children, Galton's early education took place at home, and by the time he was two-and-a-half he could read and write; by seven he was reading Shakespeare. Galton's introduction to formal education was not dissimilar from that of **Wundt** – both endured a harsh regime within a culture of corporal punishment. Galton was at boarding school until the age of sixteen, and in 1838 he went to study medicine at Birmingham General Hospital. He transferred to Kings College,

London, for a year, and later he moved to Cambridge University (1840–43), where he read mathematics but did not obtain a degree. He decided not to return to Kings College to complete his medical degree after the death of his father.

Like **Binet**, Galton's inherited wealth meant that he could pursue whatever interested him, and his interests embraced evaluations of the efficacy of prayer and quantifying the relative beauty of women from different parts of Great Britain. He invented composite photography and pioneered the use of fingerprints for identification purposes. He travelled to Egypt, the Sudan and throughout the Middle East. He was well placed within an affluent social circle and could have enjoyed a sedentary Victorian existence but for the advice of a phrenologist to pursue a more active lifestyle. At that time phrenologists were using the now discredited practice of estimating the relative strengths of a person's mental faculties and their suitability to different careers by calculating the size of bumps on different parts of their cranium. Galton joined the Royal Geographic Society and undertook a two-year trip to South West Africa, and his mapping of previously unexplored territories (now Namibia) attracted the Society's highest award. In the year he received that award, 1853, he published his first book, *Narrative of an Explorer in Tropical South Africa*. His expertise as a traveller and explorer led to the offer of a commission from the British Government to teach camping procedures to soldiers.

Galton's awareness of the importance of variation among individuals, informed by his geographical and anthropological pursuits, coupled with the publication of Darwin's *The Origin of Species* (1859), directed his enquiries to the inheritance of mental and physical characteristics and their role in determining individual differences. Galton shared the view of the philosopher Herbert Spencer that, if the doctrine of evolution is true, the inevitable implication is that the mind can be understood only by observing its evolution. Spencer set out the case for a psychology of evolutionary adaptation – how individuals adapt – and Galton developed and refined it to a point where he considered it could be applied at a societal level.

Animals come to know and adapt to their environment through their senses, and so Galton deduced that sensory acuity was the foundation of intelligence. The more acute the senses the more intelligent a person is likely to be. Furthermore, because sensory acuity was mainly a function of genetic bequest, he concluded that intelligence must be inherited. Following this line of argument, he predicted that one should expect to observe levels of intelligence running in families: intelligent parents should have intelligent children. Moreover, since people with a high degree of intelligence are likely to be more successful in adapting to their environment, he thought that reputation or eminence could be taken as a valid indicator of intelligence. Accordingly, Galton set out to measure the rate of recurrence of eminence among the children of celebrated parents (e.g. Ministers of State, Judges, Foreign Ambassadors, Governors of Colonies, etc.) as compared to the offspring of the general population. His approach to this task identifies him as a pioneer in the application of statistical techniques to psychological data. His work as an explorer and geographer had introduced him to the ideas of the Belgian astronomer, sociologist and pioneer statistician, Adolphe Quételet. Quételet's demonstration that the 'law of errors' governed variability in astronomical and social phenomena inspired Galton to use the same approach to the examination of variation in mental ability. The law of errors would now be referred to as the normal or bell-shaped curve: the fact that, for example, if one plots the height of a population of people on a chart there will be a large bulge in the middle corresponding to the average height of the majority, with fewer people who are shorter than average and fewer taller than average on either side of the bulge. The results, published in *Hereditary Genius* (1869), were clear: eminent parents were far more likely to have children who achieve recognition of their own, whereas parents in the general population are more likely to have children whose achievements are more commonplace. However, for Galton, achieving eminence required a combination of intelligence and motivation – simply being more intelligent than average was not enough because some intelligent people are lazy.

Galton's findings appeared to point to an extraordinary possibility: if intelligence is inherited, could the general intelligence of a people be improved by selectively encouraging the more intelligent among them to have more children? Galton felt that it could, and he invented and defined the term 'eugenics' as the science of improving the genetic stock. In 1865 he suggested that couples could be scientifically paired and that the government should provide financial incentives to encourage those possessing desirable intellectual characteristics to intermarry. This included the idea that one's choice of partner could be informed by an inspection of family records: the records could be used to predict the intelligence of any progeny. Over a period of time these family records might be collected for inclusion in a national genealogical archive and used to classify people as 'gifted', 'capable', 'average' or 'degenerate'. Galton's ideas enjoyed relatively little success in affecting British government policies, certainly much less than in Australia, where his ideas were used to bolster the 'White Australia Policy', or in the American eugenic movement, which was concerned about the long-term implications of interracial marriage.

Galton introduced the concept of 'regression' (which he initially called 'reversion') to describe the phenomenon whereby the offspring of parents who fall at the extremes of the distribution in the general population (e.g. very tall or very small) tend to produce offspring in the middle range (average height). For example, the offspring of very tall organisms of whatever species tend not to be taller still but closer to the average height. His attempts to quantify the degree of resemblance between the characteristics of parent and offspring led to the creation of a 'regression line', whose slope provides a measure of resemblance. However, because the slope depends on both the scale and unit of measurement, it was an imperfect device, and it was not until 1888 that he found a way of representing the measure in standardised form. The regression slope became a 'coefficient of correlation', a unit-free measure of alliance between any two variables. Karl Pearson later devised a formula that produced a mathematical expression of the strength of a correlational relationship between any two variables within the numerical range -1 to $+1$. For example, a value of $+1$ means that there is a perfect relationship between two variables (e.g. as a person's weight increases, so does their height). A value of 0 indicates there is no relationship (e.g. a person's height is completely unrelated to the size of their garden), whereas a value of -1 indicates a negative relationship (e.g. as a person's weight increases, their height decreases).

Galton's extreme nativism, the idea that the mind and its contents are innately determined, did not go unchallenged. The French philosopher Alphonse de Candolle provided cogent arguments that climate, religious tolerance, democratic government and a flourishing economy were at least as important as inheritance. In order to answer these criticisms Galton embarked on a study, published as 'Englishmen of Science', in which he distributed a questionnaire to 200 of his fellow scientists at the Royal Society. This was probably the first use of the questionnaire as a technique for collecting psychological data. While the majority of respondents indicated that they considered their interest in science to have been genetically influenced, Galton was struck, first, by the disproportionate number of Scots in his sample, and second, by the fact that they tended to attribute their achievements to the influence of the liberal Scottish educational system. This contrasted with the often very negative view of the

English educational system expressed by English scientists. Galton urged the reformation of English schools to make them more like their Scottish counterparts, and in so doing he revised somewhat his position on the inheritability of intelligence: the potential for high intelligence is inherited but it must be nurtured by propitious environmental conditions. However, his commitment to a fundamentally nativist position is indicated in his innovative study of twins, which he advocated as an approach to estimating the relative influence of nature (genetics) and nurture (environment). He showed that monozygotic or identical twins tend to be very similar to one another, even when they are reared apart, and dyzygotic or non-identical twins tend to be dissimilar, even when they are reared together.

Inquiries into Human Faculty and its Development (1883) represents the first systematic, scientific treatise on individual differences in psychological phenomena and describes the first use of the word-association test. The test involves reading words from a prepared list and recording the first word that the listener utters in reply. Galton was particularly struck by three features: first responses to stimulus words tended to be the same for the majority of people; responses were often drawn from childhood experiences; and the test appeared to reveal hitherto unobserved workings of the mind (e.g. people would sometimes respond with words that had psychological significance, such as mother–fear, rather than lexical associates such as mother–father. *Inquiries* also included the first large-scale systematic survey of the use of mental imagery. Galton showed that the ability to form images follows the 'law of errors' – it is normally distributed in the population. However, he also observed that many of the more eminent people in his sample – those he considered to be the most intelligent – were very poor at forming images. This was entirely unexpected: if intelligence is founded on sensory acuity, and sensory acuity is essential to the ability to construct images, why is it that so many highly intelligent people seem unable to form and use images? (Arthur Jensen subsequently succeeded in showing a relationship between general intelligence and measures of sensory acuity incorporated within reaction-time tasks.) Although intelligence is no longer considered to be based on sensory acuity, Galton's studies formed the beginnings of the psychological testing movement and in 1886 inspired a head-mistress in London, Sophie Bryant, to initiate a programme of psychological assessment in England. Galton's psychological testing procedures were introduced to North America by James McKeen Cattell, who had studied with both Galton and Wundt.

Galton's enthusiasm for surveying individual differences inspired his creation of an anthropometric laboratory for the study of human body measurements at London's International Health Exhibition in 1884. Over the course of about a year he took a very large number of measures of 9,337 visitors, including their head size, arm span, length of the middle finger, visual acuity and so on. He established a similar facility in the science galleries of the South Kensington Museum, and operated it for several years. Much of his capacious data archive was not analysed until the introduction of calculating machines that were adequate to the task. Those analyses revealed, *inter alia*, that people from lower socio-economic backgrounds continued their physical growth longer than those who enjoyed more privileged environments, and that the tempo of development was somewhat slower then than now.

There is little doubt that Galton was enormously influenced by his cousin, Charles Darwin: 'I rarely approached his general presence without an almost overwhelming sense of devotion and reverence and I valued his encouragement and approbation more perhaps than that of the whole world besides. This is the simple outline of my scientific history' (1908). But, while Darwin was broadly sympathetic to Galton's views on eugenics, it is also clear from correspondence between them that his extreme nativism went too far: 'Though I see so much difficulty, the object seems a grand one and you have pointed out the sole feasible. Yet I fear Utopian plan of procedure, in improving the human race' (Darwin, cited in Desmond and Moore, 1992). Comparing Galton to Wundt, the statistician and psychologist Karl Pearson opined that Wundt progressed from psychology to anthropology, whereas Galton went from anthropology to psychology. Their contributions were independent and different. Wundt pioneered experimental methods, Galton championed quantitative surveys and the application of statistical techniques. Wundt's interest was in the generalised human mind – particularly the normal, healthy adult mind – whereas Galton's interest was in variations in individual ability and in any and every mind. Regrettably, Galton's eugenics sullied his reputation as a scientist and somewhat over-shadowed his inestimable contributions in other areas.

Francis Galton's major writings

Hereditary Genius, Macmillan, 1869.
English Men of Science: Their Nature and Nurture, Macmillan, 1874.
'Typical laws of heredity', *Proceedings of the Royal Institution*, 1877, 8, 282–301.
Inquiries into Human Faculty and its Development, Macmillan, 1883.
'Regression towards mediocrity in hereditary stature', *Journal of the Anthropological Institute*, 1886, 15, 246–63.

'Co-relations and their measurement, chiefly from anthropometric data',
  Proceedings of the Royal Society, 1888, 45, 125–45.
Natural Inheritance, Macmillan, 1889.
Fingerprints, Macmillan, 1892.
Memories of my Life, Methuen, 1908.

Further reading

Desmond, A. and Moore, J. (1992) *Darwin*, Penguin.
Fancher, R. E. (1985) *The Intelligence Men*, Norton.
Forrest, D. W. (1974) *Francis Galton: The Life and Work of a Victorian Genius*, Elek.

GIBSON, JAMES JEROME (1904–79)

Gibson's 'ecological psychology' sought to understand the relationships between the way a person perceives the world and how they behave.

J. J. Gibson was born in McConnelsville, Ohio, and raised in the US Midwest. His father, Thomas, was a railroad surveyor and his mother, Gertrude, had been a teacher until her marriage. James ('Jimmy') had two younger brothers, Thomas and William. He began his undergraduate studies at Northwestern University and, after a year, he transferred to Princeton where he was influenced by Edwin B. Holt, one of the early behaviourists, and the experimental psychologist Herbert S. Langfeld, who was a strong advocate of the view that consciousness does not exist in isolation from motor actions (e.g. walking, turning, lifting) and could not be studied independently of those acts. In 1928 he completed his doctoral dissertation at Princeton. His research thesis set out to test a claim made by Gestalt psychologists such as **Wertheimer** that memories for complex visual forms change spontaneously to memories for simpler structures, in line with Gestalt principles of organisation. He demonstrated that this was not the case and showed that learning was crucially important. After completing his doctorate he went to Smith College to take up his first academic appointment, and while he was there he encountered an English translation of Kurt Koffka's *Principles of Gestalt Psychology* which greatly influenced his thinking and work. One of the students at Smith, Eleanor Jack, took his courses on experimental psychology. 'Jimmy' and 'Jackie' were married, and Jackie became his closest and most influential colleague. About their working together he wrote: 'We have collaborated on occasion, but not as a regular thing. And when we did we were not a husband-and-wife team, God knows, for we argued endlessly ... When it is assumed that whatever one Gibson says, the other will agree, we are annoyed, for it isn't so.' They had two children, James Jerome and Jean.

The influence of Gestalt thinking is indicated in Gibson's demonstration of a tilt-induction effect whereby observers report a vertical line as appearing to tilt in the direction opposite to surrounding context lines; and so, when attempting to adjust a line to true vertical, the tendency is to err in the direction of the context lines. The phenomenon is very similar to the tilted-room effect reported by another Gestalt psychologist, **Asch**. During the Second World War, Gibson directed a psychological research unit for the Army Air Force's Aviation Psychology Program. His unit implemented a new way of constructing tests for pilot selection; they used motion pictures to present the materials they used to test their candidate pilots. While working on these tests he began to develop the idea that there is more information available in moving than in static pictures. Following the war, he returned to Smith College, but then moved on to Cornell where he remained for the rest of his career.

His *Perception of the Visual World* (1950) presented his 'ground theory' of space perception. The theory suggested that gradients of texture on the ground correspond to gradients on the retina, and these are the sensory basis for perceiving depth and space. In other words the retina of the eye is sensitive to different kinds of textures in the environment and can use that textural information to estimate distances and spaces. He became dissatisfied with this theory and began to think that theories of visual perception that focus on the way the eye and brain respond to light are formulated at an inappropriate level. A new discipline, which he called ecological optics, was needed. Ecological optics is concerned with the study of optical information at the level appropriate for understanding vision. The implication of this statement is that an adequate theory of visual perception must incorporate an analysis of how organisms look and move around their environment. Animals move; they are not stationary organisms passively responding to whatever light impinges on their ocular sensing devices. In fact they often change their position in order to see things better. Thus a theory of visual perception had to incorporate a role for the movement of the organism; it should be about ambulatory vision. His new theory of visual perception and his formulation of the new discipline of ecological optics were presented in his next book, *The Senses Considered as Perceptual Systems* (1966).

The concept of invariants is essential to Gibson's theory. He considered perception to be an activity – a dynamic process. A perceptual invariant is a higher-order property of patterns of stimulation that remain constant during changes associated with the observer, the environment or both. Followers of Gibson's theory distinguish between two kinds of perceptual invariant: transformational and structural. Transformational invariants are patterns of change that can reveal what is happening to an object. For instance, when a car moves away from us at a constant speed, its apparent size reduces. The decrease in area is proportional to the square of the distance. Wherever this relationship obtains it means that the distance between us and the object is changing in a regular manner. Where the relationship does not hold, it must mean either that the object is accelerating or decelerating, or it is actually changing its size. Structural invariants are higher patterns of relationships that remain constant despite changes in visual stimulation. For instance, two cars of an identical make are parked at different distances. It is easy for us to tell that they are the same size. They will usually be viewed against a scene containing a visible horizon and it can be shown that the ratio of an object's height to the distance between its base and the horizon is invariant across all distances from the viewer.

Another essential and novel part of Gibson's theory is the concept of affordances. The notion of affordance defines a relationship between a perceiving organism and its environment. 'The affordances of the environment are what it offers the animal, what it provides or furnishes, either for good or ill. The verb to afford is found in the dictionary, but the noun affordance is not. I have made it up. I mean by it something that refers to both the environment and the animal in a way that no existing term does. It implies the complementarity of the animal and the environment ... ' (1979: 127). Affordances are the meanings an environment has for an organism; they guide behaviour. Gibson claimed that affordances can be perceived directly, without prior synthesis or analysis. This means, for instance, that the properties of objects that reveal they can be grasped can be directly perceived from the pattern of stimulation arising from them. For example, a child who is shown a novel object can instantly tell whether that object can be grasped or not because there is enough information in the object for the child to make an appropriate deduction.

Gibson's ideas are in stark opposition to a physics-based approach to the analysis of visual perception. The physics-based approach is essentially data-driven, or bottom-up, because the emphasis is on understanding the effects of photons when they strike the retina. The perception of surfaces and depth, for instance, is thought to be a composition of the information provided by these atoms of visual perception. The organism perceiving an object attaches some value to it – value is attached to an object by the perceiver, it is not directly perceived. The ecological approach takes quite a different view. It considers surfaces to be directly perceived, not constructed in the perceptual system of organisation from bits of information collected at the retinas. It also takes the view that what these surfaces afford an animal are directly perceived as well; they are not worked out or deduced by the animal. Critics have argued that Gibson's account denies a place for information processing, or even for thinking, in the processes of visual perception. Supporters counter that his ecological theory shows how the environment augments the internal processes of the mind/brain, so that information processing can no longer be understood except in terms of factors internal to an animal. Thus the environment provides structured information to a perceiving animal, reducing the amount of processing necessary for the perception of complex entities.

The theory of information that flows from Gibson's ecological theory of perception has been used in many areas of applied cognitive psychology. For example, the notion of perceptual affordances permeate much thinking in the psychology of design, where in practical use it has become synonymous with the idea of stimulus–response compatibility – the notion that what makes some tasks more or less difficult to perform is partly determined by the way in which individual stimuli and responses are paired with each other. To perform a task, or to use an object effectively, the stimulus (or object) must provide the perceiver/user with the information necessary to perform the desired action/response. Doors provide many examples of both good and poor design. Doors that provide a flat plate are clearly for pushing; however, doors with handles, though they afford pulling, should often be pushed instead. In the latter case the design has failed.

Several criticisms have been made against Gibson's theory. First, it has been argued that the theory does not specify what is meant by 'direct perception'. It is possible to build simple models that can be seen to have two distinct motions, even though the stimulus array reaching the retina does not change physically. When people view these models they notice that the perception of orientation precedes the perception of motion, which suggests that perception of the motion of the object is not 'direct' but can be decomposed into stages. Second, Gibson argued that there are invariant properties in physical events which afford the perception of those events. However, David Marr and others have attempted to create computer models of vision, and to build computers that see. These seeing computers include a role for invariant properties in physical events, but Marr has shown that the task of specifying these invariant properties is enormously more complex than Gibson supposed. This does not mean that Gibson was wrong, but it suggests that something that he considered to be relatively straightforward turns out to be extremely problematic, and this indicates that part of his theory is under-elaborated. Third, Gibson considered affordances to be the most subtle forms of perceptual invariance. However, it is extremely difficult to define affordance and to predict a relationship with behaviour. For instance, if certain objects in the world 'afford' eating, what is it in the nature of the optic array that makes explicit this affordance? Related to this is the difficulty of actually finding invariants and affordances. Gibson's theory gives little guidance on how this difficulty might be overcome.

The theory of affordances is a fundamental departure from alternative theories of value and meaning, as indicated in Gibson's extension of affordances beyond the perceptual information that surfaces provide to an animal. The more radical extension of his theory claims that surfaces can be directly perceived, and that the use of these surfaces can also be directly perceived, even those uses which do not seem to have immediate connection with visual perception. This means, for example, that how a thing tastes can be directly perceived. This is possible because 'a unique combination of invariants, a compound invariant, is just another invariant' (1979: 141), and the taste of a thing is a compound invariant. However, as Gibson himself pointed out, the more radical version of his theory cannot adequately explain how misperceptions occur. If a person is aware of an illusory perception, is the misinformation caused by the ambient light, or by the person's internal perceptual processes? The first possibility, that light in itself can be thought to have a false meaning, seems wholly untenable. The second possibility implies that some mechanism is dependent on the perceiver and this must account for the introduction of error – which implies that perception is not direct. Gibson's theory also runs into difficulties when asked to account for learning. How does the learning of affordances, not directly related to a perceiver's internal perceptual processes, come about? For example, how does an elderly man come to learn that ambient light carrying affordances information to him is carrying the same affordances information to others, such as to a toddler? The ambient light cannot carry information about the affordance an object provides to someone else. Thus, learning requires more than direct perception, which implies that some affordances are not directly perceived.

Despite these limitations and criticisms, Gibson's theory made some fundamentally important advances in the psychology of perception.

First, it placed the environment at the centre of perception research and encouraged the development of a line of investigation that used ecologically plausible or naturalistic stimuli rather than laboratory-created stimuli. Second, Gibson's concept of 'ecological optics' stimulated interest in perception in other species and thereby raised general questions about the nature of perceptual processes. His final book, *The Ecological Approach* (1979), concluded with a plea that the terms and concepts of his theory should ' . . . never shackle thought as the old terms and concepts have!'

James Gibson's major writings

'The reproduction of visually perceived forms', *Journal of Experimental Psychology*, 1929, 12, 1–39.

'Adaptation, after-effect and contrast in the perception of curved lines', *Journal of Experimental Psychology*, 1933, 16, 1–31.

'Determinants of the perceived vertical and horizontal', *Psychological Review*, 1938, 45, 300–23 (with O. H. Mowrer).

The Perception of the Visual World, Houghton Mifflin, 1950.

'What is a form?', *Psychological Review*, 1951, 58, 403–12.

'Perceptual learning: differentiation or enrichment?', *Psychological Review*, 1955, 62, 32–41 (with E. J. Gibson).

'Ecological optics', *Vision Research*, 1961, 1, 253–62.

The Senses Considered as Perceptual Systems, Houghton Mifflin, 1966.

The Ecological Approach to Visual Perception, Erlbaum, 1979.

Further reading

MacLeod, R. B. and Pick, H. L. Jr (1974) *Perception: Essays in Honor of James J. Gibson*, Cornell University Press.

Marr, D. (1982) *Vision*, Freeman.

Norman, D. (1999) *The Design of Everyday Things*, MIT Press.

Ullman, S. (1980) 'Against direct perception', *Behavioral and Brain Sciences*, 3, whole issue.

GREGORY, RICHARD L. (1923–)

Gregory's work reflects a lifelong interest in studying illusions for what they can reveal about how the brain makes sense of the information it receives about the world.

Richard Gregory's father, Christopher C. L. Gregory, was the first Director of the University of London Observatory. Richard was born in London, educated at King Alfred School, Hampstead (1931–40) and served in the RAF (1941–47) during the Second World War.

Following military service he read Moral Sciences (Philosophy and Experimental Psychology) at Downing College, Cambridge, where his interest in perceptual processes was nurtured through contact with **Bartlett** and the neuropsychologist Oliver Zangwill. After graduating, he spent two years working on methods of escape from submarines, and was then appointed to a lecturership at Cambridge and gained a Fellowship at Corpus Christi College. He started the Special Sense Laboratory and worked on a variety of topics, including recovery of sight after blindness from infancy, visual distortion illusions and the perceptual problems of moon landing and docking in space for the US Air Force. During this period he invented a number of research instruments: a telescopic camera to minimise the effects of atmospheric turbulence for planetary and lunar landing photographs, an optical depth scanning microscope, and a three-dimensional drawing machine. He left Cambridge in 1967 and moved to the University of Edinburgh, where he co-founded, with Donald Michie and Christopher Longuet-Higgins, the Department of Machine Intelligence and Perception at the University of Edinburgh. It was there that he built 'Freddie', one of the first intelligent robots, capable of recognising objects as well as handling and manipulating them. Although the work attracted considerable international recognition, failure of government funding for work on artificial intelligence prompted a move to the University of Bristol. There he established the Brain and Perception Laboratory to investigate processes in vision and hearing, with an emphasis on medical applications, and founded and directed the Bristol Exploratory Science and Technology Centre.

Broadly speaking there are three types of theory of human perception: inferential (associated with **Helmholtz**), organisational (such as that pursued by **Wertheimer** and others of the Gestalt school), and ecological (such as that developed by **Gibson**). Gregory takes as his model of human perception the perceiver-as-scientist. In this regard he follows Helmholtz, who proposed that the core of perception is based on processes involving unconscious inference, and demurs from Gibson's ecological optics: 'Current sensory data (or "stimuli") are simply not adequate to control behaviour directly in familiar situations. Behaviour can continue through quite long gaps in sensory data and remain appropriate though there is no sensory input ... In engineering terminology, we cannot monitor the characteristics of objects which must be known for behaviour to be appropriate. This implies that these characteristics are inferred, from the past. The related highly suggestive – indeed dominating – fact is that perception is predictive' (1974: xix). Thus for Gregory a central problem of visual perception is understanding how the brain interprets the patterns detected by the eye as external objects. This is important because perception involves much more than simply detecting patterns; it involves seeing objects in space and time. The act of perceiving is a dynamic process involving the brain's search for the best interpretation of the information that is being presented. The best interpretation takes the form of a 'perceptual hypothesis' or prediction which, when it is incorrect, results in a visual illusion. In other words, visual illusions are caused by the brain making incorrect calculations about how the world looks. Ambiguous pictures – pictures showing objects that look like one thing and then another – reveal that the perceptual system sometimes uses rival hypotheses about how the world looks. However, these rival hypotheses are more than mistakes, they are the inevitable consequences of the ordinary perceptual processes involved in sensing the environment around us. Gregory's work reflects his continuing interest in studying illusions – to describe them as perceptual 'anomalies' is a misnomer because they are a product of normal perceptual processes – and in understanding the lessons to be learned from studying them. He has written on a wide range of illusions, including the Ponzo illusion (sometimes referred to as the railway track illusion, whereby parallel lines appear to converge in the distance) and the Moon illusion (whereby the moon looks larger when it is positioned low on the horizon and small when it is at its zenith). He has explained a considerable number of illusions in terms of a general perspective–constancy hypothesis. The hypothesis states that in certain contexts portions of illusory figures are perceived as two-dimensional projections of three-dimensional shapes in depth. In other words, the brain normally uses a size constancy mechanism to work out that an object (e.g. a football) two metres away is the same size as an identical object fifty metres away. When presented with some kinds of images the brain wrongly calculates that the parts of the figure in the image that are furthest away are larger. The perspective–constancy hypothesis explains many illusions very well, but not every illusion. For example, when some illusions are inverted, the illusion does not disappear as would be predicted by the perspective–constancy hypothesis. This has prompted some theorists to contend that some illusions depend on the age and culture of the perceiver. However, Gregory's general approach is based on the claim that visual illusions are caused by information processing mechanisms that are normally adaptive.

Gregory's view of the perceiver as a scientist or problem solver is attractive, although it can be argued that in some respects it takes too much for granted and leaves some issues unexplained. For example, it begs the question of how it is we manage to recognise anything as being the kind of object it is. How do we know that the object before us is a table and not something else? In order to understand how we recognise the patterns detected by the eye as objects, it is first necessary to explain how we recognise patterns. To recognise something as a pattern requires much the same apparatus as is required to recognise a particular thing as an object, namely the possession of some appropriate categories of patterns and the ability to recognise instances as falling into one or other of them. Thus, at a fundamental level, the perceiver appears to require *a priori* or innate knowledge of the world in their interpretation of what they see – but this account does not indicate where this *a priori* knowledge comes from other than to imply that it must be innate.

Gregory's account of perception suggests that, in seeing something, a person relates their immediate perceptual experiences to earlier experiences and to knowledge accumulated through learning, but it says relatively little about how this might be done in a way that makes sense to others. For example, no two people have precisely the same set of experiences, but if what we perceive is influenced by our experiences, how can we be sure that people see the world in similar ways? This criticism is not specific to Gregory's position – it is germane to every 'top-down' account of perception where the perceiver is thought to be actively engaging in constructing and imposing meaning on sensory information rather than simply passively responding to sensory stimulation. How is it that people make the same interpretation of what is potentially an infinitely ambiguous visual scene? The assumption in Gregory's theory is that the range of interpretations is constrained or determined by the environment, genetic factors, or a combination of both. However, there is another possibility, namely that perceptual categories are at least partly socially contrived – they are negotiated agreements and, as such, a social phenomenon. For an example, see the discussion of studies by **Luria** and **Vygotsky** on pp. 156 and 238.

Gregory made groundbreaking advances in other areas of perception too. His studies of motion perception led to the identification and description of two interdependent systems: the image–retina movement system and the eye–head movement system. In the image–retina system, successive stimuli of adjacent retinal loci provide signals regarding the movement of an object. Information from the eye–head system is used to differentiate movements of the observer from that given by the image–retina system. These systems allow observers to distinguish between movement of the retinal image caused by eye movements and movement of the retinal image caused by physical movements of objects in relation to their background. However, there is little doubting the fact that Gregory is best known for his work on visual illusions, a reputation due in no small part to his talent for popularising and making accessible complex concepts in psychology and vision science.

Richard Gregory's major writings

Eye and Brain, Weidenfeld, 1966; fourth edition, 1990.
The Intelligent Eye, Duckworth, 1970.
Illusion in Nature and Art, Duckworth, 1973 (co-edited with Sir E. Gombrich).
Concepts and Mechanisms of Perception, Duckworth, 1974.
Mind in Science, Weidenfeld, 1981; Penguin, 1983.
Odd Perceptions, Methuen, 1986; Routledge, 1988.

Further reading

Goldstein, B. (2000) *The Blackwell Handbook of Perception*, Blackwell.
Prinzmetal, W. and Beck, D. M. (2001) 'The tilt–constancy theory of visual illusions', *Journal of Experimental Psychology: Human Perception and Performance*, 27, 206–17.
Robinson, J. O. (1998) *The Psychology of Visual Illusion*, Dover.

HEBB, DONALD OLDING (1904–85)

Hebb encouraged psychologists to think anew about how the brain functions, and reawakened an interest in the neurological basis of behaviour.

Both of Hebb's parents were practising physicians, and he spent his childhood in Chester, Nova Scotia. He was a largely indifferent student, as both a child and an undergraduate. After graduating from Dalhousie he had intended to make a living as a writer, but pragmatic considerations directed him to an early career in teaching. While a school principle in Quebec, he began reading **Freud**, **James** and **Wundt**, but his poor academic record barred him from direct entry to any of the regular university programmes. A dispensation was granted that allowed him to enrol part-time on the psychology programme at McGill University. This provided his first serious introduction to **Pavlov**'s psychology of learning, something which was not to his liking. His MA thesis was a theoretical elaboration of a radical environmentalist account of how animals learn, namely that skeletal reflexes, such as the knee-jerk reflex, are not innate but the result of learning in the womb. His thesis examiner, the neurologist Boris Babkin, encouraged him to gain more laboratory experience and introduced him to Leonid Andreyev, who had joined McGill from Pavlov's laboratory. After a tough year following the death of his wife in a car accident, Hebb left McGill in 1934 with his Ph.D. still not completed. Robert Yerkes offered him a position at Yale, but on Babkin's recommendation he went instead to work with the neurologist Karl Lashley in Chicago. It was there that he encountered the ideas and work of the comparative neurologist C. Judson Herrick and the developmental neurobiologist Paul A. Weiss. After a year, Lashley moved to Harvard and Hebb followed. Lashley's influence was important because it diverted Hebb away from mainstream debates about the relative merits of one learning theory over another and towards an analysis of whether an animal's capacity to perceive its environment is determined by genetic or environmental factors. After completing his Ph.D. at Harvard – he examined the role of innate factors in the organisation of visual perception in the rat – he returned to Montreal to work with the neurologist Wilder Penfield. With Penfield he examined the impact of brain injury on human intelligence and behaviour. These investigations demonstrated that surgical removal or accidental destruction of large amounts of brain tissue might have relatively little impact on memory and intelligence, which suggested to him that these processes may be widely distributed throughout the brain and are not located in a specific area. He also devised a series of human and animal tests of intelligence, including the Hebb–Williams maze, a procedure that was widely used to quantify the relative intelligence of different species. His studies of intelligence led him to the conclusion that experience played a greater role than was generally assumed, although he was a strong interactionist – holding the view that behaviour is the product of a complex interplay of genetic and environmental influences.

In 1942 Hebb rejoined Lashley, who was then director of the Yerkes Laboratory of Primate Biology in Florida, and worked on emotion in the chimpanzee. There he came across the work of the neurologist Rafael Lorente de Nó, which pointed to the pervasiveness of closed circuits (also called reverberatory circuits) in the organisation of the brain. Lorente de Nó suggested that these circuits could account for the persistence in memory of a stimulus that had ceased to stimulate a sensory organ. For example, reverberatory circuits could explain how brief sight of a scene can be retained in memory after the scene ceases to stimulate the retina – the sensory image metaphorically reverberates. This in turn led Hebb to the notion of a 'cell assembly', a reverberatory circuit that could be assembled by experience. The brain is composed of neurons that are connected to one another at junctions called synapses. Hebb suggested that changes in resistance at the synapse can come about through experience – these are called Hebbian synapses. Some synapses in the brain are more affected by experience than others. The ones mostly affected by experience are to be found in the hippocampus, a part of the brain that is especially important in learning, emotion and motivation. Hebb suggested that these cell assemblies are the neural equivalents of what are commonly called ideas or concepts. He introduced the term 'phase sequence' to refer to the connections that link one cell assembly to another, and, by implication, one idea to another. When a single assembly or a combination of assemblies fires, the entire sequence tends to fire, and this is experienced as a stream of thought. Pursuing this line of reasoning, Hebb suggested that what we experience as 'thinking' is due to connections of neuronal activity between cell assemblies. The implication is huge: activity within the brain that appears to involve every part of that organ can be described as networks of neural connections.

In 1948 Hebb returned to a chair at McGill, and the following year he published his classic *The Organization of Behavior: A Neuropsychological Theory*. It appeared at a time when interest in psychophysiology and psychobiology was in decline, and it provided a revitalising impetus by elaborating an approach that sought to explain behaviour and thought in terms of the organ responsible for producing them – the brain. One of the collateral consequences of this book is that it attracted to McGill some of the best researchers on brain–behaviour relationships and established McGill as a world centre for neuropsychology (the connection between neurology and psychology). In that book Hebb defined the problem of understanding behaviour as 'the problem of understanding the total action of the nervous system, and vice versa' (1949: xiv). His retirement was spent on a small farm near to his place of birth. He suffered a similar demise to **Rogers**, the result of complications following hip surgery.

Hebb's neuropsychological theory is structured around three central postulates. The first states that connections between neurons increase in efficacy in proportion to the strength of the association between pre- and post-synaptic activity: 'When an axon of cell A is near enough to excite B and repeatedly or persistently takes part in firing it, some growth process or metabolic change takes place in one or both cells such that A's efficiency, as one of the cells firing B, is increased' (1949: 62). The second postulate states that groups of neurons that tend to fire together form a cell-assembly whose activity can persist after the triggering event or stimulus and constitutes a representation of that event. The third postulate suggests that thinking is the sequential activation of sets of cell-assemblies. Taken together they form the core of Hebb's theory, which he has summarised thus:

> Any frequently repeated, particular stimulation will lead to the slow development of a 'cell-assembly', a diffuse structure comprising cells in the cortex and diencephalon (and also, perhaps, in the basal ganglia of the cerebrum), capable of acting briefly as a closed system, delivering facilitation to other such systems and usually having a specific motor facilitation. A series of such events constitutes a 'phase sequence' – the thought process. Each assembly action may be aroused by a preceding assembly, by a sensory event, or normally by both. The central facilitation from one of these activities on the next is the prototype of 'attention.' ... The theory is evidently a form of connectionism ... though it does not deal in direct connections between afferent and efferent pathways: not an S–R psychology, if R means muscular response ... It does not, further, make any single nerve cell or pathway essential to any habit or perception.
>
> (1949: xix)

Hebb's early research had shown that environmental factors could exert a much stronger influence on neural development than had previously been suggested. When rats (reared by his daughters at home) were raised in enriched environments, their performance on diversion and maze problems was much better than that of rats raised alone in cages with no 'toys' or other objects. He attributed this difference to sensory diversity and to how the brain is built up (in cell assemblies and phase sequences). Thus he suggested that there are two kinds of learning: associative and cognitive. Associative learning consists of the progressive construction of cell assemblies that occurs early in life and which can be explained using stimulus–response theories. Once cell assemblies and phase sequences are developed, they can be rearranged, and it is this activity that characterises higher thought processes of complex thinking and problem-solving.

There is a good deal of evidence that Hebb's innovative use of the concept of the reverberatory circuit post-dated by more than a decade a similar use by his teacher Karl Lashley. The issue of priority, and a recognition of Hebb's indebtedness to Lashley, may well have motivated Hebb's invitation to Lashley to appear as co-author on *The Organization of Behavior*. There were conditions attached to the offer however: Lashley would have to abandon his commitment to the idea of the mass action of the brain and revert to a position closer to one that regards changes at the synaptic junction as underpinning learning. Hebb appears to have been perplexed by Lashley's decision to decline the invitation and wondered whether it may have been due to what he considered to be Lashley's preoccupation with countering theoretical criticism. Lashley's decision may also have been due to a feeling that he had nothing substantial to contribute to Hebb's first draft. Orbach offers the following evaluation: 'Hebb ... brought Lashley's life-work to fruition in a remarkable book ... that contained in it three ideas that made a great impression on the neuropsychological community of the day: the interconnection of neurons referred to today as the "Hebb synapse"; the central autonomous process; and the cell assembly ... Lashley expressed great admiration for the book and, at the same time, he disapproved of it because of its empiricist and connectionist cast' (1998: 60).

Hebb acknowledged the speculative, ill-defined nature of much of his theory and maintained that his principle objective was to present a strong case for a new type of neuropsychological theory, of which his was one instance. The existence of the Hebb synapse is not in doubt. Other claims, such as the hypothesis that reverberatory neural activity is a kind of memory trace, are yet to be convincingly supported. Nevertheless, his ideas inspired new areas of investigation, including the role of early experience in perceptual development. Many gifted students passed through his laboratories, including James Olds who made important innovations in brain recording and brain stimulation in freely moving animals, and Ronald Melzack whose gate control theory of pain proved to be a major breakthrough in the field of pain research and therapy. The success of James McClelland and David Rumelhart in introducing Hebb's ideas into cognitive science (an interdisciplinary approach to the way the brain processes information) during the 1980s ensured that Hebb's ideas continued to figure prominently in computational representations of thought processes and language.

The history of psychology can be traced to the convergence of nineteenth-century philosophy and physiology. The philosophy of the associationists, who explained mental processes in terms of connections between more elementary units of mind, was particularly important. Hebb realised the potential in those ideas by providing a new kind of neural connectionism – associations among neurons in the brain – that sought to explain thought processes in terms of linkages between assemblies of neurons and larger models of those assemblies. While he believed that synaptic connections were the basis of mental associations, he went beyond the connectionism of **Watson** and others who argued that an association could not be localised to a single synapse and that stimulus–response relationships could be explained by simple reflex arcs connecting sensory neurons to motor neurons. His strong opposition to radical behaviourism, as espoused by Watson and others, and the importance he attached to understanding in detail what goes on between a stimulus and a behavioural response, helped clear the way for the emergence of cognitivism. (Cognitivism contends that the best way to understand human psychology is to work out the connection between what the brain does and what is experienced as thinking.)

Donald Hebb's major writings

'The innate organization of visual activity: I. Perception of figures by rats reared in total darkness', *Journal of Genetic Psychology*, 1937, 51, 101–26.
'The innate organization of visual activity: II. Transfer of response in the discrimination of brightness by rats reared in total darkness', *Journal of Comparative Psychology*, 1937, 24, 277–99.
'Intelligence in man after large removals of cerebral tissue: Report of four left frontal lobe cases', *Journal of General Psychology*, 1939, 21, 73–87.
'On the nature of fear', *Psychological Review*, 1946, 53, 259–76.
The Organization of Behavior, Wiley, 1949.
'Concerning imagery', *Psychological Review*, 1968, 75, 466–77.
Essay on Mind, Erlbaum, 1980.

Further reading

Glickman, S. (1996) 'Donald Olding Hebb: Returning the nervous system to psychology', in G. Kimble, C. Boneau and M. Wertheimer (eds), *Portraits of Pioneers in Psychology*, Erlbaum.
Jusczyk, P. W. and Klein, R. M. (eds) (1980) *The Nature of Thought: Essays in Honor of D. O. Hebb*, Erlbaum.
Orbach, J. (1998) *The Neuropsychological Theories of Lashley and Hebb*, University Press of America.

VON HELMHOLTZ, HERMANN LUDWIG FERDINAND (1821–94)

Helmholtz fundamentally altered the way physiologists and psychologists think about the nervous system when he published the first accurate estimate of the speed of a nerve impulse.

Helmholtz's mother, Caroline Penne, was the daughter of a Hanoverian artillery officer who was a descendent of William Penn, the English Quaker Reformer who founded Pennsylvania. Born in Potsdam, Germany, Helmholtz was the eldest of four children. Dogged by poor health, he was at first tutored at home by his father, August Ferdinand Julius Helmholtz, a teacher of philology and philosophy. His period at Potsdam Gymnasium, which he entered at the age of eight, was characterised by mediocre academic performance. This may be attributed more to the influence of his independence of thought rather than to any lack of ability. After graduating from the Gymnasium he had hoped to become a physicist, but lack of money meant he was unable to pursue his preferred career. Instead he entered the Friedrich Wilhelm Medical Institute, where he was given free tuition provided he agreed to serve as a surgeon with the Prussian army. After graduating from the Institute he began work in Potsdam as an army surgeon, where he also continued to work on aspects of theoretical physics. He was able to present his treatise on the law of conservation of energy at the age of twenty-six. In 1849 he went to the University of Konigsberg as a junior professor and was promoted to a full professorship two years later. He remained there for seven years, moved to Bonn for two years, and then to Heidelberg for a further two years, before finally being appointed as a professor of physics at the University of Berlin. In 1882 the German Emperor granted him noble status, and thereafter his name was Hermann von Helmholtz. In 1893 he went to the Chicago World's Fair, and while in the US he visited William **James**. On board the ship on his way back to Germany he fell, breaking his hip and sustaining a serious head injury. He never fully recovered and died the following year, but not before seeing the death of two of his children, his first wife Olga von Velten, and his illustrious student and friend Heinrich Hertz, the discoverer of radio waves. He was survived by his second wife, Anna von Mohl.

Helmholtz's invention of the ophthalmoscope in 1850 met with instant acclaim. It fundamentally altered the study of vision, as well as providing a device that transformed the diagnosis and treatment of eye disorders. The response to this innovation was surpassed only by the one that greeted his discovery, in 1852, of the speed of the neural current. It was a breathtaking scientific breakthrough. Although he was not a student at the University of Berlin, he was greatly influenced by the physiologist Johannes Müller and by one of his students Émil du Bois-Reymond, both of whom were based at Berlin. Müller had previously published three estimates for the speed of the nerve impulse, ranging from 9,000 feet per minute to 57,600 million feet per second – almost sixty times the speed of light. Helmholtz demonstrated all of Müller's estimates to be completely wrong. Working with the frog motor nerve he showed that the speed of transmission was about ninety feet per second. He then went on to measure the speed of transmission in sensory nerves and estimated these to be in the range fifty to one hundred metres per second. Although du Bois-Reymond later published more precise measurements, the importance of the discovery that nerve transmission was not instantaneous – or virtually instantaneous – is almost incalculable.

Helmholtz's work relating to the anatomy and the optics of the eye and its role in sensing and perceiving was first summarised in the *Handbuch der physiologischen Optik* (1856). It included Helmholtz's own work as well as that of other investigators. Helmholtz undertook the enormous task of replicating every experiment done by others whose results he discussed in his handbook. In a number of instances these re-examinations led to new discoveries – for instance, Helmholtz's invention of the tele-stereoscope. He continued to improve his research in optics, publishing a revised edition in 1860 and a third volume in 1867. All three volumes were published in a compendium in 1867. It contains close to 8,000 references and is still one of the standard texts in optics, having been reprinted in 1924 and again in 1964. One of his major contributions concerns his theory of colour perception.

The English physician and physicist Thomas Young had proposed that colour sensations are the product of patterns of stimulation of three different receptor types in the eye. Helmholtz rediscovered Young's relatively neglected ideas, modified them slightly, and published what became known as the Young–Helmholtz theory, or the tri-chromatic theory. Helmholtz suggested that there are three kinds of fibres in the eye – red, green and violet – and that stimulation of each kind produces a different colour sensation. A colour, other than one of the primaries, stimulates some combination of the three fibres, resulting in a perceived colour. One of the problems for the Young–Helmholtz theory is that the most common colour vision defect is the inability to differentiate red from green. According to the Young–Helmholtz theory the colour perceived as yellow results from the stimulation of red fibres and green fibres. These are assumed to be defective in red–green colour blindness. In other words the theory wrongly predicts that a person with a red–green defect should also have trouble seeing yellow. Although the theory was shown to be incorrect, it inspired Ewald Hering to develop a more successful alternative in the form of opponent–process theory, which states that there are three kinds of bipolar photoreceptors responding to white–red, red–green and blue–yellow.

Helmholtz's research in audition, which he summarised in *Die Lehre von den Tonempfindungen als physiologische Grundlage für die Theorie der Musik* (1863), was also of considerable significance. He combined his anatomical knowledge with his research on sound waves to form his 'resonance theory of hearing'. This proposed that the outer hair cells in the part of the inner ear called the organ of Corti respond selectively to different tonal frequencies. He argued that this enables the ear to discern single or combination tones from the myriad of waves impinging on it. Helmholtz was also the first physicist to investigate timbre, and to explain why the same note sounds different for different types of instrument. In contrast to Johannes Müller, who had formulated the 'Law of specific energies of nerves', Helmholtz postulated the 'Law of specific energies of fibres'. Thus, both his theory of colour vision and his resonance theory of hearing required that individual fibres within each nerve carry specific messages to the brain.

Helmholtz's explanations of sensation and perception were firmly situated within an empiricistic tradition, and to help bolster its influence he formed the '1847' or 'mechanist school' of physiology with his contemporaries du Bois-Reymond, Ernst Brücke and Carl Ludwig. In opposition to vitalism – the view that life is more than a physical process and cannot be reduced to such a process – their dictum stated that 'no other forces than common physical ones are active within the organism'. His mechanistic views met much opposition, particularly in Germany, where the prevailing climate favoured the philosophy of Immanuel Kant. Following the Kantian tradition, most German psychologists believed that certain thought processes and perceptual categories were *a priori*, or innately given. In contrast, Helmholtz argued that perceptions must be learned. In depth-perception, for example, the body must learn to correlate certain muscular tensions of the ocular muscles with the experienced distances. Helmholtz defined sensations as momentary sensory input, and perception as an input from the past. Perception modifies sensation by adding or detracting from it – a process which he termed 'unconscious inference'. This inference is an influence of which individuals are unaware, that is immediate, and that cannot be resisted. For example, when people think about making a perceptual judgement, such as estimating the number of rods they will need to use to reach an object located some distance from them, they may systematically overestimate the reaching distance. Their overestimation reflects the unconscious influence of non-perceptual processes, in this case imagining the outcome, on more fundamental thought processes. Thus, although Helmholtz was a firm empiricist, he also endorsed the idea of an active mind. The task of the mind was to create a reasonably accurate conception of reality from the various signs that it receives from the body's sensory systems. However, his view of mind differed from that of Kant because Kant believed that the mental categories of thought automatically or innately presented a conception of reality. In England, however, Helmholtz's philosophical orientation was more readily accepted since the philosophers Locke and Mill had laid the groundwork for empiricism (the view that all factual knowledge is derived from experience). However, Helmholtz's view of the mind also differed from that of most of the British empiricists, who saw the mind as largely passive. For Helmholtz, the mind's job was to construct a workable conception of reality given the incomplete and perhaps distorted information furnished by the senses. Although he found that the match between what was physically present and what was experienced psychologically was not very good, he could explain the discrepancy in terms of the properties of the receptor systems and the unconscious inferences of the observer. In so doing, he helped pave the way for the emergence of experimental psychology and, much later, of cognitive science.

The connection between Helmholtz and cognitive science (an interdisciplinary approach to the way the brain professes information) can be found in his attempts to explain why, when we move our eyes past a stationary scene, the scene does not appear to move, but when objects move in front of our eyes and our eyes are stationary, the objects are perceived to be moving. He pointed out that pressing one's finger against the side of the eyeball causes perceptions of apparent movement. However, the muscles that are stretched when this is done are the same ones used when the eyes are used normally. This suggests that motion is not based on information on what the eye muscles are doing. Helmholtz postulated, and it was subsequently established, that the visual system uses anticipatory or feed-forward information about planned eye movements to determine whether retinal displacements are due to the motion of the eye or the motion of objects in the world. A century later the philosopher and psychologist Jerry Fodor (1983) took Helmholtz's demonstration to support the proposition that thought processes are organised in a modular fashion. For example, the fact that feed-forward information about eye movements is not useful for accurate perception when the muscles are stretched manually suggests that the manual control system is functionally isolated from the visual system. In other words, the two systems can be said to occupy separate modules in the brain.

Although Helmholtz never held an academic post in psychology, his work in physics and physiology resulted in discoveries that were fundamental to psychology in general and to experimental psychology in particular. In psychology, Helmholtz worked with the physicist and physiologist Gustav T. Fechner, **Wundt** and the physiologist F. C. Donders; and in physics with Farraday, Tyndall and Kelvin. Perhaps no other individual has had as much influence, both direct and indirect, upon the establishment of psychology as a science as Helmholtz. He is associated with a series of epoch-making discoveries in the areas of thermodynamics, physiology, metabolism, optics, magnetism, electro-dynamics and geology. His research was much facilitated by the various professorships he held in surgery, anatomy, physiology and physics, and also by his invention and construction of an electro-magnetic motor, the myograph, the tangent galvanometer and the ophthalmoscope.

Hermann von Helmholtz's major writings

'Uber die Erhaltung der Kraft (On the Conservation of Energy)', *Wissenschaftliche Abhandlungen*, 1847, 1, 12–75.
'Rate of Transmission of the Excitatory Process in Nerve', *Berliner Monatsbericht, Comptes Rendus*, 1850, 30–3.
Handbuch der physiologischen Optik (Handbook of Physiological Optics), Voss, 1856.
Handbuch der physiologischen Optik Part II, Voss, 1860.
Die Lehre von den Tonempfindungen als physiologische Grundlage für die Theorie der Musik (The Theory of Tonal Sensations as the Physiological Basis of Music Theory), Dover, 1863 (reprinted 1954).
Handbuch der physiologischen Optik, Part III, Voss, 1867 (translated by J. P. C. Southall, Optical Society of America, 1924).

Further reading

Fodor, J. A. (1983) *The Modularity of Mind*, MIT Press.
Hurvich, L. M. and Jameson, D. (1979) 'Helmholtz's vision looking backward', *Contemporary Psychology*, 5, 901–4.
Koenigsberger, L. (1902) *Hermann von Helmholtz*, Dover (reprinted 1965).

HULL, CLARK (1884–1952)

Hull developed a comprehensive theory of learning based on explicit postulates that could be rigorously tested in a systematic manner.

Clark Hull's parents were married at the age of fifteen. His father was a big man with a cruel temper, while his mother was a shy woman who helped his illiterate father to read and write after they were married. Hull was born, sixteen months after his brother, in a log cabin on a farm near Akron, New York. The family moved to Michigan when Clark was about three or four, and he and his brother were raised under austere conditions, spending much of their time working on the farm. He attended a one-room schoolhouse in the tiny village of Sickels, his education occasionally being interrupted by the need to complete important chores back on the farm. At seventeen he passed a teachers' exam, and this gave him the opportunity to work as a teacher in a small rural school. He did that for about a year, during which time he experienced a crisis of religion. The teaching experience, coupled with his loss of faith, increased his self-awareness of his relative lack of understanding on a whole range of issues and motivated his decision to pursue a high-school education at Alma College. He stayed there for two years, but the graduation ceremony was followed by a special dinner after which several staff and students died from an outbreak of typhoid fever caused by eating contaminated food. Hull was seriously ill, and the fever left him with permanent amnesia about that period, as well as an especially fallible memory for the rest of his life. After a year, he returned to Alma College as a freshman with a plan to pursue a career in mining engineering. While training, he was able to secure work in the Minnesota mines, but this exposed him to an outbreak of polio that caused paralysis of his legs. Thus, at the age of twenty-four, he had to abandon his plans to pursue a career in engineering, and there was nothing he could do but return to the family farm for an extended period of recuperation. During his convalescence he decided to seek something that would allow him to combine his engineering talents with his intellectual curiosity on matters religious and philosophical. Psychology sounded promising, so he spent a good deal of his time reading William **James**'s *Principles of Psychology*, a weighty tome of fourteen hundred pages. Actually, large parts of the book were read to him by his mother because his vision was so weak he was unable to read for himself. After his recovery he returned to teaching for a period, and then enrolled in the University of Michigan where he graduated in 1913 with a degree in psychology. As a student he was particularly influenced by the experimental psychologists Walter B. Pillsbury, one of **Titchener**'s eminent students, and J. F. Shepard, and also by a course he took in logic that encouraged him to apply his engineering talents to designing and building a logic machine. At that time **Watson**'s ideas on behaviourism were beginning to filter through to undergraduate psychology degrees, and Hull was introduced to them indirectly through Shepard. After graduating, Hull was employed as an assistant to Joseph Jastrow at the University of Wisconsin, and he remained there to work for a doctorate on how people acquire and evolve concepts. He graduated in 1918 and remained at Wisconsin for a further ten years. During this period his interests in Gestalt psychology were developed through debates with Joseph Gengerelli, a graduate student at Wisconsin who, like Hull, was an talented engineer and ingenious experimentalist. Following much effort, Hull was able to bring Kurt Koffka, one of the founders of Gestalt psychology, to Wisconsin for a year. When an English translation of **Pavlov**'s *Conditioned Reflexes* became available in 1927, Hull studied it in great detail and even built a machine that simulated the conditional reflex. In 1929, at the age of forty-five, he moved to Yale University, where he remained for the rest of his career.

Although Hull is principally known for his work on the development of a mathematical theory of learning, a decade of his early academic career was spent studying hypnosis and suggestibility. Hull's interest in the latter started when he was assigned to teach pre-medical students at Wisconsin, a psychology course which included a treatment of hypnosis. His *Hypnosis and Suggestibility* (1933) was published ten years later and sets out some of the main features of his approach to understanding behaviour. Before Hull's arrival on the scene, much of the research on hypnosis had focused on the nature of the hypnotic 'trance'. Hull was not interested in speculating what this might or might not be; instead he set about using various machines to record the physiological changes that accompany hypnotic trance. This approach reflects both his basic commitment to using objective, experimental methods to collect psychological data, and the influence of his reading of Pavlov, because he considered the hypnotic state to be an unconsciously learned habit – Pavlov's conditional reflex. Staff at Yale's Medical School were concerned about Hull's work. At that time there was considerable mystery surrounding the nature of hypnosis, and many considered it an unknown and potentially dangerous technique. Pressure was brought to bear on Hull, and his research in this area was terminated. His attention turned to the analysis of learning.

Hull believed that behaviour is a result of the constant interaction between the organism and its environment, and he used the twin concepts of learning and motivation to account for the regularities in the way any living organism behaves. Specifically, he considered Pavlov's concept of the conditional reflex to provide a mechanism capable of accounting for learning, and he used the concept of drive to explain why learning occurred when it did. Although Hull was sympathetic to behaviourism, and especially to Watson's dismissal of introspection in favour of more objective, experimental methods of enquiry, he was less approving of what he regarded as the excessively dogmatic position adopted by many of behaviourism's more fanatical supporters. Their zeal sometimes acted against informed debate, and Hull felt that one consequence of this was that the behaviourists had not satisfactorily answered several of the criticisms levelled against bevaviourism by the Gestalt school of psychology. For example, the Gestalt psychologist Wolfgang Köhler published evidence suggesting that animals are capable of learning connections between stimuli, rather than just relationships between a stimulus and a response. Köhler concluded that animals are capable of creating some kind of internal mental representation of the two stimuli and of forming a link between them. Hull did not consider the Gestalt psychologists to be correct, but rather that the behaviourists had overstated their position at the level of argument and had not sufficiently pressed their case as was indicated by the facts of animal behaviour. Hull set about addressing this deficit by developing what he called a hypothetico–deductive learning theory. In general terms, a good scientific theory should consist of a logically organised set of postulates or assumptions from which theorems or propositions could be logically derived. Each proposition should then be tested under experimental conditions. If the evidence supports the proposition, then, by virtue of the logical connections between the different parts of the theory, the theory as a whole is supported. If the evidence does not support the theorem, then the theory as a whole is weakened. Hull used this general approach to develop a theory of learning. His theory makes extensive use of mathematical and logical concepts in order, first, to impose a logical structure among the basic assumptions stated, and, second, to ensure that the theorems are logically derived. His use of mathematical and logical concepts often attracted the criticism that his theory was so abstract it seemed irrelevant. However, his approach was motivated by a fervent belief that subjectivity is the source of much conflict and human misery. Rigorous methods of investigation need to be combined with the best kind of reasoning, and that, he argued, is to be found in maths and logic.

Hull's approach had its origins in a class discussion on rote learning – learning by mere repetition – during the summer of 1931. William

Lepley, a graduate student at Pennsylvania State College, provided a contribution to a small class exercise led by Hull in which he suggested that certain aspects of rote learning reported by the learning theorist Christian von Ebbinghaus seemed to be identical to some of Pavlov's ideas on the conditional reflex. Ebbinghaus had conducted a number of classical studies of memory and forgetting, in which people had to learn lists of items and recall them in the same serial order. Lepley suggested that this type of serial learning and serial recall could be explained as a sequence of conditioned responses to a set of stimuli. Hull developed this idea in an article entitled 'The conflicting psychologies of learning – a way out' (1935). That article set out a theoretical model of a small rote-learning system that consisted of eleven theorems logically derived from a statement of basic postulates. By the time Hull's *A Behavior System* (1952) appeared in print soon after his death, the theory had grown to seventeen postulates and more than 130 theorems.

The core of Hull's mathematical model of learning claims that there are two components in any behaviour: habit and drive. Habit strength ($_sH_R$) is due to associative learning, as illustrated by the strengthening of the association between a stimulus (such as a bell) and a response, such as salivation, using a reinforcement (e.g. food). Drive (D) is the motivational part of Hull's theory. The strength of drive tends to increase with the amount of time that has elapsed since the last reinforcement. For instance, the longer the period of time that has elapsed since an animal has eaten something, the greater will be the drive to eat again. Using these components, Hull developed the fundamental formula: $_sE_R = D \times (_sH_R)$, where $_sE_R$ represents excitatory potential. What this formula states is that the tendency for an organism to make a response (Hull first called this the excitatory potential, later revising it to the reaction potential) depends on habit strength, acquired through learning, and the level of drive operating at the time a particular behaviour is performed. If one translates this into an experimental prediction, then this theorem states that a hungry rat, having learned its way through a maze, will run much faster than a rat that is equally familiar with the same maze but has recently finished eating.

Hull made extensive use of subscripts in his formulae, although they do not have any mathematical meaning – they are descriptive labels. For instance, subscripts are used as follows – $_sH_R$ – in order to remind the reader that what is being referred to is an association (in this case a habit) between a particular stimulus and a particular response. One of the most influential of Hull's formulae is referred to as the law of habit formation: $_sH_R = 1 - 10^{-aN}$. This law states that habit strength can vary between a minimum (0) and a maximum (1), and that with reinforcement it increases regularly to maximum strength.

One of the major strengths of Hull's approach to theory-building is that every part of the theory is logically and transparently connected to every other part. When the theory is used to generate a theorem it can be objectively tested, and the impact of the evidence for the theory can be rationally evaluated. Of course, such a fully worked-out theory has within it the seeds of its own destruction. One could say that it is designed to be destroyed in order to advance our understanding and guide the development of better theories. So it was with Hull's theory, in two respects. First, it attracted an enormous amount of interest, precisely because of its logical coherence and its transparency. For instance, during the period 1941–50, 40 per cent of the studies published in the *Journal of Experimental Psychology* and the *Journal of Comparative and Physiological Psychology* cited Hull. Second, many of the predictions derived from Hull's theory were not supported by evidence gathered using well-designed experiments. Some of the hypotheses certainly appeared to be accurate. For example, one of the predictions one can make from the formula $_sE_R = D \times (_sH_R)$ is that an organism will do nothing if either drive (D) or habit strength $_sH_R$ is zero – because multiplying any value by zero gives a zero answer. Supposing you are really very hungry (D has a high value). Someone you know says they will give you food if you do some work for them, but when you've done this in the past not a crumb of food was forthcoming ($_sH_R$ has a value of zero, because there is no association between the verbal statement (S) and the handing over of food (R)). So, however hungry you are, you will not work for that person because you have learned that they will never feed you.

Although many of the detailed predictions deduced from Hull's mathematical theory of learning were not supported by empirical studies, his influence was nevertheless very considerable, and this was due in no small part to the efforts of Kenneth Spence. Spence completed his doctorate at Yale in 1933 and developed a close intellectual relationship with Hull, one which was both acknowledged by Hull and recorded in the detailed correspondence they maintained. After Hull's death, Spence continued to develop Hull's theory by attending to the changes required by the accumulating experimental evidence and by exploring opportunities to apply their shared ideas – just as an engineer would have wanted – to practical problems of a psychological nature. Thus their work was often referred to as the Hull–Spence theory of learning. Clear evidence of Hull's influence can be found in behavioural therapy, a collective term referring to psychotherapeutic techniques that use principles of learning to control and eliminate unwanted or maladaptive behaviours. These therapies are based on the idea that most psychological illnesses are due to the learning of maladaptive behaviours, and that those illnesses can be treated by helping the person unlearn the behaviours that caused them. Much of the practical influence of Hull's ideas has its conceptual roots in Hull's concept of drive and **Freud**'s notion of *trieb* or drive. Although Freud and Hull used the notion of drive to work out quite different theoretical positions, Hull's students John Dollard and Neal Miller were very effective in formulating a therapeutic approach that draws on core values in both. The work of Dollard and Miller is encapsulated – or caricatured, depending on one's point of view – in the frustration–aggression hypothesis. In its simplest form, the hypothesis states that aggressive behaviour is always preceded by frustration: frustration is a precondition for aggression. An extreme version of the hypothesis states that frustration always leads to aggression of one kind or another, because aggression is the only way to reduce pent-up frustration. Miller was particularly influential in promoting applications in therapeutic contexts, and he elaborated a position in which psychological therapies are considered as devices that allow people to unlearn maladaptive personal and social behaviours and acquire more effective alternative modes of living. Indirect evidence for Hull's broader intellectual influence can be discerned, for example, in the ideas of **Anderson**, who set out to specify a formal theory of learning that could be programmed into a computer and systematically broken in the best Hullian tradition.

Clark Hull's major writings

'Quantitative aspects of the evolution of concepts: an experimental study', *Psychological Monographs*, 1920, 28: 123.

'The influence of tobacco smoking on mental and motor efficiency', *Psychological Monographs*, 1924, 33: 150.

'A functional interpretation of the conditioned reflex', *Psychological Review*, 1929, 26, 498–511.

'Knowledge and purpose as habit mechanisms', *Psychological Review*, 1930, 37, 511–25.

'Goal attraction and directing ideas conceived as habit phenomena', *Psychological Review*, 1931, 38, 487–506.

Hypnosis and Suggestibility, Appleton-Century-Crofts, 1933.

'The conflicting psychologies of learning – a way out', *Psychological Review,* 1935, 42, 491–516.
'Mind, mechanism, and adaptive behavior', *Psychological Review,* 1937, 44, 1–32.
Mathematico-Deductive Theory of Rote Learning, Yale University Press, 1940 (with C. I. Hovland *et al.*).
Principles of Behavior, Appleton-Century, 1943.
Essentials of Behavior, Yale University Press, 1951.
A Behavior System, Yale University Press, 1952.

Further reading

Koch, S. (1954) 'Clark L. Hull', in W. K. Estes *et al.* (eds), *Modern Learning Theory,* Appleton-Century-Crofts (pp. 1–176).
Smith, L. D. (1986) *Behaviorism and Logical Positivism: A Reassessment of the Alliance,* Stanford University Press.

JAMES, WILLIAM (1842–1910)

Regarded as the 'father' of American psychology, James was a provocative and lucid writer who was particularly influential in shaping psychologists' thinking on the nature of consciousness and on emotion.

James's grandfather, also called William James, left Co. Cavan, Ireland, in 1789 at the age of twenty-two and settled in Albany, New York, where he started a small retail concern. His business acumen led to his accumulating enormous wealth and he became a senior figure in the state of New York, his fortune surpassed only by the German real-estate magnate John Jacob Astor. He had thirteen children by three wives. One son, Henry Sr, turned mystic and philosopher and became a Swedenborgian, a life-choice that was to leave him largely cut off from the family millions, although an annual stipend of $10,000 meant that he was not obliged to work for a living. Henry Sr was a pensive, religious man with little interest in financial affairs, and his marriage to Mary Robertson Walsh, also of Scottish–Irish descent, produced five children: William, the psychologist; Henry Jr, the novelist; Garth Wilkinson – 'Wilky', and Robertson – Bob, who both saw military service in the Civil War followed by failed ventures in farming and speculation; and Alice, a lifelong invalid with a radical intellectual fervour coupled with strident anti-British/pro-Irish political sentiments.

With a modest inheritance, Henry James Sr was able to move his family from city to city, and from America to Europe and back again. This was a hugely stimulating, cosmopolitan environment, and

William James showed considerable talent in art and in science. At the age of eighteen he started a career as a promising artist and was tutored by William M. Hunt, an American painter in the romantic tradition. This was terminated after a year, due to a combination of eye trouble and a recognition of the dismal prospects the career held. Since he was an equally gifted scientist, he enrolled on a pre-medicine course at Harvard University. This was his first time away from home for any appreciable length of time, but it didn't last for long. Poor health (which was to plague him throughout his life, and eventually led to a fatal cardiac illness) forced him to return after a year, but he went back to Harvard in 1863 in order to complete a medical degree. His studies were further interrupted by a trip to the Amazon with Harvard's naturalist Louis Agassiz; he contracted smallpox there and returned home once again, where his health further deteriorated. A further disruption involved a trip to Germany to takes courses in physiology, where he attended lectures on neurology given by Émil du Bois-Reymond in Berlin and **Helmholtz** in Heidelberg, as well as the pathologist Rudolf Virchow and the physiologist Claude Bernard. His time in Germany was punctuated by bouts of suicidal depression, and he returned to Harvard a weary man. Having graduated with a degree in medicine, James decided he was not cut out for a career as a physician. His psychological problems persisted, and he kept himself alive by reading – especially the works of the French philosopher of free will Charles Renouvire and the British associationist Alexander Bain. During 1871–72 he regularly attended the 'Metaphysical Club', a group of Harvard graduates who met in Boston to discuss the issues of the day. Its membership included the philosopher Charles S. Peirce, the jurist Oliver Wendell Holmes and the evolutionary philosopher Chauncey Wright. In 1872 he was appointed to a position in physiology at Harvard, and three years later he started lecturing on physiological psychology (experimental psychology as it would be known today). He was provided with a couple of rooms to accommodate various pieces of apparatus for measuring reaction times and sensory acuity – the first 'laboratory' of psychology in America. Shortly before his marriage to Alice Howe Gibbens in 1878, he was contracted to write the two-volume *Principles of Psychology* (1890), regarded then – and now – as one of the most provocative and lucid texts in the discipline. It took twelve years to complete, by which time James's interests had drifted from psychology, his disenchantment being indicated in the final sentence of the *Principles*: 'The more sincerely one seeks to trace the actual course of psychogenesis, the steps by which as a race we have come by the mental attributes we possess, the more clearly one perceives "the slowly gathering twilight close in utter night".' He moved to a position in Harvard's philosophy department, where he developed an extreme metaphysical position – 'radical empiricism' – and remained there until his retirement.

The *Principles* attracted much praise, although one of its reviewers, James Sully, claimed it was too brilliant – a textbook should be less exciting, less engaging. Others criticised the somewhat unsystematic arrangement of chapters. **Wundt** commented: 'It is literature, it is beautiful, but it is not psychology' (Blumenthal, 1970: 238). Much later **Skinner** opined: 'William James is generally accepted as the last important figure in the history of mentalist psychology. He was a careful thinker and a charming writer but my own feeling is that those traits are to be regretted' (cited in Thorne, 2001: 252).

James's psychology was a full-frontal assault on German structuralism, as articulated in Wundt's mission to identify the basic elements of consciousness. For James, there were no elements to consciousness, but rather a stream, an idea that found its fullest literary expression in James Joyce's *Ulysses*. There are five main tenets to his position on consciousness. First, consciousness is personal – it reflects individual experiences, so any attempt to search for a population of elements common to all minds is untenable. Second, consciousness is continuous and cannot be fractionated by experimental methods. Third, consciousness is constantly changing – one can never experience the same thing twice. (This is analogous to an adage coined by the Greek philosopher Heraclitus, who stated that one cannot step in the same river twice.) Fourth, consciousness is selective – only some of the many things entering consciousness are chosen for detailed consideration. Fifth, consciousness is functional – it exists so that a person can adapt to their environment. The implications are clear: 'For twenty years past I have mistrusted "consciousness" as an entity; for seven or eight years past I have suggested its non-existence to my students, and tried to give them its pragmatic equivalent in realities of experience. It seems to me that the hour is ripe for it to be openly and universally discarded' (1904: 477).

James is often described as being directly opposed to Wundt's search for the building blocks of consciousness, but that was only one of Wundt's psychologies. Less well-known is Wundt's Völkerpsychologie (which can be roughly translated as 'social psychology'), which is intellectually closer to James's position. Wundt argued that experimental methods can be used to describe and understand lower-level processes, such as the perception of sensations, but appeared to be less certain about their appropriateness to the investigation of higher thinking functions such as problem-solving. He appeared to take the view that higher mental processes could only be examined indirectly using concepts from culture and language, or Völkerpsychologie – but this was quite different from the natural science of experimental psychology as he envisaged it. James, too, was happy to work with the ideas of the associationist philosophers concerning the connections or associations that are supposed to exist among sensations and ideas in the brain, but he regarded them as operating at an unconscious level, and more generally in lower animal species. However, in human beings consciousness supervenes and selects those aspects of a situation required for reasoning in the service of survival. James was of the view that the capacity for consciousness is inherited rather than learned. Thus, objects in space are directly perceived and not deduced from colours and shapes, as claimed by the empiricists. In this regard, his views are very similar to those of Immanuel Kant's philosophy of mind, which says that we come to know reality through categories of thinking. Kant considered some of these categories, for example 'quantity', 'cause' and 'effect', to be *a priori* or innate. Similarly, James suggested that a great deal of behaviour, animal and human, is guided by instinct, but with an important caveat: instinct-like behaviours – he called these habits – could be learned and modified through the lifetime of an organism. He proffered a neurobiological account of the formation of habits that is broadly consonant with that favoured by **Pavlov**. As a behaviour is repeated, neurological pathways in the brain are activated over and over again, and with time the behaviours are performed with greater ease and fluency. The functional gains to the animal include a reduction in fatigue and a diminution in the level of consciousness required to perform them. James spelled out the practical implications of this in a series of maxims to guide the acquisition of preferred habits and the elimination of others:

1   put yourself in circumstances where you are likely to perform the habits you wish to acquire;
2   strive to avoid lapsing into behaviours that are contrary to the habits you wish to develop;
3   engage in the performance of new habits wholeheartedly rather than piecemeal;
4   the practice of engaging in particular behaviours will lead to the acquisition of new habits rather than any intention to perform them;
5   try to make yourself behave in ways that are advantageous to you,

recognising that this may require considerable effort in the first instance – don't give up.

These maxims capture the strong influence of philosophical pragmatism, a foundation of functionalism: any and every behaviour must be judged by its consequences. For James, the most important thing about consciousness is its purpose: to aid an animal in adapting to its environment. Wundt's voluntarism (which emphasised the goal-directed, purposeful operation of the mind) and **Titchener**'s structuralism (which focused on identifying the elementary building-blocks of consciousness) had missed this crucial point. For James, this was both a personal and an intellectual matter. An awareness that his own depression must be functional – it must be for something – was almost certainly partly responsible for helping him through bouts of suicidal feeling. His personal commitment to understanding the function of behaviour was manifested in his belief that parapsychology (the study of apparently strange or anomalous psychological experiences) must have some pragmatic value, and he was a founder of the American Society for Psychical Research.

Hardly a vestige of the psychology envisaged by James survives in contemporary introductory texts, except for his theory of emotion (cf. **Cannon** for an account). The philosophical implications of his view of psychology as 'the science of mental life' are more pervasive and underpin the professional branches of the discipline. Lightner Witmer, founder of the world's first 'psychological clinic' at the University of Pennsylvania in 1896, is associated with a view of clinical psychology that is qualitatively different from that of **Binet** or **Freud** and much closer to James's. Witmer earned his doctorate under Wundt, but his emphasis on the practical usefulness of rigorous experimental enquiry for therapeutic interventions captures a core value in James's pragmatism that many clinical psychologists would recognise today. Similarly Münsterberg, James's successor and widely regarded as the founder of industrial psychology, initiated an influential programme of applied research in organisational settings that was informed by James's philosophy. (Incidentally, the term 'industrial psychology' was first used in 1904 by the President of the American Psychological Association, William Lowe Bryan, who had intended to refer to 'individual psychology' but inadvertently wrote 'industrial psychology' and failed to spot the typographical error before it appeared in print.) The American phenomenologists (philosophers who emphasise the importance of detailed analysis of conscious experience) have also claimed James as a precursor. John Dewey and James R. Angell, regarded as the founders of the branch of philosophy known as functionalism, acknowledged their debt. More generally, James was influential through his founding of Harvard's psychology department and the large number of talented people he attracted there. James did not formulate a new psychological framework; the significance of his influence lies in the freshness of his treatment of a range of psychological questions, emblematic of the adage that the progress of psychology is often marked more by advances in the kinds of questions it asks than the completeness of the answers it gives.

William James's major writings

Principles of Psychology, Holt, 1890.
The Will to Believe, Longmans Green, 1897.
The Varieties of Religious Experience, Longmans Green, 1902.
'Does consciousness exist?', Journal of Philosophy, Psychology, and Scientific Methods, 1904, 1, 477–91.
Pragmatism, Longmans Green, 1907.
The Meaning of Truth, Longmans Green, 1909.
A Pluralistic Universe, Longmans Green, 1909.

Further reading

Blumenthal, A. L. (1970) Language and Psychology: Historical Aspects of Psycholinguistics, Wiley.
Myers, G. W. (1986) William James: His Life and Works, Yale University Press.
Thorne, B. M. (2001) Connections in the History and Systems of Psychology, Houghton Mifflin.
Wilshire, B. W. (1984) William James: The Essential Writings, SUNY Press.

JUNG, CARL GUSTAV (1875–1961)

Once regarded as Freud's heir-apparent, Jung disagreed with Freud on the primacy of the sex drive and devised an alternative position that embraced the philosophical and spiritual needs of the person.

Jung was born in the small village of Kesswil near Lake Constance, Switzerland. His father, a village parson, introduced him to Latin at the age of six, and this was the start of a lifelong interest in languages, particularly ancient languages such as Sanskrit. Until he was nine, Jung lived in a domestic environment fraught with discord between his parents Paul Jung and Emilie Preiswerk Jung. As an adolescent he was a solitary who didn't care much for school and had a strong dislike for competitive activities of any kind. He was bullied at boarding school and learned to feign sickness, including fainting, as a device to extricate himself from difficult situations. His interest in ancient languages and cultures initially suggested a career in archaeology, but he elected to enrol for a degree in medicine at the University of Basel. It was while working under the instruction of the neurologist Richard Krafft-Ebing, an expert in forensic psychiatry and sexual pathology, that he settled on a career in psychiatry. His first position after graduating was with Eugen Bleuler, an expert on schizophrenia, at the Burghölzi Mental Hospital in Zurich. On Bleuler's recommendation, Jung used **Galton**'s word-association techniques with people diagnosed with a psychosis, with a view to revealing their unconscious thought processes. His first published paper, a psychological analysis of supposed occult phenomena, was the basis of his doctoral thesis.

Jung met Emma Rauschenbach in 1896; they married in 1903, and had five children. In about 1911 Jung took a mistress, Antonia Wolff, and their relationship lasted until Antonia's death in 1952. (His wife Emma died in 1955.) This arrangement was particularly difficult for both women, because they each worked with Jung and practised as analysts. However, they tolerated it and lived with the fact that the relationship was common knowledge among members of the Zurich circle of analysts.

Jung was a long-time admirer of **Freud**, and the two met in Vienna in 1907. A couple of years later Jung, Freud and Sándor Ferenczi made a trip to America, and the itinerary included a meeting with **James**, who was particularly interested in some of Jung's ideas. It was during this trip that Jung's relationship with Freud began to cool. The main source of their intellectual disagreement lay in their respective positions on libido (a life-force energy). Jung had begun to indicate his doubts about Freud's view that libidinal energy is fundamentally sexual. Jung regarded it as a creative life-force that included sexuality but was much larger, and he extended its scope to embrace the philosophical and spiritual needs of the person. Others, such as the psychoanalytic anthropologist Abraham Kardiner, were also to take a dissonant position with regard to libidinal energy, but retained an identity with the Freudian school. So the disagreement between Jung and Freud was possibly more than an intellectual clash. By 1912 they had ceased to communicate, and two years later the friendship was at an end. Jung found the break with Freud particularly difficult, and there followed a period of three years characterised by protracted bouts of depression. This was also Jung's most creative period, during which he developed his own distinctive theory of personality.

In 1928 Jung joined the International General Medical Society for Psychotherapy; so also, that year, did Mathias Heinrich Göring, (Herman Göring's cousin). Jung was elected vice-president in 1930, and president three years later. *Zentralblatt für Psychotherapie*, the society's journal, was reorganised about this time, the intention being to publish an international edition under Jung's editorship and a German version under the management of Göring. Göring published an appeal to the readership to adopt Hitler's *Mein Kampf* as a basic reference text. Whether by error or political sleight-of-hand, the journal carried the appeal above Jung's signature. This was the primary source of a widely-held suspicion that Jung must be a Nazi sympathiser and that his presidency was part of a plan to impose a Nazi ideology on the business of the Society. Further evidence to support this view was identified in earlier statements that he – and many others swept up in the enthusiasm for the National Socialist transformation of Germany – had made. Part of the interpersonal animosity that developed with Freud was probably due to claims that charges of anti-Semitism against Jung were being fuelled by Freud, who was still resentful towards him for the damage done by his earlier resignation from the presidency of the International Psychoanalytical Association. The content of Jung's speeches given in Cologne and at Yale University during the 1930s suggests that such sympathies as he had for some of the tenets of National Socialism in its early years were well and truly banished. However, some have concluded that the weight of evidence indicates that Jung was a racist, an anti-Semite and a misogynist (McLynn, 1997).

Jung's theory, like Freud's, offers a tripartite structure of the mind. He identifies the ego with the conscious mind. His concept of the 'personal unconscious' refers to those things that are unconscious but can readily be brought to conscious awareness, such as the feeling of one's clothes against one's skin, or memories of particular things that have happened earlier in the day. Jung's concept of the 'collective unconscious' owes something to the idea of 'collective spirit', as used by the philosopher Lucien Lévy-Bruhl, and to Durkheim's 'social solidarity' whereby individuals combine to form a collective psychical existence. It is also similar to Pierre Teilhard de Chardin's 'noosphere', a global network of economic and psychic affiliations. James Lovelock's Gaia theory, which regards the planet Earth as a complete living organism, could be regarded as a fuller exposition of a similar idea. Jung uses the idea of the collective unconscious to refer to a species-specific reservoir of experiences that cannot be brought to conscious awareness and cannot be directly examined. It consists of primordial images or ancestral memory traces that extend into pre-human and animal lineage. Although the collective unconscious cannot be directly observed, evidence of its presence and influence can be detected in the consequences of our actions for ourselves and others. Some types of experience afford particularly strong insights into its presence, including *déjà vu*, near-death experiences and love at first sight. Cross-cultural examples can be detected in the many myths that share common themes and in the spiritual experiences of mystics of all religions. Jung referred to the contents of the collective unconscious as archetypes, innate tendencies to experience things in certain ways that act to organise human experience. He regarded archetypes as working in much the same way as Freud's concept of drive. For example, the mother archetype is symbolised by the primordial mother – Eve, in Western cultures. He identified numerous archetypes, including death, birth, rebirth, God, and many more. For instance, between 1931 and 1934 he offered therapy to the theoretical physicist and Nobel Laureate Wolfgang Pauli that included an analysis of some thirteen hundred of Pauli's dreams exploring the archetypal nature of mathematical symbols.

In contrast to Freud's classical position, which Jung disparagingly referred to as the 'reductive interpretation', he argued that psychological facts could not be accounted for in terms of causal connections alone and certainly not in terms of unconscious, predetermined instincts of the type favoured by the psychoanalysts. However, like Freud, he took the view that human beings are fundamentally bisexual, and that culturally-directed socialisation processes shape the creation of masculine and feminine identities. The anima is thought to reflect the collective unconscious of the 'feminine' side of the male psyche (i.e. emotionality), whereas the animus reflects the collective unconscious of the 'rational' side of the female psyche (i.e. logic and reason). The persona, which has to do with the way we manage the impressions of ourselves that we create for others, often acts to mask the influence of the animus in women and the anima in men. His thinking in this regard anticipated later psychological studies of androgynous sexual identity.

Jung's thinking on the dynamics of the psyche was influenced by the philosopher Nietzsche, whose *Ecce Homo* carries the subtitle 'How One Becomes What One Is', a phrase that is similar to Jung's notion of individuation – the act or process of giving individuality to someone or something. Both, in turn, were influenced by Schopenhauer, whose 'principium individuationis' – the way in which the forces of time and space define the uniqueness of an individual – finds expression in Jung's approach to the dynamics of the psyche. These, Jung argues, are governed by three principles. The principle of opposites states that every wish suggests its opposite. He regards the opposition between states (e.g. good–bad, happy–sad, love–hate) as the source of libidinal or psychic energy. The second principle is that of equivalence, and refers to the degree to which one is prepared to recognise the presence of opposite states: for example, the degree to which one recognises that the infant one loves is also an object of hate. The principle of equivalence is critically important for personal growth. If one recognises the presence of opposite forces, there is the potential for growth. Growth will be stifled according to the degree to which a particular state is denied or suppressed. The denial or suppression of wishes causes the diversion of psychic energy to the development of a complex. Jung's concept of the complex is a modification of an idea first postulated by Josef Breuer, one of Freud's early collaborators, who also broke away from him over a disagreement regarding the primacy of sexual drives. Jung uses the term to refer to a suppressed constellation of thoughts and feelings that cluster around a theme provided by an archetype. He pioneered the use of word association in therapeutic contexts to identify the presence of complexes. He reasoned that when a particular word (e.g. 'father') elicits a delayed verbal response from a patient and/or noticeable changes in breathing or posture, then that word had tapped a complex. Jung's third principle, that of entropy, refers to the tendency for oppositions to come together. He argued that entropy increases with age, and this accounts for reductions in libidinal or psychic energy as we get older. The goal of life is to realise the self. The self is also an archetype that represents the transcendence of all opposites, so that every aspect of one's personality is expressed equally.

A broad distinction can be made between mechanistic and teleological approaches to the explanation of human behaviour. The mechanistic approach embraces the ideas of Freud and **Watson**, and favours bio-physical explanations. The teleological approach includes humanists such as **Maslow** and **Rogers**. Jung offered a third approach, based on the concept of synchronicity – the idea that events can be intimately linked non-causally, as when close friends report having had a similar dream. Many psychologists regard such phenomena as coincidence and attribute the sense of surprise engendered by such combinations to a tendency on the part of most people to underestimate the likelihood of two events occurring at the same time. For example, **Milgram**'s 'six degrees of freedom' hypothesis predicts that any two people chosen at random from anywhere in the world can be connected to one another through a surprisingly short chain of friends or associates – just six in number.

Jung regarded 'attitudes' and 'functions' as operating at both conscious and unconscious levels of awareness. He claimed that there are two principle attitudes: introversion and extraversion. Introversion is oriented towards subjective experience, whereas extraversion is oriented towards objective experience. These definitions are somewhat broader than the popular understanding of introversion, as associated with shyness and social withdraw, and extraversion, as indicated by conviviality and sociability. Moreover, Jung regarded everyone as possessing both attitudes, these being governed by the principle of opposition. Thus the unconscious of the extravert is introverted and the unconscious of the introvert is extraverted. Whether we are introverts or extroverts, we need to deal with the world, inner and outer, and Jung suggested there are four basic ways, or functions, we use to do this: sensing, thinking, intuiting and feeling. He stated that most people develop one or two of the functions, but the goal of personal development should be to use all four. He went on to suggest that attitudes and functions interact in three ways. They may oppose one another, compensate for one another or combine in synthesis. The combination of attitudes and functions provided the basis of Jung's eight Psychological Types. These types were subsequently developed by Katharine Briggs and her daughter, the dramatist and novelist Isabel McKelvey Myers. The Myers–Briggs Type Indicator is one of the most popular and thoroughly researched tests of personality types.

Jung's limited impact within contemporary mainstream psychology contrasts with his considerable influence beyond, as reflected, for example, in the theological writings of Paul Tillich and the Dominican padré Victor White. There are several reasons for this. Like Freud's psychoanalysis, many of Jung's concepts cannot be defined in ways that allow them to be measured, and some, such as the collective unconscious, are so constructed as to make them impossible to measure. Consequently, with the notable exception of the Myers–Briggs inventory, there is a dearth of well-designed evaluations of various predictions that might follow from Jung's theory. Like Freud, Jung offers a framework for explaining every aspect of human experience, but his concept of synchronicity takes us further than psychoanalysis – into a realm of ideas more usually encountered within the domain of parapsychology or the study of paranormal, extrasensory experience. Moreover, his theoretical formulations are articulated through an extensive list of specialist terms, and readers new to that terminology may find his writing somewhat impenetrable. Even his definitions of key concepts are sometimes inconsistent. In *Contributions to Analytic Psychology* (1928), he defines the 'symbol' as the 'psychological machine which transforms energy' (p. 50), and, three pages later: 'Symbols are the manifestations and expression of the excess libido'. Elsewhere (*Modern Man in Search of a Soul*, 1933) there is tautology: consciousness is defined as 'the relatedness of psychic contents to the ego in so far as they are sensed as such by the ego' (p. 535). Five pages later: 'By ego I understand a complex of representations which constitutes the centrum of my field of consciousness and appears to possess a very high degree of continuity and identity'. Ironically, Jung's charismatic aversion to theory-building (coupled with his enthusiasm for alchemy and the mystical) deters many psychologists from broaching his work, for fear that they may find there a hotchpotch of indefinable ideas: 'Theories in psychology are the very devil. It is true that we need certain points of view for their orienting and heuristic value; but they should always be regarded as mere auxiliary concepts that can be laid aside at any time' (1946: 7).

Carl Jung's major writings

Psychological Types, Harcourt Brace, 1923.
Contributions to Analytic Psychology, Harcourt Brace, 1928.
Modern Man in Search of a Soul, Harcourt Brace, 1933.
Essays on Contemporary Events, Kegan Paul, 1946.
Collected Works, 1902–60, 18 volumes, Routledge & Kegan Paul, 1960.

Further reading

Bennet, E. A. and Storr, A. (1995) *What Jung Really Said*, Schocken.
Cohen, E. D. (1976) *C. G. Jung and the Scientific Attitude*, Littlefield Adams.
Gallard, M. (1994) 'Jung's attitude during the second World War in the light of the historical and professional context', *Journal of Analytical Psychology*, 39, 203–32.
McLynn, F. (1997) *Carl Gustav Jung*, St Martin's Press.
Welsh E., Hannah, B. and Briner, M. (translators) (1947) *Essays on Contemporary Events*, Kegan Paul.

KOHLBERG, LAWRENCE (1927–87)

Kohlberg devised a theory of moral thinking which suggests that the development of moral reasoning follows an invariant sequence of stages.

Born in Bronxville, New York, Lawrence Kohlberg was the son of a wealthy businessman. He went to prestigious schools but, instead of continuing on the path of privilege, he joined the US Merchant Marine upon leaving high school. Later he joined a ship which was smuggling Jewish refugees from Europe into Palestine through the British blockade. The moral dilemma posed by such actions – how to justify disobeying the law – was to figure in almost all of his psychological research. Kohlberg entered the University of Chicago at a time when it was possible to get credit for a course by passing the final examination. He took sufficient exams to get his BA in one year. His 1958 doctoral dissertation on moral judgement was an unusual topic for investigation at that time. The American psychologist Earl Barnes had conducted some earlier studies of children's moral reasoning, but there had been nothing on the scale of Kohlberg's thesis, which inaugurated thirty years of intellectual work. Some of Kohlberg's ideas on moral reasoning can be traced to **Piaget** and **Binet**. For example, a number of the items in Binet's and Theodore Simon's tests of intelligence were of a moral nature. Piaget's early career included time under Binet's supervision, and during this period Piaget had been particularly stricken by the qualitative difference between the ways younger and older children thought about those problems. He coined the term 'moral realism' to refer to some of these differences. Children who Piaget described as engaging in 'moral realism' believe that rules are absolute and immutable – they cannot be changed. One of the implications of this view of the world is that intention is unimportant when judging the actions of others. For example, someone who accidentally breaks three glasses should be punished more than someone who breaks just one on purpose. Kohlberg refined and extended Piaget's theory by asking ten-, thirteen- and sixteen-year-old boys to resolve a series of moral dilemmas. The dilemmas were presented as vignettes in which each boy was to choose between obeying the law or an authority figure and acting in an antagonistic fashion while serving a human need. Kohlberg was less interested in the final judgement than in the underlying structure of the child's reasoning. Analysis of children's responses to different dilemmas led Kohlberg to conclude that moral development follows an invariant sequence of three moral levels, each comprising two distinct moral stages. Each stage represents a particular method of thinking rather than a particular type of moral decision.

The defining characteristics of Kohlberg's three moral stages and six levels are as follows.

Level 1: Pre-conventional morality

At this level the child conforms to rules imposed by authority figures to avoid punishment or obtain personal rewards. Stage 1: Punishment and obedience orientation. The goodness or badness of an act depends on its consequences. Stage 2: Naive hedonism. A person at this second stage of moral development conforms to rules in order to gain reward or satisfy personal objectives.

Level 2: Conventional morality

At Level 2 the individual strives to obey rules and social norms in order to win others' approval or to maintain social order. Praise and blame-avoidance replace tangible rewards and punishments as motivators of ethical conduct. Stage 3: 'Good boy' or 'Good girl' orientation. Moral behaviour is that which pleases, helps or is approved of by others. Stage 4: Social-order-maintaining morality. The child considers the perspectives of the generalised other – the will of the community or society as reflected in law. What is 'right' is what conforms to the rules of legitimate authority.

Level 3: Post-conventional (or principled) morality

At this level, right and wrong are defined in terms of broad principles of justice that could conflict with written laws or with the dictates of authority figures. Stage 5: Morality of contract, individual rights and democratically accepted law. At this, the social contract stage, the individual is aware that the purpose of just laws is to express the will of the majority and to further human values. Laws that accomplish these ends and are impartially applied are viewed as social contracts that one has an obligation to follow, whereas imposed laws that compromise human rights or dignity are considered unjust and worthy of challenge. Stage 6: Morality of individual principles of conscience. At this, the 'highest' moral stage, the individual defines right and wrong on the basis of the self-chosen ethical principles of his or her own conscience. These principles are abstract moral guidelines or principles of universal justice (and respect for individual rights) that transcend any law or social contract that may conflict with them.

Although Kohlberg contends that his stages form an invariant and universal sequence of moral growth that is closely tied to cognitive development, he also claims that the development of thinking is insufficient to guarantee moral development. In order to move beyond the pre-conventional level of moral reasoning, children must be exposed to people or situations that introduce cognitive disequilibria – conflicts between existing moral concepts and new ideas that will force them to re-evaluate their viewpoints. So, like Piaget, Kohlberg believes that both cognitive development and relevant social experiences underlie the growth of moral reasoning.

Criticisms of Kohlberg's account of moral development can be grouped around six issues. First, do Kohlberg's stages follow a fixed developmental sequence? It took some time for a body of evidence to emerge, and the general conclusion is that Kohlberg's moral stages seem to represent an invariant sequence that is closely linked to the sequence of cognitive development described by Piaget. Second, Kohlberg posits a fundamental relationship between the development of thinking and the development of moral reasoning. In general, the psychological evidence suggests that this relationship does indeed exist. For example, proficiency at role-taking and adopting the perspective of others appears to be necessary for the onset of conventional morality. The development of what Piaget calls formal operations appears to be necessary for post-conventional, or principled, morality. However, Kohlberg emphasised that intellectual growth does not guarantee moral development. A person who has reached the highest stages of intellect may continue to reason at the pre-conventional level about moral issues. Both intellectual growth and relevant social experiences are necessary before children can progress from pre-conventional morality to Kohlberg's highest stages. Third, in the early 1960s Kohlberg's account of personality and social development challenged some of the major assumptions of socialisation – the idea that people are shaped primarily by social and cultural forces. He emphasised that, from a young age, children actively interpret and give meaning to their social experiences, and that cognitive development, the development of thinking and problem-solving, is essential to an understanding of social and moral development. Kohlberg's position has sometimes been wrongly characterised as a purely cognitive account of moral reasoning, but his 'social experience' hypothesis indicates that his theory should be considered a cognitive–social account. Most of the evidence supports the proposition that social experience contributes to moral growth. Fourth, Kohlberg's theory has been criticised for claiming that moral reasoning predicts moral behaviour. There is a good deal of research to show that the moral judgements of young children do not predict their actual behaviour in situations in which they are induced to cheat or violate other norms. Hypothetical dilemmas are just that –

hypothetical – and as such do not have important consequences of the kind encountered in real-life moral episodes. Fifth, the theory suggests that there is consistency to moral reasoning. Children and adolescents have been found to be fairly consistent in the type (or stage) of reasoning that they use to resolve different moral issues. However, it could be that this coherence simply reflects the fact that all of Kohlberg's dilemmas are abstract and hypothetical, and that inconsistent reasoning would emerge on more tangible dilemmas where consequences really count. Most of the empirical evidence indicates that there is an underlying consistency to moral reasoning – a coherence that is attributable not solely to the abstract and hypothetical nature of Kohlberg's moral dilemmas. Sixth, it has been claimed that Kohlberg's theory is gender-biased. In particular, Carol Gilligan (1982) has argued that Kohlberg's stages are based on interviews with men, and that, in some studies, women seem to have been treated as moral inferiors to men, typically reasoning at stage 3 while men usually reasoned at stage 4. She argued that females develop a different moral orientation, one that is not adequately represented in Kohlberg's theory, and she went on to argue that these different moral orientations are a product of sex typing. Although Gilligan's ideas about sex differences in moral reasoning have not been generally supported, she forcefully demonstrated that there is much more to morality than a concern with rules, rights and justice, and that reasoning based on compassionate concerns can be just as principled and mature as the moral justice orientation favoured by Kohlberg.

Stage theories can always be challenged for over-emphasising discontinuities in developmental change and for their dependence on the cultural context from which they are derived. However, Kohlberg's ideas remain at the heart of debates on the psychology of moral judgement. As well as formulating a cognitive–social account of moral development, he developed a set of developmental markers for identifying a person's stage of moral reasoning, and published this as a scoring system with a manual that has informed thousands of subsequent studies. Others have developed and elaborated his theory. For example, his early writings emphasised a general cognitive developmental perspective in which the person is regarded as unified, coherent and self-orienting to a unitary social world. Others have differentiated aspects of the self, and distinguished between different kinds of social worlds. Elliot Turiel, for example, developed domain theory, which elaborates the idea that concepts of morality and social convention emerge from the child's attempts to account for qualitatively differing forms of experience – moral experiences and social experiences.

Kohlberg asked, what is the relationship between criminal behaviour and moral reasoning? Is the moral reasoning of criminals different from the rest of us? He did not intend to formulate a theory of crime, but there has been understandable interest in exploring the implications of his theory for understanding the genesis of criminal conduct. However, its potential relevance is limited by the fact that Kohlberg was primarily concerned with moral reasoning, not moral behaviour: it is quite possible for someone to reason about moral issues and hold high moral standards but not allow those considerations to guide their behaviour. Conversely, a well-adjusted individual may find that they have been socialised to behave in morally commendable ways but they may not be engaging in high levels of moral reasoning about the principles underpinning their behaviour.

Kohlberg's impact within psychology contrasts with the scant attention paid to his work within philosophy. There are several reasons for this. Kohlberg was not trained as a philosopher, and, while philosophers have been attracted to his attempts to marry moral psychology with moral philosophy, they have often been alarmed at Kohlberg's sometimes informal use of philosophical terms. For instance, Kohlberg has argued that the six stages of moral reasoning have an inner logical order and that the sequence is logically necessary. However, if this were the case, then there would be no need to embark on a quest for evidence – something is logically necessary or it is not – hence there would be no need to conduct longitudinal studies of moral development. Another instance is the importance Kohlberg attached to the relationship between cognitive development and moral development. Philosophers take the view that it is not self-evident that more advanced thinking produces more advanced morals – a position familiar to Kohlberg, but one that, in the view of some philosophers, was not fully incorporated into his theory. For example, in one of his dilemmas one has to make a decision about the fate of three men in a boat that is capable of supporting only two occupants. One of the three is the captain, who can row and navigate; another is a healthy young man who can row; and the third is an elderly man with a broken shoulder who can neither row nor navigate. In scoring solutions to this dilemma, Kohlberg would award the highest score, Stage 6, to a decision based on drawing lots, because this is based on a principle of universal justice and respect for individual rights. However, suppose the men in the boat were raised in a culture that embraced utilitarian ethics and they all agreed that the elderly, injured man should go into the water. Is this a morally inferior way of thinking? Is the culture that produced such thinking morally inferior? Wars have been fought about the answers to such questions. These criticisms may be less important to a psychologist, but for a philosopher they suggest a lack of attention to detail that deters a more thorough engagement with Kohlberg's theory.

Lawrence Kohlberg's major writings

'The development of children's orientations toward moral order. Part 1: Sequence in the development of moral thought', *Vita Humana*, 1963, 6, 11–33.
'Moral stages and moralization: The cognitive developmental approach', in T. Lickona (ed.), *Moral Development and Behavior*, Holt, Rinehart and Winston, 1976.
The Philosophy of Moral Development, Harper & Row, 1981.
Essays on Moral Development. Volume 1, The Philosophy of Moral Development, Harper & Row, 1981.
The Meaning and Measurement of Moral Development, Clark University Press, 1981.

Further reading

Gilligan, C. (1982) *In a Different Voice*, Harvard University Press.
Hock, R. R. (1995) *Forty Studies that Changed Psychology*, Prentice-Hall.
Modgil, S. and Modgil, C. (eds) (1986) *Lawrence Kohlberg: Consensus and Controversy*, Falmer.

LEWIN, KURT (1890–1947)

Lewin was an experimental social psychologist who formulated a field theory to account for the events within a person's life space – all of the influences acting on them at a given time.

Lewin was born in Mogilno, Prussia, the second of four children. His family owned a small farm and lived above a general store run by his mother. They moved to Berlin when Kurt was fifteen. He had originally intended to become a doctor, and in 1909 he enrolled at the University of Freiberg and the following year transferred to Munich. By the end of 1910 he had transferred again, this time to Berlin, where he commenced his formal training in psychology under the supervision of the phenomenologist Carl Stumpf, who had himself been a student of the philosopher Franz Brentano. Although Lewin had completed the academic requirements by 1914 – his thesis was based on an experimental investigation of associative learning – the start of the First World War delayed the conferring ceremony by two years. In

1917 he married a schoolteacher, Maria Landsberg, with whom he had two children, Agnes and Fritz. Their marriage lasted ten years. Following several years of military service as a private and a lieutenant, for which he was awarded the Iron Cross, he returned to Berlin. There he worked with Max **Wertheimer**, Kurt Koffka and Wolfgang Köhler, founders of the Gestalt school of psychology, an approach that seeks to identify the laws governing the way we perceive the world as being patterned or organised. Lewin's first trip to America was in 1929, when he attended the International Congress of Psychologists at Yale University; in the following year he spent a period of six months as a visiting professor at Stanford University. It was during this period that he decided to settle in America, and he brought his second wife, Gertrud Weiss, and their four children to the US in 1932.

The starting point for Lewin's work is a distinction he drew between the Aristotelian and Galilean views of nature. For Aristotle, various objects fall into different categories according to their essence. Individual differences are explained as distortions caused by external forces interfering with an organism's natural growth tendencies. For Galileo, the behaviour of an object or organism is determined by the total forces acting upon it. Individual differences are understood in terms of the dynamic forces acting on individual organisms or objects. Lewin argued that much of psychology was stuck in an Aristotelian view of science. He argued that moving to a Galilean perspective would require psychologists to abandon a commitment to concepts of 'instinct', 'type' and 'average' (which imply the existence of distinct categories) and focus on understanding the complex, dynamic forces acting upon an individual. In broad terms, this approach is consistent with the ideas of Ernst Cassirer, philosopher of science and the originator of the philosophy of symbolic forms (Lewin had encountered Cassirer during his time at the University of Berlin).

The views of phenomenological philosophers such as Edmund Husserl were a formative influence on Lewin's thinking, and shaped his elaboration of the notion of 'field' in psychology. Phenomenologists place great emphasis on examining conscious experience, while trying not to be influenced by expectations or preconceptions. Lewin's phenomenological psychology may have been partly rooted in his experiences as a soldier at the front in the First World War. One of his first papers, 'Battlefield', published in the German *Journal for Applied Psychology* in 1917, suggests that he conceptualised the idea of 'field' as a phenomenon created through the action of opposing forces. Lewin's concept of 'field' referred to the totality of psychological factors acting at any particular moment to determine a person's behaviour. Reality beyond the life space is represented by perceptions of the world outside, which may be flawed to varying degrees. Thus the field embraces two factors: a person's goals and their perceived paths to those goals.

The concept of 'life space' is one of the most important in Lewin's approach. A person's life space comprises all influences acting on them at a given time. These influences, which he called psychological facts, included internal events such as hunger and fatigue, external events such as social situations, and recollections of prior experiences. In order to explain what he meant by life space, Lewin used concepts from topology. Lewin considered topology, a non-quantitative, non-Euclidean geometry, to be particularly suited to the requirements of the kind of Galilean psychology he was trying to develop. Topology focuses on understanding the relationships between the whole of an object and its individual parts, relationships that the Gestalt psychologists had established as being basic to psychology. However, being non-quantitative, topology could not handle concepts of direction and distance, both of which are essential for representing social and mental forces. Thus Lewin set about establishing the characteristics of 'hodological space' – a kind of psychological space in which, for example, the briefest distance between any two points is not the geometrically shortest but the one that involves the least effort in getting from one point to the other. Topology represents spatial relationships among objects, and thus a person's life space can be represented as an ellipse and each psychological fact as a region within the ellipse. Each region can be assigned a valence according to whether it acts in a beneficial (+ sign) or non-beneficial (− sign) way on the person. The force fields resulting for the various positive and negative influences in a person's life space is what he called hodological space. The nature of this space at any given moment determines the direction and rate of behaviour. Lewin referred to events outside the personal space as the foreign hull. Because of the dynamic nature of the forces acting on the person, events in the foreign hull could become part of the life space and events within the life space could become part of the foreign hull. One of Lewin's best known equations, $B = f(P,E)$ – which can also be written as $B = f(L)$ – summarises his argument that behaviour (B) is a function of both person (P) and environment (E), or of the life space (L). Like other Gestalt psychologists of the time, Lewin argued that people sought to maintain a balance in response to pressure from psychological needs. Motivation has its origins in the tensions induced by psychological needs (which Lewin called quasi needs), causing people to move through the life space. Consistent with this position, he regarded learning as a process of perceptual organisation and reorganisation that invariably involves some element of insight. He distinguished four kinds of learning: learning as a change in knowledge, learning as a change in motivation, learning as a planned, voluntary acquisition of some skill, and learning as a change in the sense of belongingness one feels towards particular groups. This perspective put him at odds with behaviouristic psychologies, particularly his view that all learning is goal directed and his claim that rote practice can be harmful and lead to 'unlearning'.

Lewin's move from Germany to America in 1932 presented a challenge to the continuity of his theoretical work. Essentially this was a move from an academic culture that placed a high value on theoretical science to one that emphasised practice and application. However, it also afforded him opportunities to develop aspects of his phenomenological vision through concepts of group dynamics and action research. These were expressed, for instance, in his concern with understanding the origins of social conflicts and in his determination to do something to ameliorate the suffering they caused. This is illustrated in his concern to apply social science to reform the character structure of the defeated, Nazi-trained German population. The concept of conflict figures prominently in Lewin's thinking, and he investigated three types: (i) approach–approach conflict occurs when a person is attracted to two goals simultaneously; (ii) avoidance–avoidance conflict, which refers to circumstances where the person is repelled by two unattractive goals; and (iii) approach–avoidance conflict which involves a goal about which the person has mixed feelings – e.g. 'Do I really want to be a psychologist or do I not?' – and which is often the most difficult conflict to resolve.

Lewin's thinking was well developed with respect to the structure of personality, but showed less concern with describing the internal architecture of motivations, especially unconscious motivations, or of the strength of attention to various aspects of the life space. He was not particularly interested in exploring the content of personality, and in this regard his *Dynamic Theory of Personality* (1935) is a misnomer, for he was not a personality theorist in the tradition of **Allport**, **Cattell** and **Eysenck**. This is illustrated in the seemingly trivial examples of human behaviour he would explore: two people plan to take a flight from Los Angeles, USA (LA). One wishes to travel due south to Santiago, Chile (S), the other due east to London, England (LO). Is $d_{La,S} = d_{La,Lo}$? (Is the distance from LA to London equal to the distance from LA to Santiago?) This is not the kind of question a theorist of personality would normally ask, and it illustrates how

Lewin was interested in developing a psychology in which physical space and distance is secondary to psychological space and distance. Although Santiago and London are each about 5,600 miles from Los Angeles, the psychological distances may vary according to the life space of the two travellers. In one sense Lewin could be said to have been mostly concerned with specifying what a theory of personality should be able to account for, rather than writing a theory of personality in the conventional sense. Thus it could be said that Lewin used personality as something to provide focus for his major effort to develop a new set of tools, a kind of psychological workbench, as it were, for measuring and describing psychological reality.

Lewin extended his ideas to the analysis of group dynamics, and suggested that a group could be regarded as a physical system just like a brain. Like a brain, the nature and configuration of a group can have a profound impact on its members. To test parts of his theory he devised ingenious experiments in naturalistic settings. For example, in one study (Lewin, Lippitt and White, 1939), boys were placed into one of three groups: democratic (the leader encouraged group discussion and participation), authoritarian (the leader made the decision and told others what to do), or laissez-faire (the boys did whatever they wanted). The democratic group was productive and friendly, the authoritarian group was aggressive, while the laissez-faire group was generally unproductive. He concluded that group leadership influences the organisation and dynamic of a group and this has an impact on the behaviour of its members. His ingenuity as an experimentalist sometimes earned Lewin the title of 'father of experimental social psychology'. That may be disputed, but there is no doubting his formidable influence on the first generation of experimental social psychologists – psychologists who used experimental methods to contrive social situations and systematically measure their effects on the behaviour of people on an individual and a group level.

Lewin's studies of group dynamics were to pave the way for research into encounter groups (sometimes referred to as T-groups), sensitivity training and leadership institutes. His interest in action research – studying something by trying to change it – turned his attention to psychotherapy, and he attempted to persuade the psychotherapist Jerome Frank to become involved in the development of the Center for Group Dynamics at MIT. Frank had studied with Lewin at Berlin, and his ideas drew on Lewin's concept of concreteness; namely that only factors operating at the time can have an effect – all immediate causes of events lie in the present. Although Lewin's name is strongly linked with the Center for Group Dynamics, he was its Director for only three years. Following his untimely death, the Center moved to the University of Michigan, where it prospered along the lines Lewin had envisaged.

Field theory attracted much criticism, partly because Lewin's explicitness singled it out as a prototypical phenomenological theory of personality and therefore a particularly good target for those intent on challenging that approach. The major criticisms fall into three groups. First, Lewin's topological life space diagrams are always historical – they describe what has happened and have very little predictive power in the sense that they do not provide accurate forecasts of how people will behave in the future. Second, the theory does not properly specify the relation of the life space to the external environment. Specifically, the learning theorist Kenneth Spence pointed out that Lewin's equations failed to provide principles that could be used to improve the management and control of those forces in the foreign hull that shape one's experience of the life space. Third, developmental and learning theorists have argued that field theory does not pay sufficient attention to the formative and motivational influences of childhood experiences. Lewin felt that this criticism was totally unjustified, and he pointed to the fact that he always considered historical information to be absolutely essential to an understanding of the current state of affairs within the life space of an individual.

In assessing a person's influence it can be difficult to rule out mere coincidences. Lewin's studies of social influence anticipated **Milgram**'s investigations of obedience to authority figures, although there are no clear indications that Milgram was aware of Lewin's work at the time he was conducting his own experiments. Clearer lines of influence can be discerned in the work of the clinical psychologist Martin Orne, who conducted classic investigations into the demand characteristics of psychological investigations – features of a psychological study that actively encourage participants to engage in behaviours the research psychologist hopes to observe. Orne took the term 'demand character' from Lewin. Lewin's influence can also be discerned in the work of the social learning theorist Julian Rotter, who developed the concept of locus of control, i.e. the extent to which a person feels in control of, or controlled by, external forces (this is similar to Lewin's notion of forces in the foreign hull). The limitations of Lewin's notion of field as a theoretical device to progress the development of a scientific psychology in the Galilean tradition lay in its abstractness. It was formalised to excess, most notably in his equations. An awareness of this limitation can be detected in his shift from a classic observer stance in experimentation (as he began in

Germany) to an increasingly socially immersed position, emphasising observer participation, following his relocation to America. His shift from an intellectual commitment to field theory towards a more pragmatic emphasis on action research may also be taken as tacit recognition of the limitations of his mathematical formulations.

Kurt Lewin's major writings

A Dynamic Theory of Personality, McGraw-Hill, 1935.

Principals of Topological Psychology, McGraw-Hill, 1936.

The Conceptual Representation and the Measurement of Psychological Forces, Duke University Press, 1938

'Patterns of aggressive behavior in experimentally created social climates', *Journal of Social Psychology*, 1939, 10, 271–99 (with R. Lippitt and R. White).

'Defining the "field at a given time" ', *Psychological Review*, 1943, 50, 292–310.

Resolving Social Conflicts: Selected Papers on Group Dynamics, Harper & Row, 1948 (ed. with G. W. Lewin).

Field Theory in Social Science: Selected Theoretical Papers, Harper and Brothers, 1951 (ed. with D. Cartwright).

Further reading

Heider, F. (1959) 'On Lewin's methods and theory', *Journal of Social Issues*, Supplemental Series, 13, 3–13.

Henle, M. (1978) 'Kurt Lewin as metatheorist', *Journal of the History of the Behavioral Sciences*, 14, 233–7.

Watson, R. I. and Evans, R. B. (1991) *The Great Psychologists: A History of Psychological Thought*, 5th edn, Harper Collins.

LORENZ, KONRAD ZACHARIA (1903–89)

One of the founders of ethology, Lorenz was awarded a Nobel prize for his work on the study of animals in their natural habitats.

Lorenz is probably best known in popular culture for his work on imprinting in geese: the subject matter has appeared on posters and postcards from time to time. Born in Vienna, his interest in animal behaviour can be traced to a childhood spent on his family's estate near the Danube, a rich landscape of forests and waterways. He recalled his parents, Emma and Adolf, as being supremely tolerant of his love for animals, while his nurse, Resi Führinger, had an exceptional talent for rearing animals. His early enthralment with wildlife and nature, reflected in his menagerie of birds, fish, amphibians, reptiles and invertebrates, shaped his career. His intellectual fascination was fuelled when he first encountered the idea of evolution, at the age of about ten, while reading a book by the zoologist Wilhelm Bölsche and seeing a picture of an Archaeopteryx. After graduating from high school he was convinced that his metier was in zoology and palaeontology, but his father, an orthopaedic surgeon, was eager for him to pursue a career in medicine and he reluctantly studied – first at Columbia University, New York, and then at Vienna. His father was less than enthusiastic about Konrad's love for one of their gardener's daughters, Gretel Gebhard. In time he fulfilled his father's wish and obtained an MD in 1928, although he did not become a practising physician; he also married Gretel. A couple of years after graduating he broke his lower jaw in a motorcycle accident and, in order to cover some scars, he grew a distinctive beard.

The French naturalist Alfred Giard was the first person to use the term 'ethology' as it is understood in modern use (the study of behaviour in natural – as distinct from laboratory – environments), but it was the ornithologist Oskar Heinroth who was the greater influence on Lorenz. Lorenz was particularly impressed by Heinroth's arguments for the value of comparative methods in tracing the evolution of complex social displays of animals. Lorenz's anatomy teacher at Vienna was the comparative anatomist and embryologist Ferdinand Hoch-stetter, and it was through his influence that Lorenz gained an appreciation of the suitability of comparative methods to the analysis of both behaviour and anatomical structure. It was at Vienna that he encountered the psychologist and philosopher Karl Bühler, who drew his attention to the discrepancies between the implications of Lorenz's thinking on comparative behaviour analysis and the nativistic position on instinct preferred by William McDougall and others. Discussions with Bühler emphasised the importance of formalising an explicit theory of knowledge before embarking on a systematic observation of any animal. After graduating from Vienna with a degree in medicine, Lorenz returned to managing the animals on the family estate, supported at first by an assistantship at the Anatomical Institute that funded further training in comparative anatomy and psychology, and then by his wife, who worked at a local hospital. During this period he wrote an outstanding series of papers in which he explained the philosophy, theory and observations of his approach to understanding animal behaviour. Thereafter the development of his ideas was intertwined with the work of Nikolaas (Niko) Tinbergen; it is not possible to understand the contribution of either man in isolation.

Lorenz and Tinbergen shared a number of formative childhood experiences. Tinbergen was born in The Hague in 1907. His father was a schoolteacher and a scholar of medieval Dutch. Both Niko and his elder brother were to be Nobel prizewinners: Niko for his work with Lorenz and von Frisch, in 1973, and his elder brother for his contributions to economics. Niko grew up about a mile from the sea, where he developed a childhood fascination with wildlife and nature to match that of Lorenz. Like Lorenz, he was an avid amateur naturalist. At university he took courses in zoology, although he lost interest in this for a time, mostly because of the emphasis placed on classification and the comparative analysis of dead animals. However, his interest was revived during visits to a newly-established bird observatory, and this provided an important context for his ideas on the possibility of a behavioural biology of live animals. In his doctoral work on digger wasps he established an approach to the investigation of behaviour using a novel combination of naturalistic observation and non-intrusive experimentation. Tinbergen's observations of solitary wasps nurturing their offspring in multiple burrows prompted him to ask how a foraging wasp could find its way back to a particular burrow. He used simple, ingenious experiments to demonstrate that the wasps quickly learned landmarks around each burrow. In 1932–33 he and his wife, Elizabeth Amelie, spent fourteen months on a meteorological expedition to Greenland. On returning to the Netherlands he established a laboratory at Leiden, where he studied the behaviour of stickleback fish. He also established a permanent field station at Hulshorst to study insects and birds.

In 1936 Lorenz met with Tinbergen in London, and both men were taken by the complementarity of their ideas. The meeting was followed by a two-month visit by Tinbergen to Lorenz's home in Altenberg in the spring of 1937, where Tinbergen found he could fit his non-intrusive experiments to Lorenz's intuitions and models, providing the blueprint for ethology with both an observational and an experimental base. Together they formulated a conceptual model based on the idea of an innate releasing mechanism and performed a convincing series of experiments to illustrate its action. Their efforts to establish ethology as a new discipline were supported by the zoologist Otto Köhler, co-founder and editor of *Zeitschrift für Tierpsychologie*, who published ingenious studies on pre-linguistic number sense in animals.

Lorenz was appointed to the Chair of Comparative Psychology at Konigsberg in 1940, but his work was interrupted in 1943 when he was drafted into the Psychiatric Service of the German Army. Hermann Göring, in a fit of chagrin, disbanded that service because its staff certified one of the Luftwaffe's best pilots as unfit. During the six-month period during which the Service was being run down, Lorenz occupied himself by writing on ethological matters. In 1944 he was involved in fierce fighting behind the Russian lines at Vitebsk and was captured and sent to head up a military hospital for prisoners-of-war in the Crimea. His time there was spent writing, almost entirely from memory, an encyclopaedia of animal behaviour. The book was never printed, mostly because large sections were out of date, containing no reference, for example, to American work on comparative psychology conducted during the war years. From an early age Lorenz held beliefs that came to be identified with National Socialism, including the idea that the science of eugenics could be used to enhance the human race. While he was initially sympathetic to some of the ideas of the Nazis, he was horrified by their brutality and particularly by the genocide of Jews. Later he expressed deep regret at what he saw as a personal failure to foresee those events, although his early sympathies attracted understandably harsh criticism.

Ethology survived as a scientific enterprise mostly on the basis of warm personal relations between Lorenz and Tinbergen. In 1948 Lorenz returned to Austria to resume his work on ethology, and he established an institute at the family home with the support of the English playwright J. B. Priestley, who instructed that royalties accruing from the performance of his plays in Vienna be directed to Lorenz. Within a short time Lorenz was awarded a position at the new Max Planck Institute of Experimental Physiology at Seewiesen. In the same year Tinbergen resigned his position as Professor of Experimental Biology at Leiden, despite the disapproval of his peers and a significant drop in pay and status, to become a lecturer at Oxford University. There he worked on establishing ethology as a significant movement in English-speaking science, and in 1951 he published his most famous work, *The Study of Instinct*. His position on the concept of instinct, which he regarded as innate but susceptible to influences, was originally developed by Lloyd Morgan, a European pioneer of the comparative study of animal behaviour. In *The Study of Instinct*, Tinbergen identified four questions about behaviour – immediate causation, ontogeny (the developmental sequencing of an animals growth to maturity), function and evolution – that served to unify the study of behaviour within ethology.

Among the early ethologists, Lorenz was the most philosophically and historically sophisticated, and the most interested in establishing an evolutionary and philosophical basis for a science of human behaviour – an 'evolutionary epistemology'. This approach is illustrated in the emphasis he placed on the inborn nature of behaviour patterns in all species, patterns that could be specified objectively and studied analytically. His ideas and methods attracted particularly strong criticism from American comparative psychologists, who rejected his concept of instinct and criticised both his motivational models of behaviour and his view of aggression – which placed a great deal of reliance on concepts of energy and drive. Lorenz and other ethologists tended to regard psychology as a science preoccupied with subjective phenomena and were particularly critical of American comparative psychology. For example, they accused comparative psychologists of making unwarranted generalisations from data collected from a few species (mostly rats and pigeons studied in laboratory conditions) and who regarded the use of 'comparative' as a gross misnomer.

Lorenz's position on instinct was that, in every instance of instinctive behaviour, there is a core of fixed, innate movement-forms. These instinctive movements he regarded as the central component of the whole system of instinctive behaviour. The conventional view had it that instinctive behaviour was guided by some genetically determined drive, but Lorenz argued that each instinct builds up a specific tension in an animal's central nervous system and, if the animal fails to find itself in an appropriate situation, then a reaction-specific energy is 'dammed up'. The effect of the damming-up is to lower the threshold of stimuli effective for releasing that particular instinctive movement. Robert Hinde was particularly critical of Lorenz's 'hydraulic' model, and has been credited with driving the study of motivation out of ethology. However, Hinde was not specifically concerned with exorcising the notion of motivation from ethology and was mostly calling for a more sophisticated conceptualisation of motivation capable of accounting for the increasingly complex phenomena being described by ethologists

Lorenz retired from Seewiesen in 1973 and was funded by the Austrian government to establish an institute for research on evolution and cognition, located eventually in Altenberg. An enduring contribution lies in the way he addressed the biological nature of human behaviour and thereby provided an essential backdrop for its subsequent analysis in evolutionary terms. Towards the end of his career, Tinbergen also dealt increasingly with the implications of ethology for human behaviour. For example, he worked for nearly two years on the development of a course on human biology, the emphasis of which is reflected in the title of the course's first lecture: War and Peace in Animals and Man. While Tinbergen focused more on stimulus mechanisms and Lorenz on motivation, they both envisaged a broader relevance of ethology to the study of humans. Approaching retirement, Tinbergen began work on the perceptual world of early childhood autism, while his broader interests encompassed the interaction of humans and the Earth's environment. He came to regard ethology not so much as a separate branch of science but as a phase in the evolution of the behavioural sciences that should be incorporated into further work.

While Lorenz and Tinbergen, together with Karl von Frisch, are regarded as the co-founders of ethology, their approaches differed. Lorenz was a thinker who explored his behavioural observations in the context of prevailing biological and philosophical theories. Tinbergen was more empirical, creating experimental settings in order to understand and predict how an animal, such as a bee, would behave. These differences may partly reflect differences in personality and character: Lorenz, full of ideas, would often write in anecdotal fashion, interlaced with dogmatic statements, and he was revered by his students as an authoritarian but benevolent father-figure. Tinbergen liked to listen, analyse and deduce.

Although almost all of the key concepts on which early ethology was based, such as fixed action patterns and innate releasing mechanisms, are now regarded as either vague or seriously flawed, they led to important questions being asked and to the creation of ethology as a new science of behaviour.

Konrad Lorenz's major writings

'The companion in the bird's world', *Auk*, 1937, 54, 245–73.
King Solomon's Ring, Crowell, 1952.
On Aggression, Harcourt, Brace and World, 1963.
The Evolution and Modification of Behavior, University of Chicago Press, 1965.
Studies in Animal and Human Behavior (2 vols), Harvard University Press, 1970–71.
Behind the Mirror: A Search for a Natural History of Human Knowledge, Harcourt, Brace, Jovanovich, 1977.
The Foundations of Ethology, Springer-Verlag, 1981.
The Waning of Humaneness, Little, Brown, 1987.

Further reading

Baerends, G. P. (1991) 'Early ethology: Growing from Dutch roots', in M. S. Dawkins, T. R. Halliday and R. Dawkins (eds), *The Tinbergen Legacy*, Chapman and Hall.
Krebs, J. R. and Sjolander, S. (1992) 'Konrad Lorenz', *Biographical Memoirs of Fellows of the Royal Society*, 38, 211–28.
Nisbett, A. (1976) *Konrad Lorenz*, Dent.
Tinbergen, N. (1951). *The Study of Instinct*. Clarendon Press.

LUCE, ROBERT DUNCAN (1925–)

The name 'Luce' is inextricably linked with the development of mathematical psychology.

Born in Scranton, Pennsylvania, both of Luce's parents were university graduates, although an academic career never appealed to him as a child and as a teenager he preferred landscape painting to traditional scholastic work. Writing was a significant problem for him as a child, and remained so throughout his career. It is hardly surprising, then, that he was a reluctant college applicant, and his decision to take a degree in aeronautical engineering was motivated more by a romantic fascination with aeroplanes than a desire to become an engineer. Ironically he was in his forties before he actually learned to fly. In his junior year at the Massachusetts Institute for Technology (MIT) he was enrolled in a remedial writing class and his work was often marked down for poor spelling and composition. By the summer of 1943 Luce was in the US Navy and, after Midshipman School at Notre Dame, he spent a period in the Catapult and Arresting Gear School at the Philadelphia Navy Yard. He returned to MIT three years later, this time as a graduate student in the Department of Mathematics. He never took a psychology course throughout his career and his fortuitous introduction to psychology was by way of a roommate who was tackling some of the problems posed by Leon Festinger, a social psychologist concerned with the analysis of social networks. MIT did not have a psychology department at that time, but there was a Small Groups Laboratory. He secured a position there working on the idea that many working groups have imposed upon them a communication structure that may affect the way they carry out their tasks. Within six months of Luce joining the Laboratory its director, Alex Bavelas, left to work for the State Department and handed its management to Luce and Lee S. Christie. By 1953 it was clear that the Laboratory was going to fold. Paul F. Lazarsfeld, of the Department of Sociology at Columbia University, hired Luce to manage a piece of research called the Behavioral Models Project. During this period Luce continued to work on the possibility that game theory (a part of mathematics concerned with the logical analysis of decision-making in a group of individuals) might account for some of the social interactions he had observed at the Small Groups Lab, and he commenced work on *Games and Decisions* (1957) with Howard Raiffa. During 1954–55 he was a Fellow at Stanford University's Center for Advanced Study in

Behavioral Sciences, and his interests turned to expected utility theory (a theory of decision-making based on the idea that people make decisions in order to maximise the expected benefits to themselves). When Luce returned to Columbia it became clear to him that neither the experimental methods nor the mathematical techniques that were being used there were sufficient for understanding the structures of social interaction that the staff were investigating. During this period he was introduced to psychophysics (the relationship between the physical intensity of a stimulus and its perceived intensity) and specifically to the work of Stanley S. Stevens, most of whose intellectual life had been devoted to applying mathematics to psychology.

During the early 1950s, Luce was one of only a very few mathematical psychologists in North America, the others being Richard C. Atkinson, Robert R. Bush, C. H. Coombs, William K. Estes, George A. Miller, W. J. McGill, Stanley S. Stevens and Patrick Suppes. They were drawn to the mathematical analysis of a number of psychological processes, and particularly to decision-making. Making decisions is a fundamental characteristic of any living creature. It is usually complicated by uncertainty: we cannot predict with certainty what tomorrow's weather will be, nor whether the meal we have ordered in a restaurant will be as satisfying as we hope. Mathematical psychologists were particularly drawn to the fact that people do not consistently make the same choice among a number of alternatives, even when the circumstances in which the options are presented do not change. Classical strength theory explained this by suggesting that, although a pair of options offered to a person can remain constant, the strength of the responses they could make (to accept or reject each of the options) varies in some random fashion. For example, if two alternatives, x and y, are similar to one another in terms of the strength of the response a person will make to each, then x will be stronger sometimes and y will be stronger others. Luce used classical strength theory to explain how people respond when presented with more than two alternatives, and found that the consistency with which a choice is made could not be due to differences in strength among the responses they could make. He put forward a different position: the strength of responses to different alternatives does not vary randomly, the responses are constant but the *process of choosing* among the alternatives varies. Thus his approach is based on the assumption that a person's choice between x and y should *not* change when more alternatives become available. He formulated this position in a mathematical axiom called Luce's choice axiom.

Suppose a person is offered a menu in a restaurant and we know that there is a 20 per cent chance of them choosing chicken and a 30 per cent chance of them choosing fish. That means there is a 50 per cent chance of them choosing something else from the menu (since 20 per cent + 30 per cent and 50 per cent = 100 per cent). However, if the waiter tells them that everything else on the menu is unavailable, then the probability of choosing chicken will rise to 40 per cent and the probability of choosing fish will rise to 60 per cent. The reason this happens is that, if there are only two alternatives, then, by probability theory, their probability must add up to 100 per cent and, according to Luce's choice axiom, they must maintain the same relative probabilities. Although the choice axiom does not account for all of the experimental findings on choice behaviour among multiple alternatives, several years later Amos Tversky generalised the axiom to another maxim called 'elimination by aspects'. According to elimination by aspects, a decision-maker is assumed to have a number of criteria. Each criterion has a minimum and a maximum cut-off level. The process of making a decision involves selecting a criterion and considering all of the alternatives against it. Those options not meeting the cut-off values are eliminated. The procedure is continued for the other criteria until all but a single alternative are eliminated. The sequence in which the criteria are applied is a crucial point as it has a major influence on the result. Tversky used the elimination by aspects axiom to demonstrate that, when someone is presented with a set of alternatives, each of the alternatives should be considered to have its own choice structure. Luce's choice axiom is the remarkable case in which there is no such structure. Daniel Kahneman, Amos Tversky and Duncan Luce's ground-breaking work has had considerable impact outside of psychology, as illustrated, for example, in the development and application of theory and methods for analysing choice that won Daniel McFadden a share of the 2000 Nobel Prize for Economics. Kahneman won the prize two years later.

During the 1960s, Luce worked with David H. Krantz, Tversky and Patrick Suppes on a project to generate a systematic presentation and integration of the very wide-ranging multidisciplinary publications on measurement. A major task was to find the least number of mathematical results that describe basic algebraic structures that have additive numerical representations and from which all of the results in the additive theory of measurements could be derived. This meant virtually every result in the literature had to be re-proved to fit into their scheme.

The break-up of Luce's first marriage, in 1967, marked the start of a short stay in Rio de Janeiro with his second wife, Cynthia Newby. They returned to North America to two relatively short periods of work, at the Institute for Advanced Study (1969–72) and the University of California, Irvine (1972–75), which were followed by a longer period at Harvard (1976–88) and then a return to Irvine.

Luce's interest in psychophysics derives in part from the fact that mathematics has played a significant role in the development of this field. Psychophysics is the study of the relationship between the physical magnitude of something, such as the duration of a period of time or the size of a sum of money, and its experienced magnitude, such as the perceived duration or the perceived usefulness of the sum of money. For example, place a wristwatch in front of you, check the time, and then close your eyes for 45 seconds. Open your eyes and check the time on the watch. Psychophysics is concerned with the discrepancy between the physical reality – the actual passage of time as recorded by the watch – and the subjective reality of the passage of time as you experienced it. Luce's interest in psychophysics led him to study the variability in responses people make when estimating the magnitude of a stimulus (e.g. whether one sound is louder than another) and when detecting whether or not a stimulus is present (e.g. whether or not they detected a very brief sound). The basic idea here is that subjective assessments about whether a stimulus is present or absent and about whether there is a difference between two stimuli involve some amount of uncertainty. This kind of uncertainty is an intrinsic part of a question such as 'Is there a difference in the intensity of two sounds, or am I just imagining it?' Luce proposed a mathematical model which states that the sensory attention a person gives to a set of stimuli is directly related to: (i) the number of stimuli on which decisions are based; and (ii) the influence of two decision strategies which he called timing and counting. A number of experiments on decision-making produced results that could be explained in these terms and were difficult to understand otherwise; however, the findings made clear that more was involved and that his model could not account for all of the experimental evidence.

In his later work, Luce argued that the attempts by the physiologist and physicist Gustav Fechner and by Stanley S. Stevens to place the measurement of the subjective intensity of physical stimuli (psycho-physics) on a sound scientific basis were flawed. Each had failed to justify their theoretical assumptions. Fechner used the term Just Noticeable Differences (JND) to refer to the smallest change in a physical stimulus that an organism can actually sense or the smallest difference between two stimuli that the organism can discriminate. Luce pointed out that Fechner *assumed* that JNDs are related to one another in additive fashion: one JND is added to the next, and so on. In this way the subjective intensity of a stimulus can be thought of as the addition of a numbers of JNDs: a subjectively very intense stimulus consists of many JNDs, whereas a subjectively weak stimulus consists of few JNDs. Stevens took a different view, namely that the relative subjective intensities of two stimuli have a multiplicative, not an additive, relationship. However, like Fechner, he commenced with an *assumption*. Luce formulated a theory that incorporates elements of both Fechner's and Stevens's ideas, but he specified his theory using algebra so that there are no hidden assumptions and every part of the theory is explicit and can be tested using appropriate experiments. However, Luce has added a caveat to his theory in which he points out that, being written in algebra, it does not have a probabilistic aspect. In other words he cannot yet relate his theory to probability theory, and this is important because behaviour is variable and probabilistic.

Although Luce is inextricably linked with the development of mathematical psychology and the application of quantitative techniques to the analysis of behaviour, he often expressed concern about psychologists' uncritical use of statistics. In his view, many psychologists can be trapped in a way of thinking that is dictated by their reliance on statistics rather than the problems they wish to solve: 'Statistical inference techniques are good for what they were developed for, mostly making decisions about the probable success of agriculture, industrial and drug interventions, but they are not especially appropriate to scientific inference which, in the final analysis, is trying to model what is going on, not merely to decide if one variable affects another' (1989: 281).

Duncan Luce's major writings

Games and Decisions, Wiley, 1957 (with H. Raiffa).
Individual Choice Behavior, Wiley, 1959 (co-edited with R. R. Bush and E. Galanter).
Handbook of Mathematical Psychology. Volumes 1, 2 and 3, Wiley, 1963–65 (with D. H. Krantz, P. S. Suppes and A. Tversky).
Foundations of Measurement, Academic Press, 1971.
'A neural timing theory for response times and the psychophysics of intensity', *Psychological Review*, 1972, 79, 14–57 (with D. M. Green).
Foundations of Measurement, Volumes II and III, Academic Press, 1989/90 (with D. H. Krantz, P. S. Suppes and A. Tversky).
Sound and Hearing, Erlbaum, 1993.

'A psychophysical theory of intensity proportions, joint presentations, and matches', *Psychological Review,* 2002, 109, 520–32.

Further reading

Bockenholt, U. (1992) 'Multivariate models of preference and choice', in F. G. Ashby (ed.), *Multidimensional Models of Perception and Cognition,* Erlbaum.
Bundesen, C. (1993) 'The relationship between independent race models and Luce's choice axiom', *Journal of Mathematical Psychology,* 37, 446–71.
Luce, R. D. (1989) 'R. Duncan Luce', in G. Lindzey (ed.), *Psychology in Autobiography, Volume III,* Stanford University Press.

LURIA, ALEXANDER ROMANOVICH (1902–77)

Luria devised and refined clinical tests for brain damage, and developed innovative methods for restoring brain function.

Luria was born in Kazan, a Russian university city situated to the east of Moscow. He was of Jewish extraction, but abrupt changes in the political and intellectual climate brought about by the Bolshevik Revolution allowed him to complete his school education quickly. He entered Kazan University in 1918 at a time when the university was in disarray. Luria's father wanted him to enter medical school, but Luria's ambition was to become a psychologist. Initially he graduated with a degree in social studies; he subsequently enrolled in medical classes while at the same time beginning to train in psychology at the Kazan Psychiatric Hospital. He interrupted his medical studies in order to take a position as a laboratory assistant at the Kazan Institute for the Scientific Organisation of Work, where he investigated the effects of hard work on mental activity. This took him to Moscow, where he was appointed to a junior post at the Moscow Institute of Psychology, working under the direction of Konstantin Kornilov, whose 'reactology' was emphasising the importance of studying mental effort through the systematic analysis of peripheral motor activity (e.g. reaction time, grasping, walking, lifting). There he pursued a research programme concerned with the effects of emotional stress on human motor reactions. This work owed something to **Pavlov**'s research on experimental neuroses in dogs, although Luria never accepted Pavlov's position that complex human behaviour could be satisfactorily explained in terms of reflexes and conditional reflexes.

In 1924 Luria made the acquaintance of **Vygotsky**, whose interest in the effects of nervous disease on intellectual functioning was probably partly responsible for directing Luria towards neuropsychology and motivating the completion of his medical studies. During the 1930s the two conducted a series of studies among non-literate Uzbekis that demonstrated the importance of culture in shaping cognitive processes. These people either could not or would not categorise perceptual stimuli on the basis of Gestalt laws of similarity (cf. **Vygotsky** for an account). For example, they would not classify a triangle drawn as a series of short, dotted lines with an equivalent triangle with a solid line perimeter. Instead, they categorised on the basis of objects they saw in, or associated with, the forms. For instance, the triangle with the solid line perimeter might be classified as a spearhead whereas the triangle constructed of short, dotted lines might be classified as a kind of tree. This position is somewhat similar to that proffered by the linguists Edward Sapir and Benjamin Lee Whorf, who maintained that sensory processes are subordinated to and subsumed within 'higher' functions: the language we use determines to some degree the way in which we view and think about the world around us.

After passing his medical examinations, Luria approached N. N. Burdenko, head of the Neurosurgical Institute at Moscow, in order to obtain an internship. In his autobiography, Luria described the following two years as the most productive of his life. He had no staff and no scientific responsibilities except routine medical work, and it was probably these circumstances that gave him space to devise his own approach to the neuropsychology of brain injury. In 1939 he moved to the Neurological Clinic of the Institute of Experimental Medicine in Moscow, where he became Head of the Laboratory of Experimental Psychology. When Russia entered the Second World War in 1941 he became a medical officer with responsibilities for the assessment and rehabilitation of brain-injured servicemen.

There were significant political pressures on Luria, Vygotsky and other psychologists to reconcile their intellectual positions with Marx's thesis that human beings are active participants in making and shaping their own evolution. In their efforts to create a Marxist psychology, Luria and others devised a system that sought to relate psychological theory and method to the history of cultural development, and particularly to its economic aspects. However, the constraints imposed by the Marxist philosophy that psychological phenomena are derived from and reflect physical reality meant that the most parsimonious psychological units of analysis lay not in what Luria or Vygotsky could offer but in Pavlov's conditional reflex. Stalin favoured Pavlovian psychophysiology as a model upon which all of psychology should be built, and during the 1940s the Central Committee of the Communist Party set about implementing this policy. Luria, along with many others who adhered to competing perspectives, was pressured into renouncing his activities. Thus, between 1937 and 1947, Luria suspended his interest in understanding the development of the brain and of higher thought processes and embarked on a career as a neurologist. In about 1948 he was transferred from the Institute of Neurosurgery, where he had been working for several years, to Vygotsky's Institute of Defectology. There he turned once again to the questions that had occupied the earlier part of his career. He was later restored to his post in Moscow, where he continued his work virtually until his death from cardiac failure.

Luria's approach to psychology is similar to **Allport**'s, in that it is based in part on his dissatisfaction with the need to choose between an idiographic psychology, which emphasises the importance of studying individuals, and a nomothetic psychology, which favours the formulation of general laws of human behaviour. Laboratory-based psychology, such as that developed by **Wundt**, could lead to the formulation of general principles underpinning human behaviour, but appeared to have little practical application because it could not be used to inform practice at the level of individual patients. A general law is just that – general – and can rarely be used to make decisions about what should be done to help individuals with their personal needs and problems. As Luria saw it, a new kind of psychology was required, one capable of capturing the richness of individual psychological experience while also accommodating the kinds of broad theoretical formulations that are a cornerstone of the natural sciences. Psychoanalysis seemed initially to offer a basis on which to found the kind of psychology he sought, because it focused on trying to understand and predict behaviour at an individual level. Luria hoped to create a new experimental science of individual mental life, a science that would be both idiographic and nomothetic. During his undergraduate years, and for a period of time after graduation, he was an ardent supporter of psychoanalysis and was strongly influenced by **Freud**, Adler and **Jung**. He founded a psychoanalytic circle in Kazan which he brought to the attention of Freud. Later he repudiated psychoanalysis in favour of a more rigorous experimental approach with a conceptual base that can be traced to some of the principles of Pavlovian psychology which treats the reflex as a basic building block of learning. However, Luria did not abandon his interests in psychoanalysis but exploited the properties of Jung's word-association technique by requiring research participants to give part of a response to a generic stimulus (e.g. 'house–room') and then introduced an 'impossible' stimulus word (e.g. 'moon–?'). He used delays in a person's reaction time to estimate the degree of conflict among the words, and thus their associated psychological significance. More generally, he developed what was known as the 'Luria technique', in which both voluntary and involuntary motor responses as well as verbal responses are measured. He distinguished three types of conflict arising from: (a) the prevention of excitation from extending into action; (b) lack of readiness for reacting; and (c) the diversion of suppressed activity into central processes.

Luria's innovative methods for restoring brain functioning were developed during his period as a medical officer in the Second World War and are based on his view of the brain as a complex functional system rather than a single entity. This position is summarised in Luria's three 'basic laws' of higher cortical functioning: the law of the hierarchical structure of cortical zones; the law of diminishing specificity; and the law of progressive lateralisation. He also made a substantial contribution to the development and refinement of clinical tests for brain damage that correlated with surgical and pathological reports.

The strength of Luria's approach lies in three features:

1   it is based on an explicit theoretical formulation of brain organisation, although it should be noted that parts of the model have subsequently been contradicted by empirical evidence;
2   it emphasises the qualitative aspects of performance – *how* something is done, not only the absolute standard of performance;
3   it is flexible in its approach to the diagnosis of deficits and in this respect is thought to result in greater accuracy and a more fine-grained description of a patient's problems.

These strengths found their clearest clinical expression in Charles Golden's development of the Luria–Nebraska Neuropsychological Battery. This battery consists of scales covering a wide range of problems, but, unlike other tests, items within each area were varied so as to test variations of a skill rather than one specific ability.

Against these considerations, Luria's system is sometimes criticised for its dependence on the clinical acumen of individual clinical neuropsychologists. Thus a gifted clinician such as Luria can use the system to great effect, as illustrated in the insights provided by his ground-breaking case studies, notably one of a young man with a truly exceptional memory, and another of a patient with traumatic brain injury. Although widely honoured as a founder of neuropsychology, there have been few rigorous evaluations of Luria's procedures, with the result that the validity and reliability of his 'clinical–analytical' approach are often treated with suspicion, and generally the approach has not fared well outside Europe. Although Luria published extensively over a fifty-year period, many of his publications in Russian are still unobtainable.

Alexander Luria's major writings

The Role of Speech in the Regulation of Normal and Abnormal Behaviour, Pergamon, 1961.
Restoration of Function After Brain Injury, Macmillan, 1963.
Higher Cortical Function in Man, Basic Books, 1966.
The Mind of a Mnemonist, Basic Books, 1968.
Traumatic Aphasia, Mouton, 1970.
The Man with a Shattered World, Basic Books, 1972.
The Working Brain, Penguin, 1973.

Further reading

Cole, M. and Cole, S. (eds) (1979) The Making of Mind, Harvard University Press.
Homskaya, E. D., Khomskaia, E. D. and Tupper, D. E. (eds) (2001) Alexander Romanovich Luria, Kluwer.

MACCOBY, ELEANOR EMMONS (1917–)

Maccoby made fundamental contributions to our understanding of the role of the parent–child relationship for social development and the origins of gender differences.

Eleanor Maccoby was the second daughter in a family of four girls. She was born in Tacoma, Washington, and spent her childhood there. Her father had been a farm worker from a poor family background who took pride in doing well in school and working his way to an engineering degree from Purdue University. Her mother was one of seven children. Her father established a small millwork business manufacturing cabinets, doors and windows. In an autobiographical essay Eleanor recounted that her parents were probably disappointed not to have had a son, and they cast her in the role of a son: she had a boy's nickname and wore her hair short in a boy's haircut – she was an authentic tomboy. Her parents joined the Theosophical Society when she was about nine and, with other parents from the Society, established a Theosophical summer camp where the family spent their summers from the time Eleanor was about ten. A strong teenage culture existed at the camp and teenage intellectual interests were welcomed as part of the adult discussion groups. These groups dealt with a variety of political and philosophical issues, and Eleanor was to develop intense political interests associated with the social and economic unrest of the time.

Maccoby took her first psychology course at Reed College, Portland, Oregon. It was given by William Griffith, a former student of Edwin Guthrie and an ardent behaviourist. Intrigued with the behaviourist perspective, she went to the University of Washington where, to cover her tuition fees, she worked as a secretary for one of the psychology faculty members and spent nearly all her free time at the department. There she met Nathan Maccoby, a graduate student in social psychology. They married in her senior year (and later had three children), and in 1940 they moved to Washington, DC, where Nathan took a job with the US Civil Service Commission. She joined the staff of Rensis Likert's Division of Program Surveys at the Department of Agriculture, and came in contact with **Bruner**, among others. When Likert moved his organisation to the University of Michigan, the Maccobys moved too. In the year in which she completed her doctoral dissertation on conditioning in pigeons – made possible in part by **Skinner** giving her access to his automated data-recording equipment in his Harvard lab – she joined the developmental social psychologist Robert Sears at Harvard. At that time Sears was arguing for a focus away from the analysis of individuals in a social setting and towards interpersonal behaviour and the importance of the dyad (two persons in interaction with one another) as a unit of analysis. At Harvard she worked as part of a team examining child-rearing practices that led to the publishing of *Patterns of Child Rearing* (1957), with Sears and Levin. With Bruner and Raymond A. Bauer she co-taught a course on public opinion. Although a productive researcher, gender discrimination prevented Maccoby from advancing beyond the level of lecturer at Harvard, and in 1958 she moved to Stanford University where she was appointed at the level of associate professor.

Her interactions with the developmental psychologist John Flavell led to a shift in interest from a behavioural perspective to a cognitive–developmental framework. She was particularly influenced by ideas and evidence that children can actively select, process and organise stimuli within their environment, and came to the view that the central task for developmental psychology is to understand sequences of development, including regularities and variations. She was also aware of **Broadbent**'s novel work on the role of attention in perception, and realised that there was little by way of developmental analysis in Broadbent's approach. Together with some colleagues, Maccoby embarked on a series of studies of the developmental aspects of selective perception that allowed them to trace age changes in both the ability to attend to one message while excluding another and the ability to divide attention and process more than one message at a time.

Helen Thompson Woolley carried out the first major psychological research concerned with gender differences, including differences in visual–spatial tasks, but it is Maccoby who drew all of the early work together and who, in so doing, became the leading psychological thinker on gender differentiation in childhood. In her role as a member of the Social Sciences Research Council Committee on Socialization she edited, with Carol Jacklin, a book on sex differences, *The Psychology of Sex Differences* (1974), in which some 1,600 studies of gender differences were reviewed. Reactions to the book were mixed. Some considered that their list of gender differences was overly selective and too brief, whereas others suggested that the emphasis on gender differences undervalued the considerable volume of work that pointed to gender similarities. Some critics considered that the book placed too great a reliance on biological factors in accounting for gender differences, whereas others contended that environmental factors were given too great a priority. However, there was general agreement that the research evidence they had surveyed pointed to four unambiguous differences between the sexes: verbal ability is superior in females, visual–spatial ability is superior in males, males show stronger mathematical ability, and males are more aggressive than females. Some of the debates sparked by *Sex Differences* were shaped by readers wrongly inferring that, if environmental factors could not account for observed gender differences, then biological factors should be taken as the default explanation. In fact Maccoby and Jacklin were very much concerned with pressing a third, cognitive–developmental explanation based on the concept of self-socialisation. Drawing on the idea that children are active agents in their own development, they used self-socialisation to refer to the active process whereby children make judgements about the gender relevance of various roles and activities available to them. For example, Maccoby showed that the most sex-typed parents do not have the most gender-typed children: there is no relationship between the division of household labour, parental attitudes to sex-typing, their sex-typing activities and the degree to which their children express sex-typed preferences and behaviours. Children's developmental trajectories vary because they are capable of acquiring stereotypes which they might, or might not, use to guide their own behaviour.

The magnitude of the gender differences identified by Maccoby and Jacklin more than a quarter of a century ago appears to be in decline. For example, analysis of 172 studies of parents' differential socialisation of boys and girls has shown that cognitive and social characteristics are not as large as Maccoby and Jacklin initially concluded, although this does not rule out the possibility that ostensibly small differences in the socialisation of 'gender appropriate' behaviour may have larger impacts in later life (Lytton and Romney, 1991). For instance, the verbal skills of boys have shown improvement in a number of studies conducted in different parts of the world, while North American studies suggest there is a declining trend in gender differences in mathematics. Theoretical advances now argue for placing greater emphasis on the influence of relational processes in the emergence of gender differences, specifically on how the emotional relationship between parents and children may have a differential effect on girls and boys. Such a view is consistent with, and follows from, Maccoby's argument that understanding gender differences is best accomplished by examining relationships rather than individuals in isolation from their social networks. Notwithstanding these caveats and elaborations, *The Psychology of Sex Differences* remains a landmark in the development of psychology.

Eleanor Maccoby's major writings

'Why children watch television', *Public Opinion Quarterly*, 1954, 18, 239–44.
Patterns of Child Rearing, Row-Peterson, 1957 (with R. R. Sears and H. Levin).
'Parents' differential reactions to sons and daughters', *Journal of Personality and Social Psychology*, 1966, 4, 237–43.
Experiments in Primary Education, Harcourt, Brace, Jovanovich, 1970 (with M. Zellner).
The Psychology of Sex Differences, Stanford University Press, 1974 (with C. N. Jacklin).
Social Development: Psychological Growth and the Parent–Child Relationship, Harcourt, Brace, Jovanovich, 1980.

Further reading

Golombok, S. and Fivush, R. (1994) *Gender Development*, Cambridge University Press.

Lindzey, G. (ed.) (1989) *A History of Psychology in Autobiogra*[...] Stanford University Press.

Lytton, H. and Romney, D. M. (1991) 'Parent's differential sociali[...] and girls: A meta-analysis', *Psychological Bulletin*, 109, 267–96.

Stevens, G. and Gardner, S. (1982) *The Women of Psychology: Volume*[...] *and Refinement*, Schenkman.

MASLOW, ABRAHAM H. (1908–70)

Maslow played a major role in pressing the case for humanistic psychology, and developed a theory of motivation based on the idea that needs are organised hierarchically.

Abraham Harold Maslow was the eldest of seven children. His parents were uneducated Jewish Russian immigrants and were very concerned to ensure that their children took every opportunity afforded them. Being the eldest, Abraham was placed under a lot of pressure to be academically successful, an experience he found both stressful and lonely. His parents encouraged him to take a law degree at the City College of New York (CCNY). After three semesters, he transferred to Cornell University, and then returned to CCNY. Against his parents' wishes he married Bertha Goodman, his first cousin (they later had two daughters), and they moved to Wisconsin where Maslow completed his training in psychology. His dissertation, on dominance and sexuality in monkeys, was supervised by Harry Harlow, who made significant contributions to the understanding of the development of affectional systems in monkeys and humans. Maslow returned to New York to work with the learning theorist **Thorndike** at Columbia University, where he became interested in research on human sexuality. Several years later his expertise in this area brought an invitation from Alfred Kinsey to collaborate in his classic study of sexual behaviour, but the partnership never materialised, largely because Maslow published a critical commentary of the sampling framework and procedures underlying Kinsey's work. Two years at Columbia were followed by a teaching position at Brooklyn College that brought him into contact with other European immigrants, including Erich Fromm, Alfred Adler and Karen Horney. This was followed by a move to Brandeis University, where he remained until his early retirement brought on by several years of poor health. Thereafter he was appointed resident fellow of the Laughlin Institute, California. Maslow died in 1970 from a heart attack.

The founder of Humanistic Psychology, Maslow was initially trained within the behavioural tradition and developed a strong interest in psychobiology. This was to inspire his study of human motivation, which, he argued, should be the study of the ultimate goals or desires of people. Rather than attempting to enumerate every goal and desire, he focused on their relationships and sought to identify general structures. His astute awareness of the manner in which animals seek to satisfy their needs in order of precedence provided a guide to the delineation of general structures. For example, breathing takes precedence over drinking, and drinking over eating. He identified five levels of need: physiological needs, needs relating to safety and security, the needs for affiliation and love, the need for esteem, and the need to actualise the self. The more basic needs (e.g. physiological) take precedence over higher-order needs (e.g. self-actualisation). (Maslow was aware of the existence of curiosity as an important motivational influence, but, unsure of where to place it in his hierarchy, he chose to omit it.) He used the personality syndrome – an organised, interdependent, structured group of syndromes – as his primary unit of analysis, and focused on studying two particular syndromes: self-esteem and security. He considered the inverse forms of the needs motivating these syndromes to be associated with low self-esteem and inferiority complexes. In this regard Maslow was in broad agreement with Adler's view that failure to satisfy more basic needs is at the root of many psychological problems. For example, someone whose childhood was characterised by concerns with scarcity might, in later life, manifest an obsessive neurosis by buying and storing large quantities of food. Under stressful conditions we may regress to a concern with satisfying needs at a lower level, as when a friendship ends and we may feel an intense longing to satisfy needs of belonging.

A crucial part of his theory concerns the distinction between lower ('deficiency') and higher ('being' or 'growth') needs, a division similar to one made by **Allport** between biogenic and psychogenic needs. Higher-order needs are thought to appear later, both in evolutionary terms and in an organism's development (i.e. in adulthood rather than childhood). He also regarded them as less vital to survival – satisfying these higher-order needs can be delayed – but once satisfied they are associated with a profound sense of self-fulfilment. He used **Cannon's** concept of homeostasis (the maintenance of physiological equilibrium) to explain how lower-order deficiency needs (D-needs) are satisfied. However, he also took the view that: (i) satisfying higher-order being needs (B-needs) can only be achieved given a relatively rare amalgamation of favourable environmental conditions; and (ii) satisfying B-needs does not involve homeostasis. B-needs, once satisfied or engaged, are likely to become stronger and provoke an ongoing desire to continue to fulfil one's potential and to be all that you can be. He also argued that the dynamics of personal values changes as needs are fulfilled. Specifically, we tend to overestimate the importance of those things that can satisfy the most powerful of our ungratified needs, and to underestimate the significance of the satisfiers of the less powerful ungratified needs, and the force of those needs. Conversely, we tend to underestimate and undervalue the importance of satisfiers of needs already gratified, and to underestimate the potency of those needs.

Maslow described the self-actualising person thus: 'If one expects nothing, if one has no anticipations or apprehensions, if in a sense there is no future ... There can be no surprise, no disappointment. One thing is as likely as another ... and no prediction means no worry, no anxiety, no apprehension, no foreboding' (1962: 67). His hope was that sustained effort to distil the core features of the self-actualising person would lead to the production of something akin to a periodic table of qualities, pathologies (he never regarded the self-actualised person as 'perfect') and solutions typical of the highest levels of human potential.

Maslow's criticism of the psychology he studied as a student was that it was too pessimistic: the person was regarded as enduring a hostile environment from without, and descriptive, unconscious instincts from within. Much of the criticism against his more optimistic theoretical framework concerns the approach taken to the development of his ideas on self-actualisation. He began by identifying people he regarded as high self-actualisers and then used various combinations of interviews and biographical and autobiographical accounts to distil the core characteristics of self-actualisation. The approach was based on his method of iteration, which involved obtaining information from interviews and a variety of documentary sources, using the data to refine the concept of self-actualisation, conducting additional interviews, or consulting further documentary evidence, further refining the concept and so on. The difficulty with this approach is that, by deciding *a priori* who were and who were not self-actualisers, Maslow grounded the development of his theory on his personal impressions of self-actualised people (e.g. Albert Einstein, Eleanor Roosevelt, Walt Whitman, Ludwig van Beethoven). Maslow was aware of the problems this posed, and always maintained that his approach to research was motivated principally by a concern to raise awareness of the fundamental issues involved in studying self-actualisation and demonstrating that the measurement issues were not insurmountable. A related criticism concerns the arbitrary limit Maslow imposed on the achievement of self-actualisation: he estimated that only 2 per cent of humans achieve self-actualisation, and a list he produced in 1970 contained just nine living and nine historical figures. This contrasts with **Rogers**'s view that self-actualisation is about what every organism strives to do: to grow and fulfil its biological fate. Thus, while Rogers regarded babies as the best examples of human self-actualisation, Maslow considered self-actualisation to be a rarity among the young. Moreover, Maslow contended that organisms seek to satisfy lower-order biological needs before attending to self-actualisation, yet many of the finest human achievements in arts and science are attributed to people who live an impoverished lifestyle and endure physical and psychological ill-health as a consequence.

Maslow's impact was partly a reaction against the prevailing mechanistic and behaviouristic zeitgeist, and offered an optimistic, holistic and even a mystical account of the human condition. His approach offered the prospect of refocusing psychology away from the study of behaviour towards the analysis of the whole organism – the person. Although Maslow's theory has little empirical support with respect to the order of priority of needs, it has proved a useful descriptive model of personality and a good framework from which to investigate individual differences. An enduring feature of Maslow's psychology is its concern with well-being and the realisation of potential. His interest in understanding the constituents of psychological well-being contrasted with the traditional interest in the 'abnormal' and with psychological illness. His humanistic psychology stimulated the development of new kinds of therapies that focused on realising personal resources for growth and healing and on helping people overcome barriers to achieving this. The most famous of these was Rogers's client-centred therapy. With its emphasis on personal growth and 'becoming', Maslow's theory is often described as representing a 'fulfilment' account of personality. As such, it is usually classified with other theorists, labelled 'Third Force' psychologists. ('Depth' psychologies such as psychoanalysis constitute the first force, behaviourism is the second force, and humanistic psychology the third force.) Towards the end of his life, Maslow inaugurated what he called the 'fourth force' in psychology: The fourth force refers to transpersonal psychologies which, taking their cue from Eastern philosophies, investigate meditation and altered levels of consciousness.

Abraham Maslow's major writings

Principles of Abnormal Psychology, Harper and Row, 1941 (with B. Mittelman).
'A theory of human motivation', *Psychological Review,* 1943, 50, 370–96.
'Volunteer-error in the Kinsey study', *Journal of Abnormal and Social Psychology,* 1951, 47, 259–62 (with J. Sakoda).
Motivation and Personality, Harper and Row, 1954.
New Knowledge in Human Values, Harper and Row, 1959.
Toward a Psychology of Being, Van Nostrand, 1962.
Religion, Values and Peak Experiences (lectures), Ohio State University Press, 1964.
Eupsychian Management: A Journal, Irwin, 1965.
The Farther Reaches of Human Nature, Viking, 1971.

Further reading

Goble, F. (1970) *The Third Force: The Psychology of Abraham Maslow,* Grossman.
Hoffman, E. (1988) *The Right to be Human: A Biography of Abraham Maslow,* St Martins.

McCLELLAND, DAVID CLARENCE (1917–98)

McClelland is best known for his work on achievement motivation or the 'need for achievement' and his studies of people with a particularly intense need to achieve.

McClelland was the third of five children, the son of Clarence P. McClelland, a Methodist minister and college president, and Mary E. (Adams) McClelland. He was a committed Quaker and was actively involved in many organisations, meetings and events. Born in Mount Vernon, New York, his childhood was spent in Jacksonville, Illinois. His primary degree (1938) from Wesleyan University included supervision by the learning theorist John McGeoch. His 1939 M.Sc. from the University of Missouri involved studying under the experimental psychologist and memory theorist Arthur Melton, and his doctorate in 1941 from Yale University was conducted under the direction of the social psychologists Carl Hovland and Robert Sears. During the Second World War he was assistant personnel secretary of the American Friends Service Committee and a part-time lecturer in psychology at Bryn Mawr College. Later he spent a sabbatical year (1949–50) at the Department of Social Relations at Harvard University, and another as Deputy Director of the Behavioral Sciences

Division of the Ford Foundation (1952–53). He was appointed Professor of Psychology at Harvard in 1956, where he remained until 1987, then moving to Boston University where he was Distinguished Research Professor of Psychology until his death.

McClelland's best-known work is on achievement motivation – the 'need for achievement' – a social form of motivation involving a competitive drive to meet standards of excellence that was first described by the personality theorist Henry A. Murray. The need to achieve is usually abbreviated N Ach or nAch. McClelland's interest in this area grew out of a fortuitous combination of experiences that included a contractual obligation to teach personality theory at Bryn Mawr. Donald W. MacKinnon was also at Bryn Mawr at that time. He was developing a theory of creative achievement that was also influenced by Murray, and had much in common with McClelland's own position. Murray was one of several eminent theorists, including **Freud**, **Jung** and **Maslow**, who felt that any theory of personality must commence with an explanation of why people engage in any behaviour at all – what is the source of the energy that fuels behaviour? Freud regarded behaviour as determined or motivated in order to satisfy desires. For Murray, the most important motivational questions concerned those things about a person that revealed the goal orientation of their actions. In order to reveal a person's goal orientation, it was important to profile their needs. Murray regarded 'need' as a theoretical construct denoting a neuropsychological force that organises brain processes such as perceiving, thinking and acting. McClelland's need theory of motivation was strongly influenced by Murray, and distinguishes three types of need: the need for achievement, the need for affiliation, and the need for power. Two of these needs, the need for achievement and the need for affiliation, have attracted most empirical interest, and McClelland was particularly drawn to the analysis of nAch for two reasons. First, he considered nAch to be a distinctively human motive and therefore worthy of consideration for this reason alone. Second, nAch appeared to be a value that was central to many Western societies (particularly North American society), endorsed and inculcated in children, and it seemed to be widely regarded as a crucial determinant of actual accomplishment in many achievement situations. Indeed, much of the practical impact of McClelland's work in organisational and educational settings stems from the fact that his reading of the societal significance of nAch was correct in the sense that the need to achieve is a core American value.

Much of McClelland's work focused on understanding those with a particularly intense need to achieve. He devised a number of methods to isolate and describe the behavioural characteristics of people high in nAch, including an ingeniously simple laboratory demonstration in the form of a game: people had to throw rings over a peg from any distance they chose. McClelland observed that most people tended to choose distances at random, sometimes closer, sometimes farther away, and they often alternated between extreme positions. However, a minority – those high in nAch – tended to choose a position that maximised their sense of mastery and was neither ridiculously easy nor impossibly difficult. This he likened to the principle of biological overload. Biological overload is based on evidence that muscle groups cannot be strengthened and developed by performing very easy tasks and are likely to be damaged by engaging in excessively difficult tasks. Muscle performance will develop most effectively by adopting an exercise regime that is challenging but achievable. However, McClelland also pointed out that people who are high in nAch do not behave consistently: whether they choose to engage in challenging but achievable goals depends on whether they feel they have a reasonable chance of influencing the outcome. This idea was particularly germane to psychological organisational behaviour, entrepreneurship and risk-taking, because it seemed to provide a plausible psychological explanation for variations in preference for risk-taking.

McClelland also observed that those high in nAch tended to be more concerned with personal achievement – the achievement is its own reward – and not to view their achievements as instrumental to obtaining rewards such as salary increments and promotion. Instead, they valued financial and other rewards because these provide tangible feedback that can be used to inform the level of challenge they will pursue. This idea is related to Herzberg's motivation–hygiene theory which contends that people high in nAch tend to be mostly interested in the motivators (the job itself) whereas those with low nAch are more concerned about the environment (e.g. others' perceptions of them and their performance). According to McClelland, people high in nAch behave as they do because they routinely spend time thinking about doing things better. Support for this view came from the many studies of organisational behaviour which showed that, wherever people start to think in achievement terms, things start to change. Of course, this begs the question: what leads some people high in nAch to spend so much time thinking about improving things? McClelland was convinced that achievement motivation was something that people learned, and it was therefore something that could be nurtured.

Support for this view came from studies of the family backgrounds of those high in nAch; these indicated that such people tend to have parents who encouraged the expression of relatively high levels of independence between the ages of six and eight. The parents of children lower in nAch either encouraged independent thinking and action earlier than this – too early, in McClelland's view – or suppressed the expression of independence until later childhood.

Critiques of McClelland's theory focus on the fact that, like Murray's, it does not specify how learning of nAch takes place and that the kinds of processes that can raise nAch in adulthood may not be the same as those that were formative in early childhood. Interventions in organisational or industrial settings that were derived from his theory highlighted a paradox: people high in nAch achieve success by getting things done, but their strong tendency to focus on the task means they may neglect the person-oriented issues that are required to unlock the motivational potential in others. In other words people who focus on getting things done do not always make the best managers. One of the practical implications of this is that attempting to motivate people using generic principles cannot succeed: it is necessary to match the motivational approach to the motivational needs of the person.

One factor that received relatively little attention in McClelland's earlier formulations concerned those people who seemed to manifest a particularly strong fear of failure. A growing corpus of evidence suggested that avoidance motivation also produces a complex cognitive network for dealing with reality. Later developments to the theory contend that people are motivated either to achieve success or to avoid failure. When the tendency to avoid failure is greater than the tendency to succeed, then the maximum motivation occurs when the outcome is almost certain. For example, a strong tendency to avoid failure is manifested in a preference for succeeding on a relatively simple task or failing on a very difficult one. In both circumstances there is little chance of the person being perceived to 'fail', because the outcomes are stacked either in their favour or against them. The motivation levels of these people decline when the outcome becomes more uncertain, because there is an increased likelihood that failure will be attributed to personal factors. However, for those people who are motivated when the tendency to succeed surpasses the tendency to avoid failure, then the highest levels of motivation will be observed in highly competitive situations where the outcome is strongly determined by ability levels.

One of the more controversial ideas proffered by McClelland is that those countries of which a large proportion of the population scores high in nAch tend to be more successful across a range of socio-economic, wealth creation and quality-of-life indicators. His commitment to the development of training courses to raise nAch nationally was a product of two influences: his Quaker consciousness, developed during his college years, and the implications of the numerous studies that reported support for his theoretical position. However, these interventions, coupled with the evidence that high nAch is not the same as high IQ, also led McClelland to become increasingly concerned with how little traditional tests of intelligence really revealed about what it takes to be successful in life. His position on this is similar to that of the guru of psychological testing Anne **Anastasi**.

When McClelland first began to investigate nAch it was assessed using the Murray–Morgan Thematic Apperception Test (TAT), a well-regarded projective technique comprising twenty pictures (thirty-one in later editions) depicting ambiguous emotionally-laden social situations and events. The respondent was invited to look at a picture and construct a story describing what is happening, including the thoughts and feelings of the people depicted. One of McClelland's enduring contributions was to take the test and devise a more rigorous and systematic method for scoring answers in terms of personality characteristics, emotional concerns and motives that respondents projected onto the scene. One of the relatively neglected findings to emerge from his work with the TAT concerned its poor association with self-reported questionnaire measures of nAch. It was often explained that projective measures such as the TAT are both cumbersome and of doubtful validity, but McClelland felt the difference was more than this, and that the two measures were actually tapping fundamentally different psychological processes. In this regard he anticipated a later controversy surrounding the validity and reliability of peoples' verbal reports as indicators of their thought processes, as illustrated in the work of **Simon**.

David McClelland's major writings

Personality, Sloane, 1951.
Studies in Motivation, Appleton-Century-Crofts, 1955.
The Achieving Society, Van Nostrand, 1961.
The Roots of Consciousness, Van Nostrand, 1963.
Power: The Inner-Experience, Halstead-Wiley, 1975.

Further reading

Birney, R. C., Burdick, H. and Teevan, R. C. (1969) *Fear of Failure*, Van Nostrand.

Wigfield, A. and Eccles, J. S. (2002) *Development of Achievement Motivation*, Harcourt.

MILGRAM, STANLEY (1933–84)

Milgram conducted a classic and controversial experimental study of obedience that suggests that most people are capable of heinous behaviour.

Stanley Milgram was born and raised in New York City and attended James Monroe High School – he and **Zimbardo** were in the 12th grade together – before entering Queen's College, where he studied political science. His interest in psychology emerged during his graduating year, so acceptance of his application to Harvard University's Department of Social Relations was deferred until he completed six psychology courses during the summer of 1954. His doctoral dissertation was supervised by **Allport**, who pioneered the application of social psychological approaches to the study of personality. Milgram's dissertation addressed cross-cultural differences in conformity and was based on data collected in Norway and Paris. Whereas **Asch** had previously asked participants to judge the length of lines in circumstances where there was strong social pressure to conform to the erroneous judgement of the majority, Milgram used judgements of sound duration. He concluded that pressures for conformity were greater in the relatively small, homogenous society of Norway than in France, with its greater cultural variability and stronger tradition of intellectual dissent. While teaching at Yale University, Milgram directed his interests in conformity to the study of obedience to authority and thereby developed a line of enquiry initiated by Asch, under whose supervision he worked for a short time in 1959.

Milgram was fundamentally interested in social issues as people experienced them. For example, his mother-in-law wondered why the chivalrous practice of giving up one's seat for another appeared to be in decline among the users of the New York subway system. One of his students set about testing the possibility that the citizens of New York City were inured to the needs of others. The findings, Milgram concluded, indicated that New Yorkers were not callous, but were socially inhibited from engaging with one another. His Jewish heritage undoubtedly contributed to his intellectual and personal concern for finding an answer to an even bigger question: 'If Hitler asked you, would you kill a stranger?' Milgram devised a research paradigm that sought to provide an answer. His research programme set out to examine the degree to which ordinary people will comply with the orders of authority when those orders go against their conscience. In his classic and controversial study, he created a laboratory situation that turned out to offer a very powerful way of investigating obedience. Essentially, someone taking orders from a scientist can be persuaded to deliver what they believe to be an extremely dangerous electric shock (450 volts) to someone they understand to be an innocent victim with a heart condition. In a set of twenty-one experiments, Milgram found that about two-thirds of the participants were willing to administer the shock to the victim. The study has been replicated in dozens of countries and, while there is some variation in the percentage of participants prepared to administer this level of shock, a fair summary would be that, once again, about two-thirds were obedient; this figure has become a benchmark statistic. The first published commentary on this work appeared, not in a psychology journal, but in a highly critical editorial of the St. Louis *Post-Dispatch*. Milgram was unaware of the piece until Robert Buckhout, a social psychologist based at St. Louis, brought it to his attention. Numerous critiques followed, many of them addressing issues regarding the ethics of using deception, the nature of informed consent, the dignity afforded to people who agree to participate in psychological experiments, and the extent to which Milgram's studies should be regarded as bringing the discipline into disrepute. One of the strongest claims, first articulated by the developmental psychologist Diana Baumrind, was that Milgram's study did not meet ethical standards because participants were subjected to a research design that caused them undue psychological stress that was not resolved after the study. Milgram's response was that the study was well designed and that there was clear evidence that the participants' distress dissipated after a thorough debriefing. The level of controversy was such that his application to the American Psychological Association was delayed pending the outcome of an investigation into the ethics of his studies. The conclusion was favourable, and his membership was approved in 1963. Two years later this work was awarded the annual socio-psychological prize of the American Association for the Advancement of Science. It is perhaps no accident that, when translations of this work appeared, they appeared first in Hebrew and in German.

Milgram contends that everyone has the dual capacity both to function as an individual capable of exercising their own moral judgement, and to take ethical decisions based on their personal character. However, two-thirds of us – men and women alike – are capable of heinous behaviour when, in deference to authority, we allow our own moral judgements to be over-ruled. The interpretations that can be placed on Milgram's findings, together with the ethical issues they raise, are still debated. They are often explained in terms of the presence of: (a) normative pressures induced by the experimenter's insistence that participants do what they are told – unlike the less pressured procedures adopted by **Asch** in his investigations; (b) informational influence – the tendency to allow others to reach a decision on what to do when faced with an ambiguous or crisis situation; and (c) conflicting social norms – once the first shock had been administered, participants placed additional pressures on themselves to continue to obey. Subsequent studies have shown that having peers model vicious behaviour towards others will increase the willingness of participants to inflict what they believe to be life-threatening shocks. However, victims who demand to be shocked elicit an opposite reaction from participants now reluctant to engage in a sado-masochistic rapport. Most participants decline the invitation.

Would Milgram find less obedience if he conducted his experiments today? Two reasons for thinking that fewer people would be obedient are that the mass media have alerted the general public to human susceptibility to obedience to authority and that the outcome of Milgram's own studies has found its way into popular culture (e.g. a popularised account of his experiments appeared in *Harper's* magazine in 1973, and they are the subject of Peter Gabriel's 1986 song 'We do what we're told – Milgram's 37'). Moreover, whereas Milgram found that the predictions of those unfamiliar with his experimental paradigm grossly underestimated the actual obedience rates, later studies indicate that the gap has greatly diminished (Blass, 1999). Thus, knowledge of one's vulnerability to obedience to authority might act as a protective factor against demands for compliance. However, Blass (2000), drawing on thirty-five years of accumulated research, examined the correlation between the year in which a study was published and the amount of obedience reported. He found no association: later studies found neither more nor less obedience than that reported in earlier investigations.

Milgram's methodological ingenuity is also revealed in his investigations of more benign forms of social influence. Since his laboratory looked out onto New York's 42nd Street, he arranged for various numbers of pedestrians (all of them confederates – students or colleagues) to stop and gaze up at a sixth-floor window. Behind the window Milgram filmed the crowd. He systematically varied the number of confederates and measured the size of the crowd that would gather. With one confederate gazing, about 45 per cent of pedestrians stopped to look up, but with fifteen confederates, about 85 per cent of the passers-by stopped. This is a different type of social force – contagion rather than obedience – but it is a powerful demonstration that, as the number of sources of influence increases, the intensity of their social impact seems also to increase. This is not to imply that contagion is inherently wrong: it can confer an information-processing advantage because merely noticing what others are doing and imitating their actions means that people can spend less time deciding what to do – a strategy that leads to appropriate decisions most of the time (Cialdini, 1993). Milgram's work informed a generation of experimental investigations of social influence, most forcefully articulated in the work of Zimbardo.

Milgram carried out studies of social processes based on a set of highly original experimental techniques, notably The Lost Letter Technique, The Small World Problem and the Cyranoid paradigm. The Lost Letter Technique is a procedure for investigating altruism which involves a researcher 'losing' a number of stamped and addressed letters throughout an area. The behaviour of people finding a letter (e.g. post it, read it, trash it) is covertly observed and used to indicate their altruism. In the first study, Milgram systematically changed a minor detail on the address (e.g. 'Friends of the Nazi Party' or 'Medical Research Organisation') in order to examine the impact of social and political attitudes upon willingness to help. He devised the Small World Problem to test the postulate that everyone on earth is connected together in an enormous social network. The theory predicts that any two people chosen at random from anywhere in the world can be connected to one another through a surprisingly short chain of friends or associates – just six. Originally supported by anecdotal evidence and folklore, more recent studies have suggested that the phenomenon is fundamental to structures occurring throughout nature, and it appears to be an essential component in the structural evolution of the World Wide Web. Several attempts have been made to provide a decisive test of the 'Six Degrees of Separation' hypothesis by involving several thousand people from around the world. The findings have been inconclusive, but whatever the final outcome the answer to Milgram's Small World Problem will reveal a great deal about the structure of social networks on the planet. The Cyranoid paradigm (named after Cyrano de Bergerac, who spoke eloquently on behalf of a tongue-tied suitor) involves an experimental manipulation in which one of the participants in a conversation speaks, not their own thoughts, but those of a hidden observer, the thoughts being transmitted to them via a tiny radio receiver. His interests in other areas, such as his 1972 study of the mental maps of the inhabitants of Paris and New York, anticipated the emergence of the environmental psychology of the built environment.

There is no evidence that Milgram's interests in understanding obedience and his willingness to deceive research participants were a reflection of aspects of his own personality and his treatment of others. Like his own doctoral supervisor, Gordon **Allport**, he enjoyed a reputation as a supporting rather than a demanding mentor and, while at the Graduate Center of CUNY, only one of his many doctoral students worked on the topic of obedience. The social psychologists Irwin Katz offered the following observation on the occasion of Milgram's untimely death: 'After two decades of critical scrutiny and discussion, they remain one of the most singular, most penetrating, and most disturbing enquiries into human conduct that modern psychology has produced this century. Those of us who presume to have knowledge of man are still perplexed by his findings, with their frightful implications for society' (cited in Blass, 1999).

Stanley Milgram's major writings

'Nationality and conformity', *Scientific American*, 1961, 205, 45–51.
'Behavioral study of obedience', *Journal of Abnormal and Social Psychology*, 1963, 67, 371–8.
'Some conditions of obedience and disobedience to authority', *Human Relations*, 1965, 18, 57–76.
'The small world problem', *Psychology Today*, 1967, 1, 60–7.
'The lost letter technique', *Psychology Today*, 1969, 3, 30–3, 66, 68.
Obedience to Authority, Harper & Row, 1974.
The Individual in a Social World, Addison-Wesley, 1977.

Further reading

Baumrind, D. (1964) 'Some thoughts on ethics of research: After reading Milgram's "Behavioral study of obedience" ', *American Psychologist*, 19, 421–3.
Blass, T. (1999) 'The Milgram paradigm after 35 years: Some things we now know about obedience to authority', *Journal of Applied Social Psychology*, 29, 955–7.
Blass, T. (ed.) (2000) *Obedience to Authority: Current Perspectives on the Milgram Paradigm*, Erlbaum.
Cialdini, R. B. (1993) *Influence: Science and Practice*, Harper Collins.

NEISSER, ULRIC RICHARD GUSTAV (1928–)

Neisser defined cognitive psychology as referring to all of the processes by which sensory information is transformed, reduced, elaborated, stored, recovered and used, and wrote a textbook on the topic providing a model structure that has been reproduced by numerous authors.

Niesser was born in Kiel, Germany. His parents, Hans and Charlotte, moved the family to America in 1933 when he was four. His initial academic interest was in physics, a subject he took as a major at Harvard University before switching to psychology – a change made partly due to his attraction to the lectures of Edwin G. Boring. His graduate thesis was supervised by George Miller, a young member of staff who was lecturing and writing on the psychological structure of communication and who distinguished himself by using concepts such as 'bit' and 'phoneme'. After graduating from Harvard, Neisser pursued a master's degree at Swarthmore College that brought him into contact with some of the pioneers of Gestalt psychology, notably Wolfgang Köhler and his associate Hans Wallach. When he completed his master's, he went to the Massachusetts Institute of Technology (MIT) which was at the time attempting to establish a department of psychology. Much of the intellectual discourse at MIT was about measuring 'bits of information' and the like. This was not to Neisser's liking, and in 1954 he transferred back to Harvard where he completed his doctorate; he remained there to pursue postdoctoral studies. In 1957 he was offered a post at Brandeis University, which was at that time under the direction of **Maslow** who was busy establishing a case for a 'third force' in psychology to counteract the influences of psychoanalysis and behaviourism. He was particularly impressed by Maslow's message that psychology should be a force for good and should, *inter alia*, spend more time understanding the positive side of human nature. Oliver Selfridge, a mathematician and pioneer of artificial intelligence was an equally influential intellectual force. Selfridge's work on pattern recognition completed Neisser's interest in perception and led to productive collaborations that included their widely acclaimed 'Pattern recognition by machine' (1960). More than a decade of empirical and theoretical work on visual search behaviour was punctuated by sabbatical leave at Martin Orne's laboratory at Philadelphia. It was here that Neisser wrote his *Cognitive Psychology* (1967), which gave that field its name as well as an overall conceptual framework. There he defined cognitive psychology as referring to all processes by which sensory information is transformed, reduced, elaborated, stored, recovered and used. The opening pages include the context-setting statement:

> A generation ago, a book like this one would have needed at least a chapter of self-defense against the behaviorist position. Today, happily, the climate of opinion has changed, and little or no defense is necessary. Indeed, stimulus–response theorists themselves are inventing hypothetical mechanisms with vigor and enthusiasm and only faint twinges of conscience. The basic reason for studying cognitive processes has become as clear as the reason for studying anything else: because they are there ... Cognitive processes surely exist, so it can hardly be unscientific to study them.
>
> (1967: 5)

Cognition, he argued, could best be studied by modelling the flow of information through various mental stages, and he considered the computer metaphor to offer a powerful explanatory analogue. He coined such terms as 'iconic memory' (an elaboration of an earlier concept of iconic store, referring to a sensory register that allows a visual image to persist for about half a second after the stimulus has terminated); and 'echoic memory', whereby an auditory image is supposed to persist for 1–2 seconds after the stimulus has stopped.

Neisser moved to Cornell University just after the publication of *Cognitive Psychology*, and it was here that he was influenced by **Gibson**, a strong advocate for an 'ecological approach' to understanding perception and behaviour. Neisser became convinced that the commitment to an information-processing model of cognition would not be as effective a research strategy as he had first believed. He argued that the model tends to underestimate the available stimulus information, relies too much on results obtained in artificial laboratory settings, and can divert attention from understanding how cognition really occurs in the natural information-rich environment. While *Cognitive Psychology* was a catalyst for the 'cognitive revolution', his *Cognition and Reality* (1976) posed some fundamental questions about the assumptions on which cognitive psychology was founded, and the response was strikingly different: 'the message I brought in *Cognition and Reality* was not as popular as the one I brought in .[*Cognitive Psychology*] ... now, I'm saying that what people want to do may not be worth doing; maybe they should be doing something else. That's not such a popular message' (Baars, 1986: 282). In *Cognition and*

Reality he develops the thesis that it is impossible to study a system outside of its context, a view that has much in common with those of the founder of cognitive sociology, Aaron Cicourel, and the cognitive anthropologist Roy D'Andrade. For example, memory cannot be studied in isolation from other cognitive processes, and the mind cannot be studied outside of the context in which people live their lives. Neisser was critical of the value attached to laboratory-based experimental investigations of cognitive processes, and of the mistaken belief that the processes observed therein are a pure form of the processes that operate outside the lab. He pointed out, for example, that laboratory-based investigations had failed to attend to some of the really big questions: Why do people who experience the same thing remember it differently? Why do we remember so little from the earliest years of our lives? Why are certain events remembered vividly, while others appear to be completely forgotten? The questions he posed informed the emergence of innovative studies of autobiographical memory, flashbulb memory, prospective memory and eye-witness memory. Critics of his revisionist position counter by declaring that ecologically valid studies rarely use appropriate experimental controls, tend to work within poorly articulated theoretical frameworks, and produce findings that normally cannot be generalised beyond the idiosyncratic settings in which they were observed. They are also highly critical of the emergence of speculative debates as to the meaning of findings generated by impoverished 'naturalistic' designs. In response, Neisser further articulated his conviction, and he applied it specifically to the study of memory in his book *Memory Observed* (1982). Partly as a result of these efforts, the ecological approach has become a viable alternative to the information-processing approach in many areas of cognitive psychology.

Neisser's arguments made an important contribution to a much larger debate on underlying memory metaphors that permeate laboratory and naturalistic methods of enquiry. Laboratory-based approaches tend to embrace a storehouse metaphor that leads to an emphasis on the analysis of the content of the store and access to memory content. Naturalistic studies of everyday memory favour a correspondence metaphor and pursue an analysis of the accuracy and completeness of memory for past events. However, Neisser's own theoretical position stands apart from the storehouse and correspondence metaphors, both of which pursue representational accounts of memory – how past events are represented in memory. Neisser offers a non-representational view of memory in which remembering is characterised as a form of doing. His position on this is similar to another non-representational approach, dynamic systems theory, which regards the behaviour of a system as an emergent property of the interactions between its sub-systems. Neisser's position also has much in common with Gibson's ecological orientation, but differs from it in suggesting that organisms are more active and their cognitive apparatus can direct a search for information. Neisser contends that there is a direct relation between perception and action; the action of schemata can account for the presence of adaptive behaviour while conserving the pre-eminent position of cognitive processes: schemata direct actions, actions lead to the collection of information, and information modifies schemata. His approach shares many features of the embodied mind thesis of Rafael Núñez and George Lakoff, who argue for an unorthodox perspective whereby cognition is regarded as more than a mental process. It is also thought to be founded on embodied experience. The basic idea is that the structure and function of the human organism determine how the world is experienced, including concepts that are integral to the process of thinking. Thus a human being cannot think just anything – only what its embodied brain allows. Neisser's account of the embodied mind thesis is used to explain how the brain filters the vast quantity of information that would otherwise exceed cognitive processing capacity. Thus, like **Bartlett**, **Bruner** and others, Neisser made extensive use of the concept of 'schema' and emphasised the role of schemata in setting expectations of what will happen next and what should be attended to. His use of the concept is illustrated in his explanation of skilled movement where schemata are thought to help determine what aspects of a situation should be evaluated, and to prepare an appropriate action in response to sensory information. His concept of 'anticipatory schema' implies that schema are retrieved from memory, a position which is somewhat different to that often attributed to him, namely that schema can be dynamically constructed as circumstances demand. 'Following Bartlett, I have myself often metaphorically described memories as constructions, that is, as products that are skilfully built from available parts to serve specific purposes' (1996: 204). From the outset he conceded that a 'pure' version of a reconstructive schema theory is not tenable because something must be stored for it to be reconstructed. Moreover, he was critical of Bruner's dictum on 'going beyond the information given', and felt that 'Perceiving is a matter of picking up information, not of going beyond it' (1976: 182).

Gibson's influence on Neisser's revisions to cognitive psychology are also apparent in *Remembering Reconsidered* (1988). Neisser regards remembering as a skill that must be learned, so the remembering self must have a development of its own. He divides the self into three developmental categories: the ecological self (the self as perceived with respect to the physical environment), the extended self (based primarily on personal memories and anticipations), and the evaluated self (associated with the development of a sense of social agency). In later work he differentiated this tripartite structure with the addition of the interpersonal self (associated with species-specific signals of emotional rapport and communication), the private self (awareness that one's experiences are not necessarily shared with other people), and the conceptual self (which draws its meaning from the network of assumptions and theories in which it is embedded). Self-perception is the earliest and most fundamental form of self-knowledge. The ecological self is thought to be based on direct perception of one's situation in the environment, and the extended and evaluated selves as established by social interaction with others. He postulates that we are conscious of all of our ecological selves, an awareness he refers to as 'objective consciousness' to indicate that it is an awareness immediately given of our bodies and their movements. Evidence for the 'ecological self' as a non-conceptual first person can be found in studies of neonatal distress crying and neonatal imitation. One of the attractions of the concept of the 'ecological self' is that it appears to provide a first step in resolving the paradox of the emergence of self-consciousness. Critics have contended that Neisser overstates his case however, that much sophisticated perceptual processing goes on unconsciously or non-cognitively, and that there is a substantial corpus of evidence to warrant distinguishing conscious processing from unconscious. Others, such as Bruner, argue that he does not go far enough and postulate the existence of a multiplicity of narratives: there is not a static remembered self dependent on memory, but a perpetually re-written narrative that is profoundly influenced by social and cultural factors.

One of the paradoxes of Neisser's influence relates to the pre-eminence of his *Cognitive Psychology* – the format served as a model for subsequent texts on the topic and established Neisser as the founding figure – and the reception of his *Cognition and Reality*, which he considered to have destroyed his reputation as a mainstream cognitive psychologist. Neisser's self-assessment will require revision if the prophesies concerning a second revolution in cognitivism come true. Bruner puts the case thus: 'There is no question that cognitive science has made a contribution to our understanding of how information is moved about and processed ... So let us return to the question of how to construct a mental science around the concept of meaning and the processes by which meanings are created and negotiated within a community' (1990: 10). Such an appeal implies that the ideas and arguments put forward in *Cognition and Reality* should command a significant position.

Ulrich Neisser's major writings

'Pattern recognition by machine', *Scientific American*, 1960, 203, 60–8 (with O. G. Selfridge).
Cognitive Psychology, Appleton-Century-Crofts, 1967.
Cognition and Reality, Freeman, 1976.
'John Dean's memory', *Cognition*, 1981, 9, 1–22.
Memory Observed: Remembering in Natural Contexts, Freeman, 1982.
The School Achievement of Minority Children: New Perspectives, Erlbaum, 1986.
Remembering Reconsidered: Ecological and Intellectual Factors in Categorization, Cambridge University Press, 1988 (with E. Winograd).
The Rising Curve: Long-Term Gains in IQ and Related Measures, American Psychological Association, 1988.
The Perceived Self: Ecological and Interpersonal Sources of Self-Knowledge, Cambridge University Press, 1993.
The Remembering Self: Construction and Accuracy in the Self-Narrative, Cambridge University Press, 1994.
'Remembering as doing', *Brain and Behavioral Sciences*, 1996, 19, 203–4.

Further reading

Baars, B. (1986) *The Cognitive Revolution in Psychology*, Guilford Press.
Banaji, M. R. and Crowder, R. G. (1989) 'The bankruptcy of everyday memory', *American Psychologist*, 44, 1185–93.
Bermudez, J. L. (1998) *The Paradox of Self-Consciousness*, MIT Press.
Bruner, J. (1990) *Acts of Meaning*, Harvard University Press.
Morris, P. and Hampson, P. (1995) *Understanding Cognition*, Blackwell.

PAVLOV, IVAN PETROVICH (1849–1936)

Pavlov detailed a theory of learning called classical or Pavlovian conditioning, based on the analysis of the relationship between a stimulus and a behavioural response.

Ivan Pavlov was born in Ryazan, about 120 miles south-east of Moscow. The son of a village priest, Peter Dimitrievich Pavlov, he was the eldest of eleven children, six of whom died in childhood. He suffered a serious injury as a result of a fall, and his entry to the Ryazan church school was delayed until he was eleven. After graduating, he entered the Ryazan Ecclesiastical Seminary, expecting to follow his father's career. It was there that he encountered the works of Charles Darwin, the literary critic Dmitrii Pisarev, and Ivan Sechenov, the latter being regarded as the 'father of Russian physiology'. Pavlov did not complete his studies at the seminary but pursued his interests in natural science at St Petersburg University. There he encountered the ideas of Ilya F. Cyon, a staunch critic of vitalism, the view that life is more than a physical process and cannot meaningfully be reduced to such a process, under whose direction he developed his skill in vivisection and completed his first empirical studies on the physiology of circulation and digestion. He decided to make his career as a physiologist and, after graduating, took up a position at the Military–Medical Academy with the purpose of developing his research skills and to study for a medical degree. He lectured on physiology at the Veterinary Institute and studied the circulatory system for his M.D. dissertation. He was also responsible for the management of the small-animal laboratory of the Academy's clinical director, Sergei Botkin, an eminent physician whose ideas on the importance of the nervous system to disease were later to influence Pavlov's own ideas on the matter. After completing his doctorate, he spent two years in Germany, where he studied in Leipzig with Carl Ludwig and in Rudolf Heidenhain's laboratories at Breslau. At that time Heidenhain was studying canine digestion using an exteriorised section of the stomach, but Pavlov perfected the technique by overcoming the problem of maintaining the external nerve supply (a technique termed the Heidenhain–Pavlov pouch). His appointment (in 1890) as Professor of Pharmacology in the Military–Medical Academy coincided with his marriage to Seraphima Vasilievna Karchevskaya, a teacher and the daughter of a doctor in the Russian Black Sea Fleet. The following year he was invited to organise a department of physiology in the newly-established Institute of Experimental Medicine; he was appointed to the chair in 1895. When he was awarded a Nobel Prize (1904), he received the very substantial sum of 73,000 gold roubles which he invested in Nobel's Russian company. He lost it all when the Bolsheviks liquidated its stocks and bonds during the 1917 revolution. During 1921–22, conditions were so bad in Petrograd (St Petersburg) that Pavlov requested permission from Lenin to move his laboratory abroad. The request was denied, but on 11 February 1921 the newspaper *Izvestia* published a decree, signed by Lenin, which stated that: 'In view of Academician I. P. Pavlov's outstanding scientific services, which are of tremendous importance to the working people of the world, the Council of People's Commissars decrees: To set up ... a special commission with broad powers ...

whose task is to create, as soon as possible, the best conditions to ensure the research work of Comrade Pavlov and his associates.' The same decree authorised the printing of a deluxe edition of Pavlov's work, a doubling of rations to Pavlov and his wife, and an instruction to the Petrograd Soviet 'to assure Professor Pavlov and his wife of the use for life of the flat they now occupy, and to furnish it and Academician Pavlov's laboratory with every possible facility'.

There were political pressures on Pavlov, as there were on **Vygotsky**, **Luria** and others, to reconcile Marxism with their emerging intellectual positions. At first this did not seem an intractable task, because Marx regarded the human psyche as a reflection of the physical environment but with the capacity to change that context and thereby shape its own development. Pavlov's conditional reflex appeared to be the simplest physiological event linking an organism to its environment and with the creative potential required to permit an organism to change its physical context. Pavlov, however, was less than enthusiastic, not least because of his concerns about the excesses associated with the implementation of Marxist policies. A scathing attack on the Marxist thesis delivered in September 1923 attracted a commensurate riposte from Nikolai Bukharin, editor of the official Communist newspaper *Pravda* and a member of the Central Committee. After Stalin came to power in 1924, Pavlov resigned his post in protest against the expulsion of the sons of priests from the Academy. He persisted with his critique of the prevailing political ideology, but later, with Russia under attack from Hitler, he moderated his criticism and like many others at that time got on with his scientific work as best he could. In 1927 he was diagnosed with liver cancer and endured several bouts of serious ill-health, culminating in his death on 17 February 1936. However, the political pressures persisted beyond his death, and a joint meeting of the Soviet Academy of Sciences and the Soviet Academy of Medical Sciences held in 1950 inaugurated a systematic review of teaching in psychology, medicine and cognate disciplines with the goal of ensuring the primacy of Pavlovianism.

Pavlov's research into conditioning grew from his Nobel Prize-winning work on adaptive phenomena of the digestive reflex. This focused on the mechanisms controlling the secretions of the various digestive glands and how those mechanisms were stimulated by food. His surgical skill was crucial to the success of this line of investigation – attempts at Heidenhain's laboratories had failed because the staff there lacked Pavlov's proficiency. Pavlov was able to introduce food and chemical compounds to the exposed part of the gut and observe the activity of the digestive glands. His method of 'sham feeding', in which an exit opening is made in the animal's throat so that food entering through the mouth is extracted before it reaches the stomach, allowed him to the observe the effect of food in the mouth on the secretion of digestive juices elsewhere in the gut. Using this technique he was able to show that the taste of food in the mouth causes the release of gastric juices in the stomach.

Pavlov changed the emphasis and direction of his research from digestion to the analysis of conditional reflexes following the publication of a paper by two British physiologists, William Bayliss and Ernest Starling. They coined the term 'hormone' to refer to a kind of chemical signal that seemed to be crucially important in the control of the digestive system. Pavlov had assumed that signals between the mouth and the secretory glands in the stomach were controlled by the nervous system. Bayliss and Starling's work indicated that chemical messages were also involved. Work on the conditional reflex led Pavlov to the psychology of learning, where, as a careful experimenter, he made basic advances in learning theory. (Pavlov's work is often referred to as the 'conditioned reflex', but the term 'conditional reflex' is a better English language translation because it conveys the importance of the contingent association between the neural stimulus and the response-evoking stimulus.) He had started work on his 'psychical secretions' about the same time that **Thorndike** was beginning his own studies on animal learning, but Pavlov credited him with laying the necessary experimental groundwork: 'We may fairly regard the treatise by Thorndyke (sic) ... as the starting point for systematic investigations of this kind' (2001: 6).

The essential characteristic of Pavlovian or classical conditioning is that a previously neutral stimulus, such as the sound of a bell, can elicit a response, such as salivation, because of its association with a stimulus, such as food, that automatically produces the same or a very similar response. The food can be regarded as an unconditioned stimulus and the salivation an unconditioned response. Presentation of the neutral stimulus, the bell, would not elicit the same response. However, if the sound of the bell is presented just before the food, it will, over several trials, elicit a salivatory response. At this point the bell is referred to as the conditioned stimulus and the salivation the conditioned response. This simple but ingenious paradigm allowed Pavlov to explore learning mechanisms by asking, for example, whether a conditioned response could be elicited by presenting stimuli that were similar to, but not identical with, the unconditioned stimulus. He found that it could, by a process referred to as generalisation. Using the same paradigm, he explored the capacity of an animal to recognise differences between stimuli, a process referred to as discrimination, and what happens when repeated presentation of the unconditioned stimulus is not followed by the presentation of food. Pavlov noted that the same principles could be applied to understanding human learning. For example, a child who is bitten by a dog might develop a fear response to that dog and, through a process of generalisation, acquire a fear of all dogs. However, by gradually reintroducing the child to dogs that never bite, her fear would decline, through a process of discrimination – she would come to fear only the type of dog that first bit her – and finally the fear might be extinguished. During the 1930s Pavlov began to use the concept of the conditional reflex to explicate human psychosis, which he regarded as a device by which people attempt to isolate themselves from the outside world. This led to changes in the way psychiatric patients were treated: they were placed in monotonous surroundings in order to moderate the environmental stimuli for psychosis.

(Incidentally, Edwin B. Twitmeyer, a Ph.D. student working at the University of Pennsylvania, had independently observed that the patellar or knee-jerk reflex could be conditioned to the sound of a bell. He reported his findings at the American Psychological Association's convention of 1904, but the general lack of interest among delegates discouraged him from pursing this line of work any further.)

Pavlov's identification of the conditional reflex was the impetus for an enormously productive programme of work – referred to by some as his physiology factory – which led him to postulate the existence of a complex neurophysiological system of cortical excitation and inhibition. He argued that these two fundamental processes formed the basis of all behavioural reaction. A balance was required between the two processes for an organism to behave in an adaptive manner. He went on to argue for the existence of three fundamental dimensions in neural activity: (i) the absolute strengths of excitation and inhibition; (ii) the balance between the two processes; and (iii) their susceptibility to change in a particular nervous system. These ideas, which started in his analysis of individual differences among dogs and inaugurated the field of temperament research, also informed his theory of personality types. His classification of the types of higher nervous activity, which was based on the neurological dimensions of excitation and inhibition, was mapped onto Hippocrates' four classes of temperament: Melancholic – weak in both excitatory and inhibitory processes; Choleric – dominant excitatory processes;

Phlegmatic – a state of equilibrium; and Sanguine – balanced with lively external behaviour.

Pavlov's theoretical framework is essentially an anatomy and physiology of the nervous system, but it seemed to psychologists to offer the missing link between behaviour and the nervous system. Some set about incorporating his findings into their respective systems, although it wasn't too long before the cracks started to appear: Pavlov's purpose was to understand the nervous system, not to formulate a psychological theory based on his findings. In this regard he differed from his contemporary and competitor Vladimir Bekhterev, who was less cautious in his approach and efforts to build a conceptual framework between psychology and physiology. Bekhterev was probably better positioned to take on the task, because his training had been somewhat broader than Pavlov's and included studies with **Wundt**, the neurologist du Bois-Reymond, and the psychiatrist Charcot. Pavlov regarded the views espoused by **Watson** as over-simplified applications of his own position: 'The psychologist takes conditioning as a principle of learning, and accepting the principle as not subject to further analysis, not requiring ultimate investigation, he endeavours to apply it to everything and to explain all the individual features of learning as one and the same process' (1932; 2001). Indeed, by the time Clark **Hull** was devising his mathematical representation of learning, psychologists were *de facto* pursuing an account of conditioning without reference to the nervous system.

Thorne and Henley (2001) have suggested that Pavlov's impact on psychology can be more clearly understood by structuring his influence in three phases. The first phase is associated with the impact of Pavlovian conditioning on the emergent American school of behaviourism; the second is identified with the attempts of Hull to develop a formal, mathematical model of learning; the third phase can be discerned in the differentiation of Pavlov's classical conditioning from Thorndike's instrumental conditioning and the emergence of 'two-factor' theories of learning. These theories postulated that classical theory is teaching an animal about significant environmental events, whereas instrumental conditioning enables an animal to learn to manipulate aspects of those events. Thus, Gray concluded: 'The influence of Pavlov on the study of animal learning is stronger and more direct now than at any time in the past; and it appears to be growing' (1979: 127). That Gray's assessment was not overstated is supported by two examples. First, R. A. Rescorla received the American Psychological Association's 1986 Distinguished Scientific Contribution award for his innovative work on Pavlovian conditioning and its relevance to the tenets of associationist philosophers. Second, Jan Strealau's studies of temperament, conducted within a Pavlovian framework, demonstrated the importance of temperamental features in regulating the stimulative value of an organism's surroundings and the role of behaviour in controlling the need for stimulation.

Ivan Pavlov's major writings

I. P. Pavlov: *Selected Works*, University Press of the Pacific, 2001.

Further reading

Catania, A. C. and Laties, V. G. (1999) 'Pavlov and Skinner: two lives in science', *Journal of the Experimental Analysis of Behavior*, 72, 455–61.
Gray, J. A. (1979) *Pavlov*, Fontana.
Thorne, B. M. and Henley, T. B. (2001) *Connections in the History and Systems of Psychology*, Houghton Mifflin.
Todes, D. P. (2001) *Pavlov's Physiology Factory*, Johns Hopkins University Press.

PIAGET, JEAN CLAUDE (1896–1980)

Piaget pioneered the study of the development of thinking and problem-solving in children, based on innovative methods of enquiry that focus on the analysis of errors for what they reveal about the child's conception of the world.

Jean Claude Piaget was the first child of Arthur Piaget, a professor of medieval literature at Neuchâtel University, and Rebecca Jackson. Born in Neuchâtel, Switzerland, his early education was based upon the system devised by Friedrich Fröbel who developed the first age-sequenced cognitive materials for use with young children. While a pupil at Neuchâtel Latin he developed an interest in the natural history of molluscs and in 1907 started a programme of work in collaboration with Paul Godet, Director of the Natural History Museum at Neuchâtel. Such was his reputation that, in early 1912, Maurice Bedot, director of the Natural History Museum at Geneva, offered him a position as assistant in malacology, apparently unaware of the fact that Jean was only fifteen years old. Jean explained why he had to decline the invitation, but went on to study natural sciences at the University of Neuchâtel and completed his doctorate there. A semester spent at the University of Zürich, where he attended lectures both by **Jung** and by the eminent Swiss psychiatrist Eugen Bleuler, sparked an interest in psychiatry and psychoanalysis. He left Switzerland to spend a year working in France at the Ecole de la rue de la

Grange-aux-Belles, a boys' school established by **Binet** and later directed by Théodore Simon. While working there he conducted his first experimental studies of children's thinking and reasoning, which he structured around the way they solved problems in Simon's new tests of mental ability. He was particularly struck by the fact that young children's answers to some of the items were qualitatively different from those of older children. A superficial interpretation of these differences would lead one to conclude that the answers given by the younger children were simply wrong and that, as they matured, they would learn the right answers. However, Piaget considered otherwise, and the errors made by children suggested to him that the younger ones answered the questions differently because they thought differently. This approach to understanding children's thinking was to become a core feature of his developmental theory of children's thinking processes.

In 1921 the Swiss psychologist Edouard Claparède appointed Piaget director of studies at the Rousseau Institute in Geneva. He married Valentine Châtenay two years later, and they had three children: Jacqueline, Lucienne and Laurent. Drawing on his earlier experience at Grange-aux-Belles he used a quasi-clinical method of investigation, based on careful questioning of the child during the course of a task, to study the intellectual development of his own children. His observations composed the core of much of his empirical research. The ideas and arguments that guided the formulation of his theory of cognitive development were also vital to the founding of a new discipline called 'genetic epistemology', a term coined by the American developmental psychologist J. M. Baldwin. Although Piaget's reputation and influence stem directly from his work in child psychology, he regarded his major contribution as relating to the theory of knowledge directed upon its genesis or development (hence 'genetic epistemology'). In 1955, he founded the International Center for Genetic Epistemology, and was its director until his death.

It is possible to delineate three general views on the development of thinking. One view contends that there is little 'intellectual development' and no profound underlying changes in the way a human being thinks from infancy through to adulthood. This view, as articulated by radical behaviourism, contends that it is all a matter of learning based on associations. A second school of thought can be traced to **Vygotsky** and the claim that humans are born with considerable intellectual abilities; their major developmental tasks are to do with coming to terms with the cultural artefacts that permeate the environment given to them. The third view is represented by

Piaget, who argues that for a child to come to terms with the world around them they must acquire a repertoire of intellectual mechanisms that will allow them to organise their thoughts and experiences and make reliable predictions about what will happen in that world. As a genetic epistemologist, Piaget set out to answer the question of how knowledge grows. '[His] central argument is that if rational knowledge is a fact, its development must be at least partly rational during child development and the history of science. Piaget's research programme characterizes the sequences and mechanisms by which rational knowledge develops' (Smith, 1997: 450). His explanation for the growth of knowledge contends that knowledge is a progressive construction of hierarchically embedded structures. The structures supersede one another by a process of inclusion of simpler logical modes to higher, more powerful ones. Thus, a child's way of reasoning about the world is initially qualitatively different from that of an adult, but becomes more adult-like as the child develops.

Piaget's approach stresses the claim that children actively construct their own rational view of the world. The child's mind may be lacking intellectual mechanisms but it is not a '*tabula rasa*', as has been argued by philosophers such as Aristotle and Locke and by the radical behaviourists such as **Watson**. His theory uses hypothetical constructs to describe two processes that are suggested to underlie the child's construction of the world: organisation and adaptation. To make sense of the world, a child both organises its experiences and adapts its ways of thinking to new experiences. Piaget hypothesised that this process of adaptation consists of two sub-processes: assimilation and accommodation. Assimilation occurs when children incorporate new information into their existing knowledge. Accommodation occurs when children adjust the way they think about and solve problems in order to make sense of new information that challenges, and cannot be explained by, their existing ways of thinking. Thinking develops through a number of qualitatively different, age-related stages. It is the different way of understanding the world that makes one stage more advanced than another; knowing more information does not make a child's thinking more advanced, in the Piagetian view. Piaget's theory of knowledge follows the rationalistic tradition in the importance it attaches to schemata, or thought structures, in determining a person's construction of reality. His books on the child's conception of space, time, cause, chance and morality reveal the influence of Kant's rationalist position on the categories of thought.

The following précis should be regarded as a sketch of a more elaborate exposition of Piaget's position. During the sensorimotor stage (0–24 months), infants construct an understanding of the world by coordinating sensory experiences (such as seeing and hearing) with physical, motoric actions – hence the term 'sensorimotor'. At the pre-operational stage (2–7 years) children begin to represent the world with words, images and drawings, but they lack the ability to perform mental operations. The concrete operational stage (7–11 years) is associated with ability to perform operations, and logical reasoning replaces intuitive thought as long as reasoning can be applied to specific or concrete examples: for instance, concrete operational thinkers cannot imagine the steps necessary to complete an algebraic equation; this is too abstract for thinking at this stage of development. The formal operational stage (11–15 years) indexes a world that includes understanding and explanation based on physical, concrete experiences, but moves towards a qualitatively different way of thinking based on a capacity for high-level abstraction, theorisation and a capacity for logically-driven problem-solving. Piaget's stages of cognitive development are sometimes wrongly depicted as a ceremonial progression with little individual variation from child to child. This is a misrepresentation of his position: knowledge is a progressive construction of hierarchically embedded structures, but there is enormous variety in the ways by which individuals achieve that progression.

Equilibration is a mechanism used by Piaget to explain how children move from one stage of thought – one organised system of thinking – to the next. The shift occurs as children experience large amounts of cognitive conflict (disequilibrium) in trying to understand the world. Eventually the child resolves the conflict and reaches a balance, or equilibrium of thought. Piaget suggests that there is considerable movement between states of cognitive equilibrium as assimilation and accommodation work together to produce cognitive change. For example, if a child believes that the amount of liquid in a bottle changes when it is poured into a container of a different shape, she might be puzzled. She might wonder how the amount of liquid could possibly have changed. In time she must resolve the puzzle through a qualitative change in the way she thinks. Conservation is Piaget's term for the consistent use of the criteria that define whether or not an instance is included within a concept; it involves recognising that the length, number, mass, quantity, area, weight and volume of objects and substances do not change by transformations that alter their physical appearance. Children do not conserve all quantities or all tasks simultaneously. Empirical studies indicate that the order of mastery is usually: number, length, liquid quantity, mass, weight and volume. 'Horizontal decalage' describes how similar abilities do not appear at the same time within a stage of thought development.

Piaget's theory has attracted considerable critical attention, and it provided the impetus for rapid advances in cognitive developmental psychology. Some critics have focused on his view of stages as unitary, schematic structures of thought and the implication that there is a synchrony in cognitive development. This predicts that various aspects of a particular stage of thought development should emerge at about the same time. However, several concrete operational concepts do not appear in synchrony. For example, children do not learn to conserve at the same time that they learn to cross-classify. Others have demonstrated that small changes in the procedures involved in a Piagetian problem-solving task sometimes have significant effects on a child's cognition. In other words, slight modifications in wording that appear not to substantially change the meaning of a question may prompt a child to provide significantly different answers. Clearly, this is not a fatal weakness in his theory but it identifies one of the problems associated with any attempt to test it. More generally it highlights both the value of recognising that the intended meaning of a question may not be apparent to a child and the need to ensure that the child understands both the words used in a question and the intended meaning of those words. A third criticism points to the evidence that in some cases children who are at one cognitive stage – such as pre-operational thought – can be trained to reason at a higher cognitive stage – such as concrete operational thought. This poses a problem for Piaget's theory, which suggests that such training works only on a superficial level and is ineffective unless the child is at a transitional point from one stage to the next. Possibly the greatest problem for his theory concerns his position on the causes of cognitive development. The veracity of his claim for the primacy of internal conflict as the main driver of cognitive development has yet to be established. The rate of progress on this will be contingent on the construction of an appropriate test.

Although Piaget is fundamentally linked with the developmental analysis of the child's way of thinking, his influence in other parts of psychology is often underestimated. For example, the Hawthorne Effect refers to an enormously important series of studies in the area of industrial psychology. The studies were conducted between 1929 and 1932 in the Hawthorne (Chicago) works of the Western Electric Company. When the lighting was improved, productivity improved; and when the lighting was further improved, productivity was increased still further. When the lighting was worsened, productivity gains remained level or got even better. In order to understand why this could happen, the Australian psychologist Elton Mayo designed and managed a series of studies that included interviews with tens of thousands of employees. Mayo was familiar with Piaget's methods of interviewing children, and he transferred those to the Hawthorne industrial setting. There is a good deal of controversy surrounding Mayo's explanation for the Hawthorne Effect, but that should not detract from the importance of Piaget's influence in shaping the professional toolkit of industrial psychologists during the 1930s and 1940s.

Jean Piaget's major writings

Judgment and Reasoning in the Child, Routledge & Kegan Paul, 1928.
Play, Dreams and Imitation in Childhood, Heinemann, 1951.
The Child's Conception of Number, Routledge & Kegan Paul, 1952.
Origins of Intelligence in the Child, Routledge & Kegan Paul, 1953.
Construction of Reality in the Child, Routledge & Kegan Paul, 1954.
Growth of Logical Thinking, Routledge & Kegan Paul, 1958 (with B. Inhelder).
Biology and Knowledge, Edinburgh University Press, 1971.
Equilibration of Cognitive Structures, University of Chicago Press, 1985.
Psychogenesis and the History of Science, Columbia University Press, 1989 (with R. Garcia).
Towards a Logic of Meanings, Erlbaum, 1991 (with R. Garcia).
'Commentary on Vygotsky's criticisms', *New Ideas in Psychology*, 1995, 13, 325–40.

Further reading

Evans, R. (1973) *Jean Piaget, the Man and his Ideas*, Dutton.
Smith, L. (1996) *Critical Readings on Piaget*, Routledge.
Smith, L. (1997) 'Jean Piaget', in N. Sheehy, A. J. Chapman, and W. Conroy (eds), *Biographical Dictionary of Psychology*, Routledge.

ROGERS, CARL RANSOM (1902–87)

A humanistic psychologist, Rogers developed a non-directive or person-centred method of therapy.

Carl Rogers was born in Oak Park, Illinois, the fourth of six children. His father was a civil engineer; his mother, a devout Christian, nurtured a closely-knit religious family environment. His formal education started with entry to the second grade, because he was able to read before entering kindergarten. When he was twelve his family moved to a farm thirty miles west of Chicago, and his adolescence was spent in an environment characterised by self-discipline, order and independence. His early interests in the natural sciences led him first to the study of agriculture at the University of Wisconsin. After two years he decided to enter the church ministry and, as part of his studies, he acted as the pastor for a small church in Vermont. After graduating from Wisconsin in 1924 he married Helen Elliot, against his parents' wishes. Following a trip to China and the Philippines with the World Student Christian Federation he attended Union Theological Seminary (New York City) and later transferred to Teachers' College, Columbia University, where he obtained a degree in clinical and educational psychology. The development of his clinical practice drew on diverse influences, including Otto Rank and John Dewey (the latter through the influence of W. H. Kilpatrick, a former student of Dewey's), and his later emphasis on theorising from experience, belief in the potential of human action, and the importance of considering the human organism as a whole, can be traced to some of their ideas. For example, Kilpatrick is best known for 'The Project Method', a child-centred approach to learning and teaching that is similar to Roger's notion of client-centred therapy.

As an intern at the Institute for Child Guidance, Rogers was impressed by the emphasis on eclectic psychoanalytic techniques and ideas, and much of his later work demonstrates this strong commitment to eclecticism. In 1928 he joined the staff of what was later to become the Rochester Guidance Center; following a period of nine years as the center's director, he accepted a professorial position at Ohio State University. In 1945 he became a professor at the University of Chicago, where he directed the Counseling Center and elaborated his client-centred method of psychotherapy. His successes during this period led him to be regarded as potentially posing the most serious challenge to the psychoanalytic community's dominance in American therapeutic practice. Twelve years later he returned to his alma mater, Wisconsin, where he held positions in the departments of psychology and psychiatry. While at Wisconsin he used his approach and techniques with people suffering from schizophrenia, but did not achieve the same level of success he had had with student populations while at Chicago. In 1963 he moved to La Jolla, California, where he joined the staff of the Western Behavioral Sciences Institute and later helped to found the Center for Studies of the Person. He was actively involved with its work there until his death following surgery for a broken hip.

Carl Rogers is best known for the development of a method of psychotherapy characterised as non-directive or person-centred, and for his pioneering research on the therapy process. As a theoretician, Rogers was primarily concerned with the development and growth of the person, and consequently his theory of personality is not as structurally explicit as many others. Two concepts are fundamental to his theoretical framework: the organism and the self. The organism is the physical creature that actually experiences the world. The totality of experiences constitutes the organism's phenomenal field. It is impossible to know another's phenomenal field except through empathic inference. Thus, according to Rogers, behaviour is not a function of external reality or of surrounding stimuli but of the phenomenal field. Within a phenomenological framework it is necessary to determine how people can separate fact from fiction and construct a correct representation of reality. The only way to test reality is to check the correctness of the information on which one's hypothesis about the world is based against other sources of information. In other words, the person uses sensory information to supplement information stored from previous experiences. Through experience, a part of the phenomenal field becomes differentiated – this is the self. Rogers defines this as the 'organized, consistent conceptual gestalt composed of perceptions of the characteristics of the "I" or "me" and the perception of the relationship between the "I" or "me" to others and to various aspects of life, together with the values attached to these perceptions' (1959: 200). He distinguishes between the self as it is (the self-structure) and the ideal self (what the person would like to be). The degree of congruence between the self and the organism determines maturity and psychological wellbeing. When the person's perceptions and interpretations reasonably reflect reality as perceived by others, the self and the organism are said to be congruent. When there is a significant discrepancy, people feel threatened and anxious and tend to think and behave in stereotypical or constricted ways. The organism is thought to have a single motivating force, the drive to self-actualisation. Two important needs that are linked with the organism's drive to maintain and enhance its self are the need for the positive regard of others and the need for self-regard. In treating the person as oriented towards growth, self-actualisation and fulfilment, Rogers is similar to **Jung** and **Maslow**.

Rogers's chief concern is with understanding how incongruence develops and how self and organism can be made more congruent. In his person-centred psychotherapy the therapist enters an interpersonal relationship with the client, rather than adopting the role of doctor (as in the doctor–patient model) or scientist (as in the scientist–subject model). Therapists are expected not to hide behind a professional facade but to let the client know their thoughts and feelings. Entering this relationship unconditionally allows the client to explore increasingly strange and novel feelings in themselves. This 'unconditional positive regard' shares some features with the theological concept of 'grace', or unmerited favour, and the similarity may be due in some small part to Rogers's early theological training. A feeling of safety is essential for the therapeutic process to work. Rogers came to the view that the therapeutic process is a model of all interpersonal relationships. He formulated a general theory of such relationships, which he summarised as follows: if (a) two people are minimally willing to be in contact, (b) each is able and minimally willing to communicate, and (c) contact continues over time, then the greater the degree of congruence of experience and communication in one person the stronger the tendency towards reciprocal communication and mutual understanding. His client-centred (later to be called person-centred) therapy is distinctive in three ways. First, it is founded on a belief in the capacity and potential of the client. Second, the therapeutic relationship is seen as pivotal – everything follows from the quality of the person–therapist relationship. Third, there is a belief that the progress of therapy follows a predictable pattern based on the interpersonal characteristics of the person–therapist relationship: in other words, when certain conditions exist a certain process will occur.

The confidentiality of therapy sessions had hitherto acted as a barrier to research and fostered the growth of a mystique about counselling and psychotherapy. In order to test and develop his ideas, it was essential for Rogers to subject the therapeutic process to systematic scrutiny. In this regard he was a pioneer in the scientific investigation of the therapeutic process. He introduced the practice of recording therapy sessions with the client's permission, and he demonstrated that this neither interfered with nor jeopardised the process or the outcome. He applied content analysis procedures to classify and count a client's statements, in order to explore hypotheses about their personality, self-concept and growth through the therapeutic process. Having a permanent record of a therapy session made possible the systematic analysis of therapist–client dialogue, and opened up ways of identifying complex relationships that could not be detected in a session itself or from the therapeutic outcome. This approach was to inform the development of widely used rating scales for the measurement of process and change during psychotherapy.

Although many of Rogers's ideas are now regarded as being relatively uncontentious, his early efforts to publish and lecture on his person-centred ideas attracted considerable criticism. He was promoting the systematic quantitative investigation of therapeutic processes at a time when there were no examples of comparable research in psychoanalysis. What he was proposing was regarded by some as impossible, because it was thought that therapists and their patients would never let anyone listen in to and measure their sessions. Thus, criticisms were directed against his efforts to redefine the role of the 'patient', the perceived threat to the integrity of the therapy session by the use of recording apparatus, his relative neglect of unconscious processes, and his efforts to demystify the psychotherapeutic process. Rogers argued that diagnostic measures tended be inadequate, prejudicial and often misused. His policy of eliminating them from the therapeutic process was regarded by some as disturbing and profoundly unwise. His championing of 'non-directive' therapy was often dismissed as conceptually muddled and impossible to attain. However, towards the end of his career he introduced a pragmatic caveat to his position on unconditional positive regard: 'I have learned that in any significant or continuing relationship, *persistent* feelings had best be expressed. If they are expressed as *feelings*, owned by *me*, the result may be temporarily upsetting but ultimately far more rewarding than any attempt to deny or conceal them' (1980: 44). Much of the disapproval of Rogers's ideas and work has diminished with the growth in interest in the comparative analysys of different therapeutic processes, and the incorporation of person-centred sympathies in a wide range of therapies, although the somewhat naive phenomenology underlying his theory of the person continues to attract criticism. (Phenomen-ologists place great emphasis on examining conscious experience while trying not to be influenced by expectations or pre-conceptions.) Moreover, the successes of others, notably Heinz Kohut, in integrating many of Rogers's ideas into their own version of psychoanalysis were important in achieving a rapprochement between humanistic psychology and psychoanalysis.

Rogers's numerous contributions can be summarised as follows:

1   He developed a mode of psychotherapy which is built around a growth model, rather than a medical model; this model is based on the hypothesis that the individual has within him/herself the capacity for self-understanding and self-direction; it demonstrates that these capacities are released in a relationship with certain definable qualities; and it incorporates the view that the human organism is basically constructive and trustworthy.

2   He formulated a theory of the necessary and sufficient conditions
    which initiate a definable process in a therapeutic relationship and
    the changes in personality and behaviour which occur as a result
    of this process.
3   He developed an approach to therapy characterised by the terms
    'non-directive', 'client-centred' and 'person-centred'.
4   He lifted the veil of mystery from psychotherapy, and opened it to
    scrutiny and study, by recording therapeutic interviews.
5   He completed a number of important studies on the process and
    outcome of therapy, and the connection between the qualities in
    the relationship and the changes that occur.
6   He encouraged the application of the dynamic principles learned
    in therapy to a wide variety of fields: teaching and learning;
    marriage relationships; family life; intensive groups; administra-
    tion and management; resolution of conflict; community
    development.

Carl Rogers's major writings

Counseling and Psychotherapy, Houghton Mifflin, 1942.
Client-Centred Therapy, Houghton Mifflin, 1951.
'The necessary and sufficient conditions of therapeutic personality change', *Journal of Consulting Psychology*, 1957, 21, 95–103.
'A theory of therapy, personality and interpersonal relationships as developed in the client-centred framework', in S. Koch (ed.), *Psychology: A Study of a Science. Volume 3: Formulations of the Person and the Social Context*, McGraw-Hill, 1959.
On Becoming a Person, Houghton Mifflin, 1961.
A Way of Being, Houghton Mifflin, 1980.

Further reading

Cohen, D. (1997) *Carl Rogers. A Critical Biography*, Constable.
Kirschenbaum, H. (1979) *On Becoming Carl Rogers*, Delacorte Press.
Rogers, C. R. (1967) 'Autobiography', in E. G. Boring and G. Lindzey (eds), *A History of Psychology in Autobiography. Volume 5*, Appleton-Century-Crofts.
Thorne, B. (1992) *Carl Rogers*, Sage.

SIMON, HERBERT ALEXANDER (1916–2001)

A Nobel Prizewinner in economics, Simon blended economics with psychology in experimental studies and computer simulations of problem-solving and decision-making.

'Herb' Simon's father, Arthur C. Simon, was an electrical engineer, inventor and patent lawyer, and his mother, Edna M. Simon, was a skilled pianist and homemaker. His childhood was spent in Milwaukee with his older brother Clarence, his grandparents, and for a short time his uncle. His family was fond of the outdoors and spent holidays in Wisconsin's North Woods wilderness. During his teens, Simon spent several summers farming on a Wisconsin marsh in which his family owned an interest. After high school he went to the University of Chicago, where he preferred to study on his own and attend what lectures he chose. He married Dorothea Isabel Pye in 1937 and they had three children: Kathie, followed two years later by Peter, and two years after that by Barbara. Despite his prolific academic career, Herb Simon lived simply: one car, one hi-fi, no TV. At international conferences he was easily recognised by his distinctive beret – he only ever owned one at a time and bought each replacement from the same shop. He and Dorothea lived in the same house for 46 years, never wishing to move to anything more extravagant. Their car was something of a luxury – Simon would walk a mile to work each day, and another one home.

Simon's education and career began in political science and economics. His undergraduate work included a study of recreation administration in Milwaukee. After graduating, he continued his research into the performance of municipal governments with reference to the quality of procedures involved in budgetary decision-making, first as an assistant to Clarence E. Ridley of the International City Manager's Association, and then as director of administrative measurement studies in the Bureau of Public Administration at the University of California, Berkeley. Although Simon's doctorate was in a department of political science, the climate was one that favoured a liberal training and he completed courses in economics, logic and mathematical biophysics. His doctoral dissertation, on organisational decision-making, was later published as *Administrative Behavior* (1947). The development of this line of work was to win him the Nobel Prize for economics in 1978. From 1942 to 1949 he was a faculty member at the Illinois Institute of Technology and chairman of the Department of Political and Social Science. Second World War developments in operations research and cybernetics paralleled Simon's interests in decision-making processes, and he was involved in the development of decision models of management. In 1949 he joined the Graduate School of Industrial Administration at Carnegie Institute of Technology (now Carnegie-Mellon University), where he pursued empirical investigations of organisational decision-making while continuing to work in management science. He became a consultant to the RAND Corporation's Systems Research Laboratory (in about 1952), which was to lead to a significant collaboration with Allen Newell.

Simon was particularly struck by the fact that the adaptive behaviour of organisms falls short of the rational ideal of 'maximising', as postulated in economic theories. Why is it that organisms 'satisfice' rather than 'optimise'? What is the most parsimonious way to account for 'satisficing' behaviour? Newell and Simon pursued answers in their studies of human problem-solving and, in so doing, formulated and developed several concepts which have had a profound influence both within cognitive science and more broadly. Research on decision-making processes in organisations had originally led Simon to a concern with problem-solving processes; and later, through early contacts with electronic computers, he came to recognise that they could be used to simulate human thinking. Simon and Newell proposed that problem-solving involves trying to select operators (the means) that can be applied to a particular problem state in order to achieve a goal state (an end). Means–end analysis is thought to proceed within a problem space, comprising the potential states of knowledge and operators that transform one state of knowledge into another. Means–end analysis makes heavy demands on controlled processing: the goal state and relevant intermediate states must be considered jointly. But this is more of a technical consideration, for the real breakthrough implied that the prevailing penchant for economic and probabilistic models of decision-making was misguided because they were vastly more complex than what was actually required to explain the behaviour of an organism.

Returning to Simon's original question: What is it about an organism and its environment that makes its choice so simple? First, Simon starts by positing a single goal: to find food. Second, the organism needs only to maintain a certain average intake of food to survive and has no need to maximise – Simon referred to this as a fixed aspiration level. Third, what an organism is capable of perceiving, together with the nature of its environment, constrain its planning horizon. Fourth, the nature of an organism's needs and environment creates a natural separation between means and ends: 'As long as aspirations are fixed, the planning horizon is limited, and there is a sharp distinction between means and ends, the existence of multiple goals does not create any real difficulties in choice' (1956: 131). Of course, considerable complications arise if any of these conditions are relaxed, but Newell and Simon started with a computational implementation of their simpler position because, from a philosophical perspective, it was the most parsimonious way to proceed, and pragmatically they were constrained by the engineering limitations of the day. Their 'General Problem Solver' provided a reference model for numerous subsequent efforts to specify formally the information processes that define cognition. Their theory of problem-solving performs the process it explains: their computer programme thinks rationally but without recourse to a deductive logic. Simon once defined rational decision-making as the process of choosing a finite number of acts in a series of steps that (1) lists the acts, (2) determines all of their consequences, and (3) makes a comprehensive evaluation. The conceptual simplicity of this definition is its major weakness, but it is also a strength that has made it particularly useful in the computational implementation of a rational decision-making agent.

Adriaan de Groot had published a ground-breaking text on problem-solving in chess wherein he introduced and elaborated on the idea that the ability to 'chunk' information is crucial to the development of expertise. During the 1960s, Simon explored the implications of this thesis through collaborations with Barenfeld, Gilmartin and Chase on the knowledge component of skilled performance in chess-playing, and the evocation of expert knowledge by recognition of cues in the task situation. Other research, with J. R. Hayes, explored how people understood verbal task instructions; and later research focused upon simulating and explaining the processes of scientific discovery and analysing learning processes in physics, mathematics and other school subjects. Thus, trying to broaden, step by step, the range of cognitive processes that could be explained within the information-processing paradigm, Simon addressed an ever-widening array of cognitive tasks that face people in school and their professional work. While embracing a progressively greater number of cognitive processes, Simon and Newell's approach is constant in its emphasis on the relative invariance observable in people's strategies on domain-free problems. They postulate that this similarity reflects the fact that the human information-processing system is neither as complex nor as sophisticated as is often supposed: people have a few basic heuristics for dealing with a wide variety of problems. (In many respects, the simplicity of Simon's lifestyle is emblematic of this theoretical position.) For example, 'Perception in chess' (Chase and Simon, 1973) showed that 50,000 visual configurations are sufficient to describe all of the board positions that could arise in normal chess play. Thus the ability to detect a particular configuration can be used as a sound basis for planning sequences of moves. Expert chess players learn to recognise common configurations as single perceptual units. When considering a particular position, experts would recall six or seven configurations, each containing from three to five pieces. Six or seven items is within the information processing range of working memory, and the intellectual skill of chess players could be explained in terms of memory due to perceptual learning.

Newell and Simon's approach to the analysis of problem-solving places considerable emphasis on mapping the task environment. They argue that a complete understanding of a problem's task environment is commensurate with an understanding of all the ways in which a problem could be represented. They also argue that the task environment exerts a powerful influence on the apparent complexity of what a problem is doing and, since the human information-processing system is not very complicated, if problem-solving behaviour appears complex it is probably because the task environment is complex. Numerous questions have been raised about their approach. For example, a complete mapping of the task environment can be achieved in artificial domains but not in more naturalistic environments. Another question concerns the significance Simon and Newell attach to the verbal reports that research participants are required to produce while solving problems set for them. Nisbett and Wilson (1977) have argued that people have little or no introspective access to higher mental processes and that their verbal descriptions of how they are thinking cannot be accurate. Simon counters this by stating that people will have an awareness of their mental processes when reporting about something of which they are truly aware – namely, something that is currently stored in working memory. Criticisms have also been directed against the nature of the problems used by Newell and Simon. Their artificial scenarios seem to have little relationship with problem-solving ability in the real world, and the kinds of verbal reports that can be elicited within clearly defined problem domains rarely, if ever, appear in more complex settings. The sort of strategising used in abstract problems may not routinely occur in the knowledge-rich domains of everyday life. Thus, powerful though it is, the 'General Problem Solver' has been mainly applied to artificial, puzzle-like problems such as the Tower of Hanoi, and much less successfully to 'real-world' problems involving a considerably greater amount of more generalised background knowledge.

In spite of these criticisms, three aspects of their approach endure: searching a problem space, goal-directed problem-solving, and context-free problem-solving methods.

Herbert Simon's major writings

Administrative Behavior, Macmillan, 1947.
'Rational choice and the structure of the environment', *Psychological Review*, 1956, 63, 129–38.
'Elements of a theory of human problem-solving', *Psychological Review*, 1958, 65, 151–66 (with A. Newell and J. C. Shaw).
'Computer simulation of human thinking', *Science*, 1961, 134, 2011–17 (with A. Newell).
'Human acquisition of concepts for sequential patterns', *Psychological Review*, 1963, 70, 534–46 (with K. Kotovosky).
'Motivational and emotional controls of cognition', *Psychological Review*, 1967, 74, 29–39.
'Information-processing analysis of perceptual processes in problem-solving', *Psychological Review*, 1969, 76, 473–83 (with M. Barenfeld).
Human problem-solving, Prentice-Hall, 1972 (with A. Newell).
'Perception in chess', *Cognitive Psychology*, 1973, 4, 55–81 (with W. G. Chase).
Models of Thought, Yale University Press, 1979.
Protocol Analysis, MIT Press, 1984 (with A. Ericsson).

Further reading

Anderson, J. R. (1985) *Cognitive Psychology and its Implications*, Freeman.
Nisbett, R. E. and Wilson, T. D. (1977) 'Telling more than we know: Verbal reports on mental processes', *Psychological Review*, 84, 231–59.
Posner, M. I. (ed.) (1989) *Foundations of Cognitive Science*, Bradford.

SKINNER, BURRHUS FREDERICK (1904–90)

A staunch proponent of behaviourism, Skinner developed a theory of learning known as operant conditioning, based on the relationship between behaviour and reward or reinforcement.

Skinner's father, Walter Skinner, was a drummer in the final year of the American Civil War who settled in the dusty railroad town of Susquehanna, Pennsylvania, where he secured a position as a carpenter and later became an attorney, and where he started his family. Skinner's mother was Grace Burrhus Skinner. The eldest of two boys, he was present when his brother Ebbie died of a cerebral aneurysm at the age of sixteen. Autobiographical accounts describe his childhood as warm and stable. His childhood creativity and his skill in inventing and building extended to designing a system for extracting oxygen from seawater. This creativity was also evident throughout his adult life, and at one point Skinner opined that his greatest contribution to psychology would be the cumulative recorder, a machine invented while he was a graduate student to record discrete actions, such as key-presses made by a subject, as a continuous cumulative line. From the cumulative record generated by this machine it was possible for an experienced observer to identify patterns in a subject's response as it changed over time.

Skinner graduated from the same high school as both his parents. It was a schoolteacher, Mary Graves, who influenced his decision to pursue a degree in English literature and afterwards to embark on a career as a writer. He spent some years as a journalist, mostly writing copy on labour problems, travelling and pursuing a bohemian lifestyle. However, he developed an interest in psychology, and described the moment when he decided to pursue his interest academically by quoting H. G. Wells's dilemma: If Shaw were drowning on one side of a pier and **Pavlov** on the other, and you had only one life preserver, to which would you throw it? 'Wells's decision to throw it to Pavlov confirmed my decision to abandon literature for behavioral science' (1976: 91). He decided to return to college, and it was at Harvard that he became convinced that behaviourism as expressed by **Watson** was the only way forward for psychology. He completed his master's degree there in 1930 and gained his doctorate the following year. He remained to pursue post-doctoral research until 1936, when he moved to Minneapolis to teach at the University of Minnesota. It was there that he met and married Yvonne Blue. They had two daughters, Julie and Deborah. (Deborah became something of a celebrity when it became known that she was being raised in one of Skinner's inventions – the 'air crib' or 'baby tender'. This sounds fancier than the reality of the contraption, which consisted of a crib and a playpen with glass sides and air-conditioning. It combined safety with comfort, but the idea never caught on because it looked as though one was trying to rear a baby in something resembling an aquarium.) In 1945 he was appointed to the psychology department at Indiana University. Three years later he returned to Harvard, where he remained for the rest of his life. He retired in 1974 but remained active until his death, from leukaemia, in 1990.

Skinner's contribution to psychology took the form of an intellectual revolution against the Germanic academic psychology imported to America in the ideas of **Titchener** and Hugo Münsterberg. Indeed, his preference for building innovative machines rather than developing theories reflects the American tradition of pragmatism associated with the philosophers **James** and C. S. Peirce and the educationalist John Dewey. The tone of Skinner's influence reflects the logic of Percy Bridgman, a physicist whose quest for operational definitions was motivated by an attempt to safeguard concepts against meaninglessness by defining them with reference to clearly defined experimental operations. Skinner's work also followed from Pavlov's in its commitment to the primacy of behavioural data and to the analysis of individual organisms rather than groups. However, there are both theoretical and empirical differences between the two. Skinner's theoretical argument was for the primacy of the analysis of behaviour in its own right, rather than treating behaviour as a diagnostic window for the exploration of underlying psychological and physiological processes. His methodological innovation was to devise a way to study environment–behaviour interactions in their own right, and he introduced the term 'operant' to refer to those interactions. For Skinner, physiological processes are fundamentally important because of what they allow organisms to do, but they are not the primary subject of a science of psychology. However, Skinner fully acknowledged the influence of Pavlov on the development of his own ideas and, when Horsley Gantt and Howard Liddell, two Americans who had worked with Pavlov, established the Pavlovian Society, Skinner readily accepted their invitation to join and soon afterwards found himself its president.

Skinner was particularly influenced by the neurologist Sir Charles S. Sherrington, who thought of the nervous system as focusing on a diverse stimulus array in what he called a 'final common pathway'. He postulated that the focus of a reflex, or its 'final common pathway', could not possibly be located 'within' an organism but must be at the boundary between the organism and its environment. Skinner regarded a reflex as being not a neurological entity but a correlation between a stimulus and the organism's observable behaviour. But how can one explain the many instances of observable behaviour in the absence of a correlation with an environmental stimulus? Skinner argued that the conventional Cartesian position on this, that the stimulus is 'internal', is wrong, and he suggested instead that what is termed 'voluntary behaviour' is not due to an 'act of will', for example, but determined by its environmental consequences. These are what Skinner referred to as 'operants', and he initially regarded them as another type of reflex but quickly dropped that idea in favour of an explanation of operant behaviour as a function of an organism's history of reinforcement. For example, when an animal is observed performing a particular behaviour Skinner looked for its cause, and its source of control, in its history of reinforcement rather than the content of its nervous system. For Skinner, the important questions are: which of an organism's past actions were rewarded, and when? A history of reinforcement is a radical theory based on observable events rather than on unobservable events internal to the organism.

Skinner also wanted to distance himself from **Thorndike**'s law of effect, which refers to strengthening by reinforcement or weakening by punishment, and from what Sechenov, the Russian physiologist, referred to as the 'reflexes of the brain'. His attempts to dissociate himself from the analysis of 'internal reflexes' supposed to underlie his stimulus–response correlations were often less successful than he would have wished. He regarded Thorndike's 'internal connections' within the brain as pre-computational versions of the kinds of internal representations that are particularly influential in cognitive science. Skinner pursued this line of analysis to a trenchant critique of cognitivism, an approach to psychology that places exceptional importance on understanding thought processes, because it commences by assuming that people have internal processes and then proceeds to contrive modes of investigation that purport to explain those hidden processes. A staunch critic of the 'cognitive revolution' and of the emergence of cognitive science (a multidisciplinary perspective focusing on the way people acquire and process information), he accused cognitivists of unwarranted speculation about internal, unobservable processes, of emasculating the experimental analysis of behaviour, of reviving a discredited theory in which states of mind are treated as the causes of behaviour, and of inventing explanations which, like those of psychoanalysis, cannot be properly tested.

Skinner was an enormously productive scientist. Between 1958 and 1962 there were more than twenty experiments, mostly with pigeons, running concurrently seven days a week in his laboratories. His theoretical work makes three basic assumptions: that behaviour is (a) lawful, (b) can be predicted and (c) can be controlled. A functional analysis of behaviour working from these assumptions will disclose that the causes of any observed behaviour lie in antecedent events occurring in an organism's environment. His theoretical system is based on the concept of operant conditioning. In classical or Pavlovian conditioning, a previously neutral stimulus, such as the sound of a bell, can elicit a response, such as salivation (unconditioned response), because of its association with a stimulus, such as food (unconditioned stimulus), that automatically produces the same or a very similar response. If the bell is presented just before the food, it will, over several trials, elicit a salivatory response. At this point the bell is referred to as the conditioned stimulus and the salivation the conditioned response. Operant conditioning regards every organism as being involved in the process of 'operating' on its environment – it goes about doing what it does. During the course of operating it encounters a special kind of stimulus – a reinforcing stimulus (a 'reinforcer'). The reinforcer has the effect of increasing the operant – the behaviour immediately preceding it. A behaviour followed by a reinforcer increases the likelihood that the behaviour will be repeated, whereas a behaviour that is not followed by a reinforcing stimulus decreases its probability of recurrence. The way in which a reinforcer is delivered to an organism can be varied systematically according to 'schedules of reinforcement', and these are fundamentally important in maintaining behaviour. In continuous reinforcement, for example, the organism is rewarded every time it performs a particular behaviour. Under a fixed-ratio schedule, the ratio between behaviours and reinforcers is stable: for example, performing a certain behaviour three times will lead to one reinforcer. Skinner also investigated variable reinforcement schedules and found that behaviours rewarded under these were very slow to extinguish. He suggested that, in humans, they are the mechanism that accounts for compulsive gambling. Behaviour modification is a therapeutic technique that follows directly from Pavlov's, Watson's and Skinner's accounts of the lawful, predictable and controllable nature of human behaviour. At its simplest, it involves the selective reinforcment behaviour to be repeated, and the extinguishing of undesirable behaviours by identifying and removing the reinforcers that cause those behaviours to be elicited. While the technique enjoyed considerable popularity during the heyday of behaviourism, as reflected in Nathan Azrin's application of operant principles in the design of token economies and A. E. Kazdin's work with socially withdrawn adults, disappointing evaluations as to its effectiveness led to its decline. However, Arnold Lazarus who coined the term 'behaviour therapist' in 1958, and Daniel O'Leary who used behaviour modification techniques in the classroom, achieved some success in arresting that trend by arguing for a broader characterisation of behaviour modification than that implied by a strict stimulus–response view of behaviourism.

Shaping, part of Skinner's theory, is the mechanism whereby complex behaviours are thought to be constructed from simpler ones. Skinner's most radical application of his theory, including the concept of shaping, related to his account of the acquisition of language. An infant's vocal responses are selectively conditioned as operants leading to the shaping of words, then phrases, then sentences and so on. Cultural variations in reinforcing practices account for the variety of languages that emerge around the world. **Chomsky**'s devastating critique of this explanation in his 1959 review of Skinner's *Verbal Behavior* (1957) is, like *Verbal Behavior* itself, regarded as a classic in its own right. Thus the publication of *Verbal Behavior* played an important part in popularising Chomsky's rationalist and, in his own terms, Cartesian alternative to the study of language and language acquisition – precisely the type of approach Skinner regarded as fundamentally unsound because of its almost theological commitment to assumptions about the existence of 'internal' mental processes. In some respects Skinner's clarity of thought and expression made his ideas particularly easy targets, and thereby hastened the demise of his influence. For example, his theory of learning places great importance on understanding the processes whereby reinforcers cause connections to be formed between stimuli and responses. However, the Garcia effect, also referred to as the food aversion effect, demonstrated that animals will learn in ways that are not consistent with his theoretical predictions. Named after John Garcia, this refers to the phenomenon whereby an animal that falls ill after eating a novel food may acquire a permanent aversion to it – even if the food is eaten just once, the illness occurs several hours after eating the food, and the food was not the cause of the illness. In a similar vein, Keller and Marian Breland tell an interesting story which they refer to as 'the misbehaviour of organisms'. During the early 1950s they made several attempts to take Skinner's laboratory findings on pigeons and rats and apply them to other species in more naturalistic conditions outside the laboratory. Their early attempts were wholly affirmative and optimistic. However, later efforts to control and shape the behaviour of pigs, racoons and cows were startling failures. Why? 'Instinct', said the Brelands. Many animals are trapped by strong instinctive behaviours and the influence of instinct is particularly noticeable when attempting to condition new behaviours that are very close to existing instinctive behaviours. In many cases the novel behaviours simply could not be conditioned. Skinner's behaviourism had no place for instinct, and this is one of its most substantial limitations. The Brelands concluded: '[T]he behavior of any species cannot be adequately understood, predicted, or controlled without knowledge of its instinctive patterns, evolutionary history, and ecological niche' (1961: 684).

Notwithstanding these criticisms, Skinner's legacy remains in the predominance of the view that psychology is about the study of overt, observable behaviour, a position widely held even by many psychologists within the cognitive tradition who rely on observable behaviour to index and infer the operation of underlying processes.

B. F. Skinner's major writings

'The concept of the reflex in the description of behavior', *Journal of General Psychology*, 1931, 5, 427–58.
Behavior of Organisms, Appleton-Century-Crofts, 1938.
Walden Two, Macmillan, 1948.
Science and Human Behavior, Macmillan, 1953.
Verbal Behavior, Appleton-Century-Crofts, 1957.
Schedules of Reinforcement, Appleton-Century-Crofts, 1957 (with C. B. Ferster).
Cumulative Record, Appleton-Century-Crofts, 1959.
The Technology of Teaching, Appleton-Century-Crofts, 1968.
The Contingencies of Reinforcement, Appleton-Century-Crofts, 1969.
Beyond Freedom and Dignity, Knopf, 1971.
About Behaviorism, Knopf, 1974.
Particulars of my Life, Knopf, 1976.

Further reading

Bjork, D. W. (1993) *B. F. Skinner: A Life*, Basic Books.
Breland, K. and Breland, M. (1961) 'The misbehaviour of organisms', *American Psychologist*, 16, 681–4.
Chomsky, N. (1959) 'A review of B. F. Skinner's verbal behavior', *Language*, 35, 1, 26–58.
Lattal, K. A. (ed.) (1992) 'Special issue: reflections on B.F. Skinner and psychology', *American Psychologist*, 47: 1269–533.
Modgil, S. and Modgil, C. (eds) (1987) *B.F. Skinner: Consensus and Controversy*, Falmer.
Smith, L. D. (1986) *Behaviorism and Logical Positivism: A Reassessment of the Alliance*, Stanford University Press.

SPEARMAN, CHARLES EDWARD (1863–1945)

Spearman developed a theory of intelligence that distinguishes between a general factor, 'g', and specific factors, and devised novel statistical techniques to test his theory.

Spearman's grandfather was Sir Alexander Young Spearman, a senior official in the British Treasury. Charles's father died in 1865 at the age of thirty-three. Charles was his younger son by his marriage to Louisa Mainwaring. Louisa remarried, but her second husband, Henry H. Molyneux-Steel, died in 1882, just as Charles was embarking on a career as an infantry officer in the Royal Engineers. During his fifteen years of military service he was involved in several colonial wars, before leaving in 1897.

Spearman's first intellectual commitment was to philosophy, but his reaction to the associationists, a school of thought with which he was most familiar, was less than enthusiastic: 'Sensualism and association tend strongly to go with hedonism; and this latter was (and is) to me an abomination' (1930: 301). He was loyal to the idea that if ever a genuine advance was to be made in philosophy it would come mainly by way of psychology. Thus he took himself to Leipzig, where he learned much of his experimental psychology not directly from **Wundt** but from his two assistants, Felix Krueger, with whom he co-published and who succeeded Wundt at Leipzig, and Wilhelm Wirth. Otto Klemm arrived in the year of Spearman's departure from Leipzig, something Spearman regarded as a missed opportunity. Wundt's influence was indispensable, although Spearman was critical of what he considered an unwarranted emphasis on the analysis of fundamental sensations.

His time at Leipzig was interrupted by the Boer War, which prompted a return to active service as the Deputy Assistant Adjutant General to Guernsey, a position of political significance because of the ambivalent attitude of the Government of France. A two-year stint in the Channel Islands, during which he met his life-partner Frances Aikman, was followed by a brief return to England, but the cost of living in Berkshire prompted the Spearmans to move to Leipzig where Charles completed his doctoral thesis on spatial perception (with minors in history and political economy). From there he proceeded to Würzburg where, for three months, he studied under Wundt's former pupil Oswald Külpe, although the greater influence on his thinking was due to the phenomenology of Karl Bühler – a philosophy that focuses on examining conscious experience while trying not to be influenced by expectations or pre-conceptions. This was followed by a period at Göttingen under George E. Müller, whose rather narrow intellectual vision contrasted with that of Külpe. At Göttingen he attended Husserl's lectures, and expeditions throughout Germany included brief encounters with Carl Stumpf and Hermann Ebbinghaus, Ebbinghaus being one of the first to support his later work on general intelligence. The year 1907 saw his departure from Germany to take up a position as Reader in Experimental Psychology at University College London (UCL). That role included responsibility for a small laboratory set up a decade before by James Sully when UCL had secured a considerable part of Hugo Münsterberg's apparatus shortly before he emigrated from Germany to America. Spearman's next appointment at UCL was the Grote Chair of Mind and Logic, a position he took on the retirement of its previous holder Carveth Read – whose epistemology had influenced **James**'s ideas on pragmatism. Spearman held that position until 1931, although the title was changed to Chair of Psychology in 1928. After his retirement he spent some time working for **Thorndike**'s Unitary Traits Committee, attempting to establish a consensus view on the nature of intelligence.

Although **Galton**'s approach to the measurement of psychological phenomena, and the importance he attached to the development of intelligence testing, were not particularly popular in German thinking of that time, Spearman considered them inspirational, and it was from Germany that he mailed his own ground-breaking manuscript '"General intelligence" objectively determined and measured' (1904b) for publication in the *American Journal of Psychology*. There he set out the case for 'correlational psychology' 'for the purpose of positively determining all psychical tendencies, and in particular those which connect together the so-called "mental tests" with psychical activities of greater generality and interest' (1904b: 205). Spearman used his statistical background to set about estimating the intelligence of a group of children aged ten and thirteen-years old in a village school, but he quickly realised that an empirically derived correlation between any pair of variables would yield an incorrect estimate of the actual or 'true' association, to the extent that there is error in the measurement of those variables. However, if the quantity of error could be calculated, then it should be possible to correct the observed correlation according to the formula: r (true) = r (observed)/reliability of variable 1 × reliability of variable 2. Using this 'correction formula', Spearman observed what he considered to be the true relationships among pairs of variables and inferred that 'general intelligence' or 'g' was in fact something real, and not merely a statistical artefact. He also noticed that the correlations among the many measures he had taken on children's performance were almost all positive and hierarchical. Both concepts guided his development of the two-factor theory of intelligence.

According to this theory, the performance of any intelligent action requires a combination of 'g', which is available to the same individual to the same extent for all intelligent acts, and of 'specific factors' or 's' which are particular to each act and which vary in strength from one act to another. Thus Spearman argued that, if one knows how a person performs on one task that is highly saturated with acts requiring 'g', one can accurately predict a similar level of performance for any other task requiring comparably saturated 'g' acts. The prediction of performance on tasks with high 's' factors would, by definition, be less accurate. However, Spearman regarded 'g' as pervading performance on all tasks, so the prediction of performance on tasks with high 's' factors will nevertheless be significantly better than random. Thus Spearman concluded that the most important information to have about a person's intellectual ability is an estimate of their 'g'.

Spearman was unaware of remarkably similar work conducted seven years earlier by the Norwegian psychologist and schoolteacher Thomas Parr. In 1897 Parr had published his analysis of the relationship between grades achieved in handwriting and grades obtained in all other subjects. His sample population of 234 was much larger than Spearman's, though his analysis was based on an examination of average scores rather than correlations. He found that children with superior handwriting also tended to achieve high grades in all other subjects. His explanation for the relationship is closer to Galton's than to Spearman's – he took the view that higher intellectual achievements, for example in science and literature, were determined by one's ability to perform simpler tasks, such as handwriting, to a very high level.

One of Spearman's greatest achievements is associated with his success in operationalising his theory through the development of a statistical procedure, the method of tetrad differences, for reducing very large sets of data and elucidating latent structures therein. The procedure, now known as factor analysis, led to the identification of underlying patterns in his data that Spearman interpreted as supporting his two-factor theory. The purpose of factor analysis is to examine the correlations between a large number of tests and reduce them to a smaller number of underlying dimensions or factors. An analogy sometimes used to illustrate this idea is the observation that all of the colours of the visible spectrum can be reduced to just three primary colours. When Spearman examined patterns of correlations among various psychological tests, he found that almost all correlations were positive, a phenomenon he referred to as the 'positive manifold'. The effect of the positive manifold was such that, when he factor-analysed his data, there was a large first factor. Spearman derived from this the 'principle of indifference of the indicator'. This means, for example, that scores on a vocabulary test correlate with scores on a test of numeracy because both tests are tapping general intelligence or 'g' – the indifference of the indicator means that either measure can be used to index general intelligence.

The general factor postulated by Spearman was supported by some psychologists, notably Sir Cyril Burt and **Cattell**, and proponents of 'g' are still to be found within the ranks of prominent psychologists, notably Arthur Jensen. Critics, such as Louis Thurstone, Cattell and Joy P. Guilford, presented plausible arguments for a multi-factorial view of intelligence, while others, such as David Wechlser (who had studied under Spearman at UCL) felt that Spearman's general approach seriously underplayed the importance of motivational and personality factors. However, it was Thurstone who provided the first serious challenge to Spearman's 'g' in his claim that this was merely a hypothetical construct that should not be accorded any special significance over alternative candidate constructs. The empirical basis for Thurstone's challenge was grounded in his observation that Spearman's factor analysis could reduce the patterns of associations in a very large correlation matrix but it nevertheless left a substantial proportion of the variation in the original correlation matrix unexplained. Although Spearman could produce a simple two-factor structure, there was often a good deal of unexplained variation in the original correlation matrix. Why was this? Thurstone developed a set of statistical techniques he considered to be superior to those used by Spearman. These had the effect of maximising the linking or 'loading' of any particular test on a specific factor while minimising its connection with any other factor. When he applied his technique, he found that the factor Spearman called 'g' disappeared. Thurstone suggested that his factor analysis supported the view that intelligence should be thought of as a group of many independent abilities. The ensuing debate resulted in a stalemate, because Spearman's and Thurstone's approaches were mathematically equivalent. The only reason for preferring one over the other is that a variation in the sequences of mathematical operations applied to a data set led to solutions that preferentially supported either the two-factor or the multifactor view of intelligence. During the late 1930s **Eysenck** re-analysed some of Thurstone's data, using a statistical technique developed by Burt, and reported evidence suggesting that Spearman's 'g' was indeed present in Thurstone's own data. There were, Eysenck concluded, no inherent contradictions in the approaches taken by Spearman and Thurstone.

Although Spearman's influence is associated with his two-factor theory and his contribution to factor analysis, he also published on the nature of intelligence and the laws of cognition. Although his arguments for the development of a systematic psychology of cognition were well founded, his often grossly exaggerated claims for his 'neogenetic scheme' were at least partly responsible for their poor reception. He suggested that all human cognition could be explained by three laws, each of them derived from older principles espoused by the associationists: the law of the apprehension of experience, the law of the education of relations and the law of the education of correlates. According to these laws the mind comes to be aware of its experience and of relations between the contents of experience, and creates new items based on, but additional to, the original experience. Naive assertions such as 'The entire range of cognition whatsoever, as regards both form and material, would appear to receive its definite and final boundaries' (1923: 354) were often regarded with incredulity. His 'laws of cognition' were essentially empirical generalisation, and included statements such as: 'mental events tend to recur more easily than when they first occurred', and 'fatigue tends to diminish mental processes'. The law of perseveration, 'the tendency for inertia or lag in the beginning and ending of mental events', prompted some of his colleagues and students to pursue a line of enquiry which led them to postulate the existence of a second universal factor, 'p', alongside 'g'.

Spearman is credited with establishing a dynamic, internationally recognised school of psychological research in Great Britain, and the extent of his formative influence on its development is indicated by the fact that twelve of the first twenty Monograph Supplements of the *British Journal of Psychology* were authored by people who had studied under or worked with him. His death after a fall from his hospital bedroom (he always believed that everyone has the right to determine the timing of their own demise) left Cyril Burt as the standard-bearer of factor analysis in Great Britain and successor to Steadman's Chair at UCL.

Charles Spearman's major writings

'The proof and measurement of association between two things', *American Journal of Psychology*, 1904a, 15, 72–101.
' "General intelligence" objectively determined and measured', *American Journal of Psychology*, 1904b, 15, 202–93.
The Nature of 'Intelligence' and the Principles of Cognition, Macmillan, 1923.
The Abilities of Man, their Nature and Measurement, Macmillan, 1927.
Creative Mind, Cambridge, 1930.
Human Ability, Macmillan, 1950 (with L. Wynn Jones; published posthumously).

Further reading

Burt, C. (1940) *Factors of the Mind*, University of London Press.
Lovie, P. and Lovie, A. D. (1996) 'Charles Edward Spearman, F.R.S. (1863–1945), *Notes and Records of the Royal Society of London*, 50, 77–88.
Spearman, C. (1930) 'C. Spearman', in C. Murchison (ed.), *A History of Psychology in Autobiography, Volume 1*, Clark University Press.

SPERRY, ROGER WOLCOTT (1913–94)

A Nobel Prizewinner, Sperry devised ingenious experiments to examine the organisation of the brain and the effects of breaking the connections between the left and right hemispheres.

Born in Hertford, Connecticut, Roger Sperry's father Francis Bushnell was in banking and his mother, Florence Kraemer Sperry, had a business school training. His father died when he was eleven, leaving Florence to care for Roger and a younger brother, Russell Loomis, who went on to pursue a career in chemistry. She supported the small family unit through her work as the principal's assistant at the local high school. Sperry completed his early education in Elmwood, Connecticut, and at William Hall High School in West Hartford, and it was during his time at William Hall that his athletic talent was marked through his establishing an All-State Record in the javelin. Sperry graduated from Oberlin College with a degree in English literature, after which he took a decisive turn to neuroscience while completing the two-year MA programme in psychology at Oberlin under the supervision of Raymond H. Stetson. He attended Stetson's lectures in psychology, and it was during one of those lectures that he got the idea for a paper he published some twenty years later, *On the Neural Basis of the Conditioned Reflex*. This short paper had significant theoretical implications for those interested in understanding central nervous system pathways and conditioned learning. Although Stetson specialised in motor phonetics and the analysis of rhythm, his breadth of scholarship encouraged in Sperry an interest in philosophy and the humanities as well as in empirical research.

While completing his Ph.D. at Chicago with the developmental neurobiologist Paul A. Weiss, Sperry developed surgical techniques with the stereomicroscope which he applied and developed in much of his later work. Weiss had demonstrated that movement patterns of amphibia were self-created in the embryo, and were apparently independent of specific nerve connections. Sperry felt Weiss's results with amphibia might be explained by a more specific type of control in the growth of nerve circuits than the theories of the time suggested. In his doctoral research he examined related questions in rats, testing fibre connection versus impulse specificity theory by transplanting the insertions of extensor and flexor muscles of the limbs and cutting and interchanging their nerve supply. He found that this mammalian motor system, contrary to the prevailing doctrine of the time, was hard-wired and highly resistant to re-education. In other words, unlike Weiss's amphibia, the wrongly connected nerves or muscles continued indefinitely to produce maladaptive reversed limb movements.

Ramon y Cajal's descriptions of developing axons had suggested that growth cones moved in an ordered and directed manner, work that was to win him a share of the 1906 Nobel Prize alongside Camillo Golgi. However, it was Sperry's investigations of the spectacular regenerative capacity of axons in the visual pathway of amphibia that provided the strongest evidence that the formation of neural pathways in the brain is very precise. From 1941 to 1946 Sperry worked in Karl Lashley's laboratories, first as a Fellow of the National Research Council at the Harvard Biological Laboratories and then as a Fellow of Harvard University at the Yerkes Laboratories of Primate Biology in Orange Park, Florida.

In a series of brilliant experiments involving the rotation of eyes in amphibians, the optic nerves were sectioned and the eyes rotated through 180 degrees. Would vision be normal after regeneration, or would the animal forever view the world as upside down and right–left reversed? The animals saw the world as upside down and reversed from right to left. No amount of relearning could modify those responses (despite the remarkable capacity of the amphibian nervous system to regenerate when altered), suggesting that they were not organised through a learning process. The chemo-affinity theory Sperry developed in the early 1940s attempted to account for his findings by linking the functional interconnections of neuronal elements to developmental principles of differentiation and cyto-chemistry. The existence and regulative role of preferential cell-to-cell affinities which he postulated was confirmed by experiments motivated by this theory. Although a number of more recent studies have challenged the chemo-affinity theory, it still stands as one of the most important insights in developmental neurobiology.

It was during this period with Lashley that Sperry developed his ideas on the use of corrective nerve and muscle surgery for motor losses in humans. At that time it was commonplace to transplant nerves surgically to antagonistic muscle groups, and then to subject the patient to an intensive programme of rehabilitation designed to re-train the transplanted nerves. During a period of military service he persuaded surgeons that motor-nerve transplants were being carried out too liberally in the mistaken belief that the human brain could easily learn any number of new uses for motor nerves after they had been surgically connected to foreign muscles. This resulted in significant modifications to the conventional treatment protocols of the time.

Shortly after moving to the Department of Anatomy at Chicago, Sperry began to work on the function of the corpus callosum, a part of the brain connecting the two hemispheres. The year 1949 brought mixed fortunes: he contracted tuberculosis from a monkey he had been dissecting in order to obtain tissues for nerve transplants; more happily, he married Norma Gay Deupree and they had a son, Glenn, and a daughter, Janet Hope. Sperry's studies on the corpus callosum elucidated some of its major functions in interhemispheric memory transfer and eye–hand coordination. Joseph Bogen suggested that the split brain work might be extended to humans suffering severe epilepsy – earlier studies indicated that commissurectomy appeared to have little adverse impact on general levels of intelligence and motor coordination. The first callosalectomy was performed in 1962 on a Second World War veteran with progressively worsening fits. The procedure was followed by a dramatic reduction in the number and severity of the man's seizures. Later work on humans allowed investigators to compare cognitive abilities between the two separated halves of the brain, something which had been impossible before that time. The left half of the brain appeared to be superior to the right in analytical, sequential and linguistic processing, while the right half appeared to perform better in holistic parallel and spatial processing. Thus his findings supported the German physiologist Gustav Fechner who, nearly a century before, had predicted that splitting the brain would reveal two spheres of consciousness within a single cranium.

The idea that the right hemisphere was not an unconscious and minor part of the brain, subservient to the elaborate control of the left, was first articulated by Hughlings Jackson. However, the idea was largely ignored, except in the work of Russell Brain, Oliver Zangwill and some others, until Sperry demonstrated that the right hemisphere has its own consciousness and that it can be conscious and intelligent (for example, in non-verbal and visual–spatial tasks) in a way different from the left. His work on human split-brain studies stimulated additional research by many of his prominent collaborators, such as Jerry Levy who has suggested the reason the brain has two halves is that the cognitive processes for language and for spatial–perceptual functions are incompatible and need to be kept apart. Sperry's groundbreaking studies on the functional specialisation of the cerebral hemispheres won him a share of the 1981 Nobel Prize for Physiology or Medicine.

Sperry's first published paper begins '[T]he objective psychologist hoping to get at the physiological side of behavior is apt to plunge immediately into neurology trying to correlate brain activity with modes of experience ... the result in many cases only accentuates the gap between the total experience as studied by the psychologist and neural activity as analysed by the neurologist' (1939). Although this theme runs throughout Sperry's work, he returned to it very explicitly some thirty years later in his explorations of the emergence of consciousness from the unified brain. He proposed that subjective experience plays a principle role in brain function and, in pursuing this argument, he contended that behaviourism and other reductionistic perspectives need to be replaced by a new approach to the concept of consciousness. In formulating this new approach he placed considerable emphasis on the concept of 'emergence'. Emergence occurs whenever the interaction between two or more entities (for example, atoms or molecules) creates a new entity with new laws and properties that did not previously exist. Consciousness in Sperry's view is a product of, and dependent on, neural activity, but is nevertheless separate from it. It is generated by the activity of cerebral networks as an interacting entity. This newly emerged property – consciousness – continuously feeds back to the central nervous system, resulting in a dynamic process of emergence, feedback, newly emergent states, further feedback and so on. Thus, in Sperry's view, reducing consciousness to its separate neural components eliminates the emergent phenomenon of consciousness.

One might imagine that the original questions posed by Sperry would have long been settled. For example, how is it that neurons become so precisely interconnected in development? Is neural activity important for the development of patterned connections? These and other questions have yet to be fully answered, but it is testament to the significance of his work that many of his early studies are frequently cited alongside contemporary investigations. More generally, Sperry was quick to recognise the wider implications of the evidence that many mental abilities are carried out, supported and coordinated predominantly in one cerebral hemisphere or the other. He was a staunch critic of the prevailing educational systems of the West, as well as science in general, for their neglect of non-verbal forms of intellect. Society, he argued, discriminates against the right hemisphere.

Roger Sperry's major writings

'Action current study in movement coordination', *Journal of General Psychology*, 1939, 20, 295–313.

'Effect of 180-degree rotation of the retinal field on visuomotor coordination', *Journal of Experimental Zoology*, 1943, 92, 263–79.

'Neurology and the mind–brain problem', *American Scientist*, 1952, 40, 291–312.

'Preservation of high order function in isolated somatic cortes in callosum-sectioned cats', *Journal of Neurophysiology*, 1959, 22, 78–87.

'Some functional effects of sectioning the cerebral commisures in man', *Proceedings of the National Academy of Science*, 1962, 48, 1765–9 (with J. E. Bogen and M. S. Gazzaniga).

'Language after section of the cerebral commisures', *Brain*, 1967, 90, 131–48.

'A modified concept of consciousness', *Psychological Review*, 1969, 76, 532–6.

'Changing priorities', *Annual Reviews in Neuroscience*, 1981, 1–15.

'Mechanisms of neural maturation', in S. E. Steven (ed.), *Handbook of Experimental Psychology*, 2nd edn, Wiley, 1988.

Further reading

Schmitt, F. O. and Warden, E. G. (eds) (1974) *The Neurosciences. Third Study Program*, MIT Press.

Voneide, T. J. (1997) 'Roger Wolcott Sperry', *Biographical Memoirs of Fellows of the Royal Society*, 43, 463–71.

THORNDIKE, EDWARD LEE (1874–1949)

Thorndike laid the foundation for modern learning theory by formulating a theoretical position that led to the specification of laws of learning that could be empirically tested.

Thorndike was born in Williamsburg, Massachusetts, the second son of four children. His father was a Methodist minister and his mother a homemaker. He was a diligent schoolboy who first heard the word 'psychology' during his junior year at Wesleyan University. When he was admitted to Harvard his intention was to take a degree in English, but he was gradually drawn to psychology. His research work was supervised by Edmund B. Delabarre, founder of the experimental psychology laboratory at Brown University. While at Harvard, Thorndike took a course offered by **James**, and the two became good friends. When he first moved to Cambridge, Massachusetts, he raised chicks in his bedroom to use in his psychological studies. Not surprisingly his landlord disapproved and James attempted to help by getting laboratory space for him at Harvard. He was unsuccessful, so James allowed Thorndike to continue his research in the basement of his home. A rejected marriage proposal, coupled with a lack of interest in tutoring work to pay for graduate school, motivated a wish for a change, and he accepted a fellowship from James McKeen Cattell at

Columbia University. In 1897 he moved to New York, taking with him two chickens which he planned to breed in order to test J. B. Lamarck's thesis on the inheritability of acquired abilities (the idea that any characteristic acquired by an animal during its lifespan would be passed on to its offspring). Practical considerations forced him to abandon the project when he realised how long it would take to train and breed several generations of chickens. His doctoral thesis, an experimental investigation of learning in animals, was supervised by Cattell, and is the foundation document of modern comparative psychology (the study of behaviour in different species). He knew it too, writing to his fiancée he opined, 'My thesis is a beauty ... I've got some theories which knock the old authorities into a grease spot' (Joncich, 1962: 146).

It was at Columbia that Thorndike began the research that firmly established his reputation in psychology. He devised a classic experiment in which the core apparatus was a puzzle box with various ropes, ladders, levers and so on. An animal (usually a cat) was placed in the box and encouraged to escape by the offer of food placed outside. Thorndike observed the behaviour of the animal: through trial and error it would escape from the box and eat the food. Initially it might take a cat between three and five minutes to escape, but each time it was returned to the box it escaped after shorter and shorter periods. It was pretty clear that the animal had learned to escape, the first attempt being a matter of chance, later attempts guided by previous experience. Although this explanation may seem blatantly obvious, it was crucially important because Thorndike used the findings to challenge the claims espoused by **Wertheimer** and other Gestaltists that animals can learn by a process of problem-solving and almost instantaneous insight. If that were so, the cat, having solved the problem once, would escape in no time at all when returned to the box. Thorndike went on to formulate a position from which he argued that learning is a process of trial and error (he later preferred the terms 'selection' and 'connection') common both to lower species and to humans. At that time associative theories of learning proposed two mechanisms that might account for Thorndike's findings. The first arises from the consequences of behaviour: a behaviour becomes associated with its result. **Skinner** made much of this type of learning and focused on the analysis of the effects of reinforcers on the probability that an antecedent behaviour will be repeated. A second mechanism suggested that the presentation of two or more stimuli, spatially and temporally adjacent, influences the association an organism makes between them. Thorndike regarded both explanations as primitive, but good starting points none the less. Much of his career was concerned with the formulation of empirically testable laws of learning that elaborated, modified and refined these basic positions. His thinking on this can be structured into two phases bisected by the early 1930s.

The British associationist philosopher Alexander Bain had developed a primitive neurological theory of connections that was taken up by both Thorndike and **Pavlov**. Thorndike was particularly attracted to the physiological basis of Bain's treatment but, being a student of James, he considered that physiological principles alone could not account for the processes of learning that were essential to a functionalist, adaptive account of behaviour. Thus, his theoretical position is essentially a combination of associationism and functionalism. Thorndike's pre-1930s theory of learning postulated that learning is a mechanism whereby bonds are formed between stimuli and behaviours. He suggested that these bonds have a physical representation in the form of neuronal connections within the brain, and he developed a connectionist theory of learning which, crudely stated, regards learning as the making of connections, and unlearning – or 'forgetting' – as the breaking of connections. Three variables – contiguity, frequency and recency – are combined to form the basis of his theory, and their relationships were formalised in three basic laws. The Law of Exercise stated that, all other things being equal, repeated performance of a task makes the task easier to complete and reduces the likelihood of error. The law is considered problematic not least because of uncertainty regarding Thorndike's use of the phrase 'all other things being equal', but it was for a time influential in educational circles because it was consistent with the pedagogic view that practice and repetition improve learning. His more famous 'Law of Effect' states that a stimulus–response connection is strengthened when a response is followed by a satisfier. Elimination of incorrect responses is attributed to the occurrence of annoyers. Taking these two claims together, the Law of Effect postulates that one learns or retains responses that are followed by satisfiers and refrains from responses followed by annoyers. One of the necessary additions to his Law of Effect, the 'Law of Readiness', was introduced to explain why some behaviours are more likely to be learned than others. The Law of Readiness was never clearly defined, which accounts for its demise, but basically it states that in order for an organism to learn it must attend to specific stimuli of consequence in a situation. A difficulty with this law is that is does not make clear how an animal could work out which of the many novel stimuli surrounding it might be 'of consequence' before commencing a behavioural response. For example, how would an animal work out whether it was safe to enter a dark hole which it had not previously encountered?

In addition to the three primary laws, Thorndike had five specific ancillaries:

1   multiple responses: an organism will respond in a variety of ways if its first response does not immediately lead to a satisfier;
2   set or attitude: the predisposition of an organism to behave in certain ways;
3   prepotency of elements: organisms learn to react selectively to significant elements of a problem;
4   response by analogy (also referred to as the theory of identical elements): the speed at which an organism may learn in new situations is determined by its resemblance to prior experience;,
5   associative shifting: organisms respond in similar ways to similar stimuli.

Thorndike's theory attracted considerable empirical interest and the accumulating corpus of evidence informed revision from 1930. His ideas regarding trial and error were replaced by processes of selection and connection respectively but the most important change was his retraction of the Law of Exercise because studies with humans indicated that it did not apply. Work with people suggested that covert, cognitive processes such as problem-solving must be implicated in human learning. These were subsequently embodied in his principle of 'learning by ideas'.

Thorndike took the view that psychological evidence should and could be related to the functioning of the nervous system. He suggested that connections between neurones determine the flow of neuronal current, and that this underpins all psychological processes. Thorndike was not a developmental psychologist: he considered the phenomena referred to as 'developmental' as explicable within his laws of learning and viewed the term 'developmental psychology' as completely unnecessary. Although his theoretical framework is reductionistic, his case for the primacy of stimulus–response connections, and the implications of that thesis for educational policy, is richer than might be supposed. For example, Thorndike and Robert S. Woodworth conducted an empirical evaluation of the educational policy of 'formal discipline', the doctrine that exercising the mind by requiring children to learn Latin and Greek would greatly benefit their learning of wholly unrelated subjects. They trained people on various tasks and measured their achievements on other tasks of varying similarity to the original. The evidence indicated that the benefit was slight and seemed to be principally due to the number of identical elements shared by the various tasks. These findings helped shift educational practices towards specifically task-oriented teaching and away from a policy based on formal discipline. Incidentally, Thorndike's son, Robert, went on to have a successful career in the development of psychological tests for use in schools. One of Thorndike's students, Leta Stetter Hollingworth, took these ideas forward in her classic studies of children and adolescents with exceptionally high or exceptionally low intelligence. Her work persuaded Thorndike to relax his strong nativistic stance with its emphasis on genetic influences and to embrace a more prominent role for environmental factors in shaping behaviour.

Thorndike was a prolific author, penning more than 500 publications including fifty books. His work attracted particular notice because it represented the first serious attempt by a psychologist to study animal behaviour for its own sake rather than as a vehicle to shed light on the nature of human processes. The arguments of earlier writers, such as George J. Romanes' work on animal intelligence, had been mostly anecdotal. Conwy Lloyd Morgan had rectified Romane's penchant for anthropomorphic accounts of the mental lives of animals, and the American psychologist Margaret Floy Washburn systematised Morgan's efforts to quantify levels of consciousness in different species. In this context Thorndike's work was breathtakingly innovative, because it inaugurated the experimental analysis of animal behaviour as an enterprise of value in its own right. However, the reception of his ideas was not universally positive. Wesley Mills, a senior figure in American animal psychology, was sharply critical of Thorndike's methods, arguing that the study of animals outside of their natural habitat made no sense. Others considered Thorndike's connectionism to have gone too far, but for a different reason. Edwin Guthrie argued that learning is about linking stimuli with motor and glandular movements (a position similar to, but simpler than, **Pavlov's**), and he concluded that just one principle is required: contiguity in time between stimuli and movements. Thorndike, Guthrie argued, had engaged in unwarranted theory-building and in devising so-called laws of learning that missed what learning was really about. Much of Thorndike's work with animals, particularly his insistence on detachment when making behavioural descriptions, was prescient of ideas promulgated by **Watson** and Skinner. Thus the tendency is to classify Thorndike as a behaviourist, although his studies of learning in humans were also informed by, and spoke to, the functionalist tradition of James and were influential in establishing the idea of a science of education.

Edward Thorndike's major writings

'Animal intelligence: an experimental study of the associative processes in animals', *Psychological Review Monograph Supplements*, 1898, 2, 8.
'The influence of improvement in one mental function upon the efficiency of other functions', *Psychological Review*, 1901, 8, 247–61 (with R. S. Woodworth).
Animal Intelligence, Macmillan, 1911.
Educational Psychology: Vols I & II. The Original Nature of Man, Teachers' College, 1913.
The Fundamentals of Learning, Teachers' College, 1932.
The Psychology of Wants, Interests and Attitudes, Appleton-Century, 1935.

Further reading

Joncich, G. (ed.) (1962) *Psychology and the Science of Education: Selected Writings of Edward L. Thorndike*, Teachers' College.
Lattal, K. A. (1998) 'A century of effect: legacies of E. L. Thorndike's Animal Intelligence monograph', *Journal of the Experimental Analysis of Behavior*, 70, 325–6.

TITCHENER, EDWARD BRADFORD (1867–1927)

The founder of a school of thought referred to as structuralism, Titchener emphasised the importance of understanding the structure of experience by using analytic introspection to reveal the building blocks of mental life.

At the time of the American Civil War, Titchener's father, then a young man, travelled from England to America to fight on the side of the Confederates. On his return he married and settled down in the ancient, Roman-established town of Chichester in Sussex. Edward was born soon afterwards. Titchener's father died in his thirties, but E. B. was a bright child, and a scholarship secured a good education at Malvern College, a prestigious secondary school. He then went to Oxford where he developed an interest in experimental physiology under the influence of Sir John Scott Budon Sanderson, and in experimental psychology through a reading of the third edition of **Wundt**'s *Principles of Physiological Psychology*, which he translated into English and took with him to Leipzig where he studied with Wundt for two years. Titchener returned for a very brief period to Oxford before he received an invitation from Cornell University to fill the position vacated by James R. Angell – it was Angell who suggested that he would be a good replacement. He was also offered an appointment at Oxford, but Cornell offered laboratory facilities and wanted to develop experimental psychology whereas Oxford showed considerably less interest. Although it seems that he intended his stay at Cornell to be temporary, possibly hoping that Oxford's attitude towards experimental psychology might change, he remained there for the rest of his career, establishing the largest doctoral programme in psychology in North America. He is often described as the 'dean of experimental psychology' in America, and was hugely influential in bringing the experimental psychology of Wundt and the German tradition to America and thereby contributing to the transition from a concern with the philosophy of mental life to a psychological science of the mind. His most important contribution was undoubtedly establishing the scientific status of psychology, and he did so in the autocratic style of Wundt. He knew what needed to be done and who was best placed to undertake the work. Thus it was his practice to design research studies and assign his students to them as he saw fit.

Anecdotes about Titchener abound and, whereas the passage of time often imposes embellishments, the details of most biographical accounts reveal a striking consistency in their descriptions of his values and style. His position on science was clear-cut: 'Science deals not with values but with facts. There is no good or bad, sick or well, useful or useless, in science' (1914: 1). Evans (1984: 18) characterises his attitude to psychology thus: 'To Titchener, the American psychologies prior to the 1880s – and much since then – were little more than watered down Cartesianisms, codified phrenologies, or worst of all, thinly disguised theology'. Like Wundt, Titchener was strongly committed to establishing a science of psychology based on well-founded laboratories equipped with the standard apparatus required to fractionate consciousness. However, he regarded **Watson**'s efforts to establish a school of behaviourism as little more than an apparatus-driven technology of behaviour and quite distinct from pure experimental psychology as he understood it.

In 1894, Titchener married Sophie K. Below, who gave him invaluable assistance in his laboratory and prepared drawings for his book. His attitude to women was complex, or at least inconsistent, and controversial. The American Psychological Association admitted women almost from its foundation, but when Titchener established an informal group of directors of psychology laboratories, The Experimentalists (later reorganised as the Society of Experimental Psychologists), he excluded women from its membership. This brought accusations of chauvinism and misogyny. Christine Ladd-Franklin was at the time conducting important work on colour vision, and her fury is recorded in communications between them. Paradoxically, there is other evidence that he was often well disposed to women, as in the case of Celestia Suzannah Parrish who joined his summer school in 1893 and who, with his encouragement and support, went on to the chair in psychology and pedagogy at the State Normal School (later part of the University of Georgia). Margaret Floy Washburn was his first doctoral candidate and the first woman to receive a doctorate in psychology. Half of his first twelve doctorates were given to women, and 'More women completed their Ph.D. degrees with him than with any other male psychologist of his generation' (Evans, 1991: 90).

Other examples of the controversies that surrounded Titchener's life relate to the difficult relationship between the American Psychological Association and The Experimentalists. He founded the latter partly out of dissatisfaction with the Association and partly from his displeasure in its failure to censure E. W. Scripture, head of Yale's Psychological Laboratory, for what he regarded as plagiarism of his translation of one of Wundt's texts (*Human and Animal Behaviour*). He was for several years one of the senior editors of the *American Journal of Psychology*, which was purchased by one of his students, Karl Dallenbach, in 1921. He resigned when Dallenbach proposed introducing advertising material. The historian of psychology, Edwin G. Boring, has suggested that some of Titchener's difficulties with the American establishment were almost entirely of his own making. He retained a strong English identity – often referring to Americans as 'you' and the English as 'we' – and even seemed hostile to the notion of adopting American citizenship. (Incidentally, similar observations have been made concerning the patrician mannerisms of **Cattell**.) Ironically, his values and personal style were so strongly shaped by his period at Leipzig that he was sometimes mistakenly taken to be of German origin.

Titchener promulgated a view of psychology as the science of the normal adult human mind. By systematically applying the technique of analytic introspection the mind could be disaggregated to its basic elements: sensations, feelings and images. He regarded images as the elements of feelings, and feelings the elements of emotions. By the end of his career he had catalogued more than 44,000 different sensations. His penchant for taxonomy was also reflected in his home, which resembled a museum, comprising an enormous collection of objects including many kinds of live reptile. Much of Titchener's career was spent differentiating and naming psychological elements with respect to five attributes: quality, intensity, duration, clearness and extent.

Quality allows us to differentiate sensations, and intensity describes the strength of an experience. Duration refers to the period an experience lasts and clearness indicates how much an experience stands out from its background. Extent refers to experience in terms of spatial dimension. A goal of psychology is the production of an encyclopaedia or thesaurus of elementary sensations where the entry for each sensation is structured under five attribute headings. In Titchener's structuralist framework, attention is synonymous with clearness, and meaning is something we attribute to our experience based on context. But while Wundt considered it important to distinguish immediate experience (for example, one's immediate reaction to a visual stimulus) from mediate experience (for example, measurements of the same stimulus taken by light meters), Titchener's insistence on treating psychology as a natural science led him to focus on the analysis of immediate experience but from the perspectives of different people. Psychology should be concerned with the analysis of consciousness, the total of immediate experience at any given moment, and mind, the accumulated experiences of a lifetime. For Titchener, a psychology that attends both to the systematic analysis of a thing as it is experienced, such as a visual illusion, and to the thing as it is described or measured by a physical device, is doomed to fail because it is committing the 'stimulus error'. This entails describing the stimulus itself rather than the analysis of the experience of the stimulus. In Titchener's view, the distinction Wundt makes between immediate and mediate is wrong because it is unnecessary; there is but one experience viewed from different perspectives.

To view Titchener as Wundt's double would be something of a misrepresentation. The stylistic likenesses between them are conspicuous: both were autocratic and insisted that colleagues and students working within their laboratories conform to their theoretical positions. But there were substantial intellectual differences too, though Titchener was eager to emphasise that 'if my recent writing has seemed rather to be directed against Wundtian doctrines, that is but the natural reaction of a pupil who cannot swear to the literal teaching of the Master' (1901: vii–viii). Among these differences was Wundt's position on the need for two psychologies: one to investigate lower mental processes, such as sensations, using experimental methods; and another to study higher mental processes such as language and thinking. Wundt did not consider the latter to be tractable using experimental techniques, whereas Titchener considered it an entirely feasible enterprise. Titchener took a strong position on the importance of using introspective techniques in a value-free manner that would yield meaning-free descriptions of the elements of consciousness (a position referred to as structuralism), whereas Wundt stressed the voluntary, goal-directed, purposeful operation of the mind (a perspective coined voluntarism). Their respective viewpoints can be contrasted in Wundt's position on the concept of apperception, or attention through an act of will, and Titchener's argument that attention is merely an attribute of clarity that can be applied to elementary sensations and images.

While on the subject of misrepresentation, it is worth commenting on the phenomenon known as the 'Titchener illusion' – it was not discovered by Titchener. The visual illusion often appears in introductory texts on psychology and can be created by drawing two identical circles with a space of about five inches between them. When a ring of large circles is drawn around one of those circles and a ring of small circles drawn around the other, the two original circles are perceived to be of slightly different sizes. Although frequently attributed to Titchener, he neither sought nor claimed authorship, and the illusion is almost certainly due to Hermann Ebbinghaus who first described it during the 1890s.

In many respects Titchener was responsible, directly and indirectly, for the demise of structuralism. He was directly responsible in the sense that it was the inevitable consequence of the lines of investigation he pursued – they quickly exposed the theoretical and methodological weaknesses underpinning structuralism. For instance, introspection appeared to be indistinguishable from retrospection and seemed to beg the question whether Titchener was actually examining memories of sensations rather than the sensations themselves. He was indirectly responsible for its decline in the sense that he eschewed practical applications of psychology, and this caused a gap to emerge between professional practice and the pure, experimental approach which he advocated for the analysis of the normal adult human mind. Some of Titchener's more eminent students, such as Walter B. Pillsbury, watered down the more extreme tenets of structuralism and were very successful in disseminating sound experimental psychology to subsequent generations of students through well-received textbooks. However, Titchener's exclusivity had the effect of distancing his structuralism from several important developments in other parts of psychology. For example, his focus on the normal adult mind meant that structuralism appeared to have little to offer clinical psychology and there were few points of contact with psychoanalysis. Moreover, the study of animal behaviour had little relevance to a structuralism committed to a quite different approach to revealing the elements of human consciousness. What could structuralism learn from behaviourists publishing findings indicating that much could be learned about humans by studying other species? Here is another of the Titchener paradoxes – as a student at Oxford he was particularly interested in comparative studies of animal behaviour. Titchener's focus on the adult mind also meant that there were few interactions with child psychologists such as Arnold Gesell, who was using modes of systematic observation and measurement that were potentially sympathetic to structuralist aspirations for psychology. Similarly, the structuralists either ignored or could find few bridges that would allow them to engage with the breakthroughs in the study of personality, learning and individual differences. Another crucial factor in the demise of Titchener's structuralism lay in its failure to assimilate ideas and evidence emerging from the study of evolutionary processes. This is all the more surprising because Titchener was for a time a devotee of the evolutionary theorist Herbert Spencer. Although the school of structuralism was short-lived, and essentially died with Titchener, the survival of historical interest is due to the emergence of functionalism – the name Titchener gave to a hugely influential school which emerged as a reaction to structuralism and which emphasised the role of consciousness and behaviour in understanding how organisms adapt to, and are influenced by, their environments.

Edward Titchener's major writings

'The postulates of structural psychology', *Philosophical Review*, 1899, 8, 290–9.
Experimental Psychology, 4 volumes, Macmillan, 1901–5
Lectures on the Elementary Psychology of Feeling and Attention, Macmillan, 1908.
Lectures on the Experimental Psychology of the Thought Processes, Macmillan, 1909.
A Text Book of Psychology, Macmillan, 1910.
'On "Psychology as the Behaviorist Views It" ', *Proceedings of the American Philosophical Society*, 1914, 53, 1–17.
Systematic Psychology: Prolegomena, Macmillan, 1929.

Further reading

Boring, E. G. (1927) 'Edward Bradford Titchener', *American Journal of Psychology*, 38, 489–506.
Evans, R. B. (1984) 'The origins of American academic psychology', in J. Broek (ed.), *Explorations in the History of Psychology in the United States*, Associated University Presses (pp. 17–60).
Evans, R. B. (1991) 'E. B. Titchener on scientific psychology and technology', in G. A. Kimble, M. Wertheimer and C. L. White (eds), *Portraits of Pioneers in Psychology*, Erlbaum (pp. 89–103).

TULVING, ENDEL (1927–)

Tulving developed a theory of memory that introduced the concept of episodic memory, a type of long-term memory for personal experiences and events.

Endel Tulving spent his childhood in a small town in Estonia. He really liked sports but showed no particular interest in science. His father was a judge, and the family lived in relative comfort until Estonia was forcibly incorporated into the USSR in 1940. In 1944, at the age of seventeen, Tulving and his younger brother Hannes were separated from their family and taken to Germany; the separation lasted for twenty years. After the war he completed his high-school education and then worked for a while as a teacher and interpreter for the American Army. He studied medicine for a period at Heidelberg before emigrating to Canada in 1949, where he worked for a short time as a general labourer. The following year he married Ruth Mikkelsaar – they had been at high school together – and they had three daughters: Elo Ann, Ruth and Linda. With his wife's support he completed a psychology degree at Toronto, followed by a master's degree and then a doctorate at Harvard; his doctoral thesis was on movement of the eyes and visual acuity. He returned to a position at Toronto and in a few years found himself in the company of several newly-appointed senior staff including Daniel Berlyne, who made innovative contributions to the psychology of creativity and exploration, and the cognitive psychologist George Mandler. Tulving's first research work at Toronto drew on seminar material taught by George Miller and Edwin B. Newman at Harvard. It focused on devising a method for measuring the quantity of sequential constraint on items recalled on successive trials in a multi-trial free recall situation. With Mandler's encouragement he adopted the term 'subjective organisation' to describe what his method measured. In 1970 he accepted a chair at Yale, but a variety of factors conspired to provoke a return to Toronto and he held a joint professorship at Yale and Toronto until 1974.

Tulving's approach to the analysis of memory was formulated at a time when the consensus view was that psychologists needed to refine their thinking and distinguished between various sub-systems of memory. The best known of these is due to a classification made by Tulving between procedural (for example, memory for the performance of movements including classical conditioned responses), episodic (for example, memory for personal experiences and events) and semantic memory (for example, commonsense knowledge and knowledge of language). Tulving's first formulation of the hypothetical distinction between semantic and episodic memory focused on different types and sources of information – personally experienced events versus general facts. The idea was well received, but development of a research programme based on this distinction had to deal with the obstacles presented in a tradition based on the analysis of memory for language, or verbal learning as it was called, and the complete absence of any pertinent empirical data. A little over a decade later there were sufficient data to conclude that the distinction corresponds to a neurological reality and to provide evidence for his hypothesis that episodic and semantic memory represent two functionally separable memory systems.

At the time when Tulving introduced the distinction between semantic and episodic memory, most psychologists were using methods to exploring memory that dated back to von Ebbinghaus's work during the 1880s. Ebbinghaus argued that, in order to study memory in its purest form, it was necessary to establish experimental conditions that would remove potentially confounding variables. His experiments were designed to uncover rudimentary laws of memory by using nonsense syllables to create situations where the memory content was meaningless and therefore isolated from other memories and prior experience. Tulving gave two reasons why these methods could not capture what was going on in episodic memory. First, episodic memory is about happenings in particular places – about 'what', 'where' and 'when' – whereas laboratory conditions attend only to the 'what'. For example, research participants were asked questions of the general form: 'What do you remember of the material presented to you earlier?' Second, previous studies assumed that, when someone is shown a list of items and later asked whether a particular item appeared on the list, their response was a reliable index of the content of their memory. The reasoning seems straightforward: if someone recognises an item from a list it is because they have a conscious recollection of its appearance in the list. However, the activity of recalling something from memory can be fallible – some items in memory may not be recalled on demand.

Tulving is recognised as the cognitive psychologist who, more than any other, drew attention to one of the most important issues in the analysis of memory: the relationship between the encoding (converting information into a form that allows it to be stored in the brain) and the retrieval of mental events. Tulving and Craik (1975) argued that what is encoded into memory is influenced by the particular conditions pertaining at the time. For example, every time we see a near-miss between a car and a pedestrian we do not encode as part of that memory everything we know about cars, only the specific characteristics of the car in question. In order to recall the details of a particular car it is necessary that there is sufficient overlap between the information being recalled at a particular time and in a specific place and the details of the original event encoded in memory. Hence, when we see another near-miss, it may evoke the memory of an earlier incident in ways that seeing tens of thousands of different cars would not. Tulving's claim that recall will be improved in contexts that successfully reproduce features of the original encoding environment is a fundamental principle of a technique called the cognitive interview. This notion was taken up by Edward Geiselman as a police interviewing technique: witnesses are brought through the minutiae of the day in which they witnessed a particular incident, and in so doing they recall a great deal more than the evidence elicited by direct questioning about the incident in question.

Tulving's account of memory is sometimes summarised as the encoding-specificity principle: a cue or hint will help someone to retrieve a piece of information from memory if it provides them with information that had been processed during the encoding of the to-be-remembered material. One of the difficulties confronted by Tulving's position is caused by the way the principle of encoding specific is applied. Memory is thought to depend on the amount of information overlap between information being processed at the time it is being recalled and the details of the original event encoded in memory. It is usually impossible to obtain an independent measure of information overlap between the two – the exception being very tightly controlled laboratory situations of the kind that Tulving criticises for excluding episodic memory. An appealing alternative is to use a calculation of the overlap based on a measure of a person's level of memory performance at the time they are encoding something and the time they are recalling it. But there is a problem: this is circular, because the second measure of memory (performance when recalling something) is used as a proxy for a direct index of information overlap with the encoding of the information. Tulving addressed this issue through the development of a mathematical formulation predicting the degree of encoding specificity. However, that formulation has been criticised on several grounds, *inter alia* that it does not take into account the considerable priming effects of the recognition task on recall. In other words, performance on a recall task may be artificially high because on many of the experimental trials in which people had seen the to-be-remembered material they may have spontaneously generated memories of incidental things they were doing during the recognition phase. This would give them an unfair advantage on some of the recall trials. Other criticisms have focused on the generality of recognition failure among different types of materials. For example, recognition failure tends to be greater when people are given pairs of abstract nouns (e.g. honour–anxiety) and 'typical' instructions than when they are given 'elaborate' instructions. This suggests that when paired-associate terms are abstract or unrelated to one another they do not provide much context for one another and the effects of encoding specificity are weaker. When the paired-associates are strongly related, either because of the semantic links between the two terms or through a person's efforts to learn, then the effects of encoding specificity will be stronger. Despite these criticisms, Tulving's claims about the relationship between encoding and retrieval have been supported.

Tulving has made important contributions to the analysis of long-term memory and suggests that it involves two sorts of knowledge: procedural and propositional. Procedural knowledge involves knowing *how* to perform skilled actions, such as riding a bicycle or driving a car. Propositional knowledge involves knowing *that* certain things have happened or are true – this is factual knowledge. **Anderson** used very similar ideas when developing computer simulations of memory and problem-solving. Tulving further defined propositional knowledge as involving episodic and semantic memory. Episodic knowledge involves memories for things that have happened to a person – their personal experiences of the world – and has motivated much of the later development of research and theory on autobiographical memory. Semantic knowledge involves the store of knowledge remembered independently of time and place – general information about the world. Tulving has used an 'onion model' to describe the relationships between the three major memory systems: procedural memory is regarded as the most basic sub-system; out of this arises semantic memory; and finally episodic memory from the semantic. In terms of human evolution, he considers episodic memory to be the most recently evolved. It suggests that, in terms of individual development, it is relatively late-developing and early-deteriorating; one develops this memory system in late childhood and it is the first to go as part of the ageing process. It is also exceptionally vulnerable to any kind of brain damage.

Working with Daniel Schachter, Tulving formulated a fourth type of memory, the perceptual representation system (PRS), of which people are largely unaware and which contains a kind of sensory memory of the environment. The PRS is thought to operate at a pre-semantic level and is often studied in experiments on priming. Priming refers to a procedure whereby a person is given some contextual information, such as the general appearance of an object or the time at which they saw it. It was while conducting priming experiments that Tulving and Schachter noted that impossible objects, such as those depicted in the drawings of the Dutch artist Maurits Escher, cannot be primed. In other words, providing people with contextual information usually helps them recall details concerning a particular object, but not in the case of pictures of objects that cannot physically exist. Their conclusion, that the PRS 'has evolved to perform only ecologically valid computations' (1990: 303), would have pleased **Gibson**.

Endel Tulving's major writings

'Episodic and semantic memory', in E. Tulving and W. Donaldson (eds), *Organization of Memory*, Academic Press, 1972.

'Structure of memory traces', *Psychological Review*, 1975, 82, 261–75 (with M. J. Watkins).

'Depth of processing and the retention of words in episodic memory', *Journal of Experimental Psychology: General*, 1975, 104, 268–94 (with F. I. M. Craik).

'Encoding specificity: Relation between recall superiority and recognition failure', *Journal of Experimental Psychology: Human Learning & Memory*, 1976, 2, 349–61.

'The measurement of subjective organization in free recall', *Psychological Bulletin*, 1977, 84, 539–56 (with R. J. Sternberg).

'Retrieval independence in recognition and recall', *Psychological Review*, 1978, 85, 153–71 (with A. J. Flexsor).

Elements of Episodic Memory, Clarendon Press, 1983.

'Priming and human memory systems', *Science*, 1990, 47, 301–16 (with D. L. Schachter).

'Episodic memory: from mind to brain', *Annual Review of Psychology*, 2002, 53, 1–25.

Further reading

Collins, A. F. *et al.* (eds) (1995) *Theories of Memory I*, Psychology Press.

Conway, M. A., Gathercole, S. E. and Cornoldi, C. (eds) (1998) *Theories of Memory II*, Psychology Press.

Tulving, E. and Craik, F. M. (eds) (2000) *The Oxford Handbook of Memory*, Oxford University Press.

VYGOTSKY (VYGOTSKII), LEV (LEO SEMEONOVICH (1896–1934)

*Vygotsky formulated a theory of cognitive development bas~
between social–historical factors, as reflected in educational systems, a~
a more immanent, interpersonal nature, such as parent–child interactions.*

Vygotsky was born the second eldest of eight children in a middle-class Jewish family, and grew up in Gomel (his father was the bank manager), near the borders between Belarus, Russia and the Ukraine. His mother, Cecilia, was fluent in several languages; although trained as a teacher, she never taught for any appreciable length of time. Though greatly interested in the arts and humanities, the fact that Jews were prohibited from teaching in public schools directed Vygotsky to a career in medicine, and he entered Moscow's medical school by dint of academic merit and good luck, the Jewish entry quota having been altered from selection to lottery. He transferred from medicine to law after about a month and took several courses on which Zinaida, one of his sisters, had also enrolled. At that time it was possible to register at more than one university, and in 1914 he also registered for a degree in humanities at Shanavsky's University – though the degree was not a qualification recognised by the government of the day. There he found an opportunity to read widely – his thesis was on Shakespeare's 'Hamlet' – before returning to Gomel in late 1917. Much of his time at home was spent caring for his mother, who had contracted tuberculosis, and for his thirteen-year-old brother who died from typhoid before the year was out. Vygotsky himself was diagnosed with tuberculosis in 1919, a disease that was to kill him at the age of thirty-seven. In Gomel he also taught at various institutions, established a psychology laboratory at a teachers' college, and wrote a psychology text for teachers. During this period he read widely and familiarised himself with the works of **James** and **Freud**. He also pursued his interests in the arts and founded the literary journal *Verask*. In January 1924 he presented three papers at the Second Psychoneurological Congress in Leningrad. These argued against **Pavlov**'s 'reflexology' as a psychology of consciousness, and in support of the less mechanistic 'reactology' (the study of mental effort as reflected in peripheral motor activity, such as the speed with which a person would react to a physical stimulus) favoured by K. N. Kornilov, director of the Institute of Experimental Psychology at Moscow. Vygotsky was offered a position at the Institute and there he encountered neuropsychologist

ria, who was at that time a psychoanalyst. During his time there ygotsky wrote his doctoral thesis on the psychology of art. Like Luria, he had a wide range of interests including 'defectology', a term which does not have a literal English-language equivalent but which loosely refers to the education of children with sensory, physical and learning impairments. At this time Vygotsky was promoting applications of a version of Kornilov's reactology, as reflected in his use of reaction-time measures, to the analysis of a range of problem-solving activities. Kornilov was an advocate of a version of psychology broadly similar to **Watson**'s behaviourism, although he did not reject a consideration of psychological states to the same degree. Vygotsky's adaptation of Kornilov's position was based on less mechanistic principles, reflecting his attempt to incorporate a place for social and cultural influences in the analysis and explanation of behaviour.

Vygotsky's most influential work is his conceptualisation of the representation of knowledge and the significance of inter-relationships between macro- and micro-social influences. His analysis is directed by the importance of the linkages between social-historical factors, as reflected in the educational systems into which a child is introduced, and those of a more imminent, interpersonal nature, such as parent–child interactions. For example, Vygotsky took the view that language is not simply a tool whereby the mental activity of one individual, the parent, interacts with that of another, the child. It is a contrivance that has shaped cultural change and is integral to the environment given to both adults and their children. This position on the nature and function of language partly reflects the influence of a more radical position that had been formulated much earlier by Wilhelm von Humboldt. Humboldt formulated the *Weltanschauung* (worldview) hypothesis: thought is impossible without language, and language determines thought. How people come to think is a product of the particular language that is the prevailing medium of expression for their society. Vygotsky's constructivist framework demands a very significant role for social and cultural factors, and in this regard it is a good deal more sophisticated than the extreme determinism favoured by Humboldt. It is somewhat similar to **Piaget**'s in its claim that learning and development involve fusing new information with existing knowledge structures and adjusting prior understanding. Unlike Piaget, Vygotsky considered the development of thinking, cognitive development, as more than a progressive construction of complex structures on simpler ones. Cognitive development is a socio-genetic process: it is carried out in the social activities of children with adults who have the potential to generate and lead development. The essence and uniqueness of human behaviour lies in the intercession of social tools and social signs, particularly language. Vygotsky's theory is based on four main tenets: (i) children construct their knowledge of the world; (ii) development cannot be isolated from its social and cultural context; (iii) learning can lead development; and (iv) language plays a crucial role in cognitive development.

Vygotsky places thinking and problem-solving in three groups: some kinds of thinking can be performed independently by the child; others cannot be performed even with help. Between these two are things a child can do with assistance. He referred to the difference between what a child can do with assistance and what she can do independently as the zone of proximal development (ZPD). With the assistance and guidance of adults a child will develop the ability to complete tasks on her own. The ZPD is central to Vygotsky's framework and captures his belief that learning is a socially and culturally mediated activity. The ZPD can be thought of as the difference between the actual development level of a child, as determined by independent problem-solving, and their level of potential development, as determined through problem-solving under adult guidance or in collaboration with more capable peers. Development is nothing less than a dialectical process of mastering cultural tools and resources. Drawing on his knowledge and experience in the area of defectology, Vygotsky opposed the ideas of William Stern, who devised the notion of mental age and intelligence quotient (IQ), in preference for a view of intellectual disability as a process rather than a static condition with which a child is lumbered from birth. Pursuing this line of argument, and consonant with the ideas of Luria, he suggested that psychological assessment should focus on understanding mental processing and, specifically, the strategies employed by the child to solve a whole range of problems with which she is confronted. Like Piaget, he valued the analysis of errors for what it could reveal about a child's problem-solving strategies and inform the beneficial interventions of the teacher.

Vygotsky was strongly committed to the development of a Marxist psychology consonant with the characteristics of a natural science. Neither the founders of Marxism nor the contemporary Soviet psychologists of his time had made much progress in completing this task, though not for the want of trying. For example, Aleksei Leontev spent much of his career attempting to formulate a position based on the Marxist thesis and Vygotsky's psychology, and in so doing he developed a theoretical position not dissimilar from **Gibson**'s ecological optics. Vygotsky's efforts were directed to formulating a psychology based on laws that establish the concepts through which human activity might be described. In his view, **Watson**'s behaviourism was correct in its assertion that a scientific psychology is only possible as a natural science, but, while recognising and defining the task, it failed to complete the Marxist task by virtue of its neglect of social, historical and cultural forces. The Gestalt proposition, as developed by **Wertheimer** and others, could be regarded as an improvement because, in introducing the concept of structure to the analysis of experience, it combined both descriptive (behavioural) and functional (adaptive) accounts of behaviour. Gestalt theory is a materialistic psychology that approximates behaviourism but offers more because it can accommodate internal, mental processes such as 'ideas' and 'thought'. Vygotsky took the view that contemporaneous Marxist formulations, while achieving a degree of conceptual purchase on the contribution of social forces, had failed to reach the achievements of the behaviourists in America and Gestalt psychologists in Germany. What Vygotsky was attempting imposed a requirement to identify a new unit of study for psychology as well as a new way of thinking about method: 'The search for method becomes one of the most important problems of the entire enterprise of understanding the uniquely human forms of psychological activity. In this case, the method is simultaneously prerequisite and product, the tool and the result of the study' (1988: 65). Vygotsky's conception of method is closely lined with that of praxis – his method is not just about the systematic application of technique, it is about something to be practised. Vygotsky could have pursued his alternative to Watson's behaviourism and the Gestaltists in its theoretical form, but his concern with method almost certainly influenced his preference to follow an empirical, evolutionist route that explored cultural differences in thinking. This work was strongly influenced by his collaboration with Luria, and it included a series of studies of peasant communities in Uzbekistan (see p. 156). Those studies showed that Uzbekis either could not, or would not, categorise perceptual stimuli on the basis of Gestalt laws of similarity. For example, they would not classify a triangle drawn as a series of short, dotted lines with an equivalent triangle with a solid line perimeter. Instead, they preferred to categorise on the basis of the objects they thought they could associate with the forms. For instance, the triangle with the solid line perimeter might be classified as a spearhead whereas the triangle constructed of short, dotted lines might be classified as a kind of tree. One reading of this research contends that this was an intellectually motivated investigation of thinking as a culturally embedded activity. Another points to the absence of any discernible resistance to the politicisation of the findings (Uzbekis who had received Soviet education showed signs of the higher mental process typical of the Russians, whereas others did not) as so-called 'scientific' support for Soviet policies directed to the extermination of millions of Islamic people living in Uzbekistan.

Vygotsky's work was slow to have an impact on European and American psychology. There were several reasons for this. First, his work was banned from publication under the Soviet regime until 1956. Kornilov's reactology, Bekhterev's reflexology and Vygotsky's constructivism were viewed as failing to adequately represent Marxist–Leninist psychology and were rejected in favour of Pavlov's model of brain functioning. Second, his death at the age of thirty-seven meant that his international presence was not well established. For example, he was aware of Piaget's work and commented on it in his own writing, but Piaget was unaware of Vygotsky's until late in his own career. Third, differences between the Russian and American psychological traditions imposed a combination of ideological and terminological barriers. **Bruner** and others were instrumental in introducing Vygotsky's ideas to the attention of psychologists in the English-speaking world, but even the timing of that was a matter of coincidence: Bruner first heard of Vygotsky's ideas at a party in the home of neurologist Wilder Penfield. Bruner was particularly struck by the parallels between his own ideas on language and thought and those of Vygotsky, and he incorporated many of Vygotsky's positions into his cultural account of a naturalistic developmental theory.

Lev Vygotsky's major writings

Rieber, R. W. and Carton, A. S. (eds) (1988) *The Collected Works of L. S. Vygotsky* Plenum.

Further reading

Luria, A. R. (1935) 'Professor Leon Semenovich Vygotskii', *Journal of Genetic Psychology*, 46, 224–6.
Van der Veer, R. and Valsiner, J. (1991) *Understanding Vygotsky: A Quest for Synthesis*, Blackwell.

WATSON, JOHN BROADUS (1878–1958)

Watson founded a school of thought called behaviourism which focuses on the prediction and control of behaviour.

In a popular article written in 1928 for the *Saturday Review of Literature*, Watson opined: 'Many biographers take their characters back to infancy and childhood, in order to secure a certain continuity in the life trends of the person biographer. View any of these biographies now, in the light of what the behaviorist has taught us about conditioning and slanting in infancy and their inaccuracies become apparent at once.' It is somewhat ironic, therefore, that a good deal of what has been written about Watson has focused on his early childhood and its consequences for the sometimes tragic events of his adult life. Watson's great-great-grandfather left County Down, Northern Ireland, in 1752 (a Scottish–Irish ancestry he shared with **Cannon**). His grandfather left the family farm to his son Pickens, who married Emma Kesiah Roe. They had three children, Edward, Thomas Stradley and Mary Alice, before John was born in Travellers Rest, Greenville, South Carolina. Watson's parents lost most of their money during the American Civil War. Watson was reared in a home that his mother endeavoured to sustain as a pious, Baptist environment. His father, a womaniser with a serious drinking problem – his daughter Polly Hartley alleges he had a couple of Indian wives in the Greenville area – left the family home in 1891 when John was thirteen. It is not clear whether Emma threw him out or whether he elected to leave to pursue a more hedonistic lifestyle, but the traumatic effect – the young J. B. Watson felt betrayed – was acted out in John's aggressive attitude towards peers and schoolteachers and occasional bouts of trouble with the law. Watson's entry to Furman University was a personal turning point, and he spent more of his time in academic pursuits. When he was admitted to the graduate programme at the University of Chicago he met up with one of the ex-Furman staff, Gordon Moore, and took Moore's course on thinking, consciousness and the psychology of **Wundt**. James R. Angell encouraged him to pursue a major in experimental psychology (with a minor in philosophy), and he soon developed an enthusiasm for the study of animal behaviour and comparative psychology. His philosophy minor included courses from the educationalist John Dewey, who favoured reflection and the development of skills of independent, critical enquiry and considered learning-by-doing to be vastly superior to the prevailing preference for education based on learning the facts and regurgitating them at examination time. His doctoral thesis, supervised by Angell and the neurologist Henry Donaldson, was on the relationship between observed behaviour and the development of the nervous system in the white rat. The focus of the work involved examining the cortex of rats killed after short periods of time, such as a day, and longer periods, such as thirty days, and relating behavioural changes with physiological changes. Supervision by Donaldson brought the bonus of contact with the German–American biologist Jacques Loeb, who was proffering radical ideas about control mechanisms in animal behaviour. At that time Loeb was extending the theory of tropisms, formulated by the German botanist Julius Sachs, from plants to animals by way of demonstrations that the movements of simple animals were determined by physical forces such as light and gravity.

With his doctoral thesis completed, Watson was offered a position as an instructor at Chicago, and it was there that he met Mary Ickes, whom he married and with whom he had two children. Like his father, he embarked on a series of extramarital affairs that almost cost him his job. James Baldwin, a founder of developmental psychology, offered him a post at Johns Hopkins University in Baltimore. Soon after Watson's arrival, Baldwin resigned following a scandal arising from his discovery in a brothel, and he handed Watson the headship of the department as well as the editorship of several journals, including the renowned *Psychological Review*. At that time research on animals of the type pursued by Watson, the comparative psychologist Yerkes and a small number of others, did not seem pertinent to the burgeoning pressures for an objective psychology capable of mounting a serious intellectual challenge to the ideas of **Titchener** and others. Watson's genius was expressed in his 'Psychology as a behaviorist sees it', a manifesto for redefining psychology as the science of the control and prediction of behaviour. He proposed the idea of an objective psychology of behaviour called 'behaviourism', concerned with the description, prediction and control of behaviour. It was a stark articulation of a number of intellectual forces: Auguste Comte's positivist philosophy of science, **James**'s contention that consciousness does not exist, McKeen Cattell's call for an objective psychology, Loeb's claim that tropisms account for much of the behaviour of animals, George Herbert Mead's critique of dualist (mind–body) philosophy and Addison Moore's instrumental pragmatism (thinking is a way of doing things – a means of action). There was also the considerable influence of Knight Dunlap, who completed his doctorate under James's successor Hugo Münsterberg, whose time at Johns Hopkins overlapped with Watson's. Dunlap took the view that it is impossible for a person to be aware of their own state of awareness; one cannot observe the process of observing.

Watson's rejection of mentalism, introspectionism and everything that went with these traditions was total. He regarded thought as nothing more than a sub-vocalisation process, and suggested that it could be measured by recording movements of the larynx. Speech is nothing special – it is just like any other kind of behavioural movement, and he suggested that the acquisition of language is probably subject to **Thorndike**'s Law of Effect which states that a stimulus–response connection is strengthened when the response is followed by what Thorndike called a 'satisfier' and weakened when followed by an 'annoyer'. There being no end to the number of experiences one can have, he regarded Titchener's structuralistic enterprise as committed to a mission that could not succeed because it could never end – one could forever fractionate human experience into more and more basic elements. Philosophically closer to James's functionalism, he nevertheless admitted that he was never sure what it was supposed to be, but that this hardly mattered because it clearly failed to offer a plausible alternative to the deficits of the doomed structuralism. For Watson, the suggestion that consciousness has a place in the psychology of behaviourism is as absurd as suggesting it has a natural home in molecular biology. Similarly for meaning: 'I should like to say frankly and without combativeness that I have no sympathy with those psychologists and philosophers who try to introduce a concept of "meaning" ("values" is another sacred word) into behavior. At every point we would describe all of psychology in terms of what we see the organism doing' (1919: 103). Up until 1919 Watson regarded instincts as having an important role in learning, but his position on this was weakened by Zing Yang Kuo's work on learning in cats that suggested otherwise. By the mid-1920s he had downgraded the importance of instincts in favour of a less-nativistic, or genetically-based, position.

Watson summarised the practical implications of his psychology thus: 'Give me a dozen healthy infants, well-formed, and my own specified world to bring them up and I'll guarantee to take any one at random and train him to become any type of specialist I might select – doctor, lawyer, merchant-chief, and yes, even beggarman and thief, regardless of his talents, penchants, tendencies, abilities, vocations, and race of his ancestors'. His autobiography includes an apology for his *Psychological Care of Infant and Child* on the ground that 'I did not know enough to write the book I wanted to write' (1936: 280). Supporting evidence for this conclusion can be found in some of the advice offered on how to raise children: 'Never hug and kiss them, never let them sit on your lap. If you must, kiss them once on the forehead when they say goodnight. Shake hands with them in the morning' (1928: 81–2).

Watson and Rayner's study of 'Little Albert' was a powerful demonstration of the potency of the kinds of simple learning principles he considered to underpin seemingly complex behaviour. 'Little Albert' was an eleven-month-old baby who showed no obvious signs of specific fears or phobias except for sudden loud sounds. Watson brought along a tame white rat and Albert would play with it quite happily. On another occasion the familiar rat would be placed on Albert's lap and then Rayner would make a loud, unexpected noise directly behind the startled Albert, who would immediately become distressed. After a time the mere appearance of the rat would cause Albert to become troubled, particularly when the sudden unexpected noise was repeated. After a period of time the little boy would become distressed at the presentation of any furry object. For Watson, this was a devastating demonstration of the bankruptcy of any explanation of fear responses based on unobservable internal processes of the kind preferred by the psychoanalysts: it was all a matter of learning by association. This archetypal example of the behavioural line of investigation provoked strong reactions: it was emblematic of what follows from a complete rejection of internal mental processes. It seemed to signal an almost amoral regard for Albert's hapless plight that encapsulated what some opponents concluded formed a rebarbative ethical vacuum at the core of behaviourism. Watson countered that one demonstration of the principle he was seeking to establish was enough, and thereafter he promoted the use of learning principles to extinguish fears and phobias in children manifesting such maladaptive behaviours. (The fears of 'Little Albert' are reported to have been extinguished by Mary Cover Jones, Watson's last graduate student and coincidentally a Vassar classmate and friend of Rosalie Rayner.) Nevertheless, arguments *ad hominem* abounded, as illustrated by Henry Murray's description of Watson as a persuasive, one-track, charismatic, timely publicist. Others were less personal in their attacks, but even intellectual supporters of the behaviourist project were critical of Watson's radical position. For example, the learning theorist Edward C. Tolman coined the term 'twitchism' to convey his view that Watson's theory placed too great an emphasis on a tropistic analysis of individual responses to specific stimuli while it neglected higher units of analysis that were required to account for the organisational features of complex instinctive behaviour. Intermingled with balanced intellectual criticism and personalised rants were the messages of moral censure in Watson's salacious departure from Johns Hopkins and his decision to follow a career in advertising.

It was at Johns Hopkins that Watson met and commenced a relationship with Rosalie Rayner, a graduate student under his supervision. The inevitable divorce from Mary Ickes was acrimonious and widely publicised – the contents of love letters were leaked to the press and articles appeared in the *New York Herald* and the *New York Times*, as well as in other national and regional newspapers. Media interest was fuelled by the fact that Mary was the sister of the politician Harold Ickes, who later became President Roosevelt's Secretary of the Interior. (Harold Ickes had always been opposed to his sister's marriage, and it had taken place in secret in December 1903, the Watsons living apart until formally announcing their marital status in late 1904.) Rosalie Raynor was the niece of Senator Rayner, responsible for public enquiries into the sinking of the *Titanic*. The media attention surrounding the affair was considered to have tarnished the reputation of Johns Hopkins, and by 1920 Watson was out of a job. Cognisant of the potential damage that could be done to Mary Cover Jones's academic career, he declined her invitations to co-author much of their then-unpublished collaborative work. Watson's own career in academia was in tatters, and he spent the rest of his life in the advertising business, first with the J. Walter Thompson agency and then with the William Esty Agency, where he remained until his retirement.

After leaving academic life Watson reoriented his writing to the production of books for the lay reader, in which he revealed the mechanisms whereby fears and other emotional reactions are learned and provided instruction in their control and elimination. Watson and Rosalie had two sons, James and William, and by all accounts their marriage was a happy one, although Watson was emotionally distanced from both children. The death of his beloved Rosalie in 1935 was an incalculable loss, and Watson reverted to bouts of drinking that further damaged his burdened relationship with his sons. Watson was furious when he heard of William's announcement of his intention to pursue a career in psychology; father and son rarely communicated thereafter. William shot himself in the head four years before his father's own death. Watson's daughter Mary (nicknamed Polly) made half a dozen suicide attempts throughout her life, and his granddaughter, actress Mariette Hartley (she appeared *inter alia* in the TV soap opera 'Peyton Place' and later in the sitcom 'Caroline in the City'), partly attributed her own addiction problems to her dysfunctional relationship with her grandfather. Watson's hermit-like retirement in rural Connecticut was spent tending livestock and maintaining a workshop. Shortly before his death from cirrhosis of the liver he gathered all of his unpublished work and set fire to the lot, the act apparently motivated by his conviction that 'when you're gone, you're gone'.

Watson's contribution to psychology would probably not have achieved its deserved recognition – or at least the acknowledgement would have been delayed – but for Bergmann's critical appreciation. This encouraged others to turn their attention to Watson's original texts and examine anew some of the core ideas and terminology that was *de rigueur* study for American psychology of the 1950s. It also helped arrest the tendency on the part of some authors to position **Skinner** as the perceived founder of radical behaviourism. In many respects Watson's behaviourism had gone the same way as the functionalist movement – both had become truisms: 'Virtually every American psychologist, whether he knows it or not, is nowadays a methodological behaviorist' (Bergmann, 1956: 270). Watson's ideas have had at least three enduring impacts. First, he established a convincing case for regarding psychology as a science concerned with the study of observable behaviour. Second, he reoriented psychology away from the analysis of the structure and content of consciousness to the prediction and control of behaviour. Third, many of his ideas have become obliterated from the visible map of psychology because they have become incorporated in various guises into the day-to-day lexicon of many psychologists.

John Watson's major writings

Animal Education: An Experimental Study on the Psychical Development of the White Rat, University of Chicago Press, 1903.
'Psychology as the behaviorist sees it', *Psychological Review,* 1913, 20, 158–77.
Behavior: An Introduction to Comparative Psychology, Holt, 1914.
Behaviorism, Norton, 1914.
Psychology from the Standpoint of a Behaviorist, Lippincott, 1919.
The Psychological Care of Infant and Child, Norton, 1928 (with R. R. Watson).

Further reading

Bergmann, G. (1956) 'The contribution of John B. Watson', *Psychological Review,* 63, 265–76.
Cohen, D. (1979) *J. B. Watson: The Founder of Behaviourism*, Routledge & Kegan Paul.
Samelson, F. (1981) 'Struggle for scientific authority: the reception of Watson's behaviorism', *Journal of the History of the Behavioral Sciences*, 17, 399–425.
Watson, J. B. (1936) 'John Broadus Watson', in C. Murchison (ed.), *A History of Psychology in Autobiography*, vol. 3, Clark University Press.

WERTHEIMER, MAXIMILIAN (1880–1943)

Wertheimer's studies of apparent motion made him one of the founders of Gestalt psychology, a school of thought that claims the mind has innate organisational abilities that influence how the world is perceived.

Max Wertheimer's father was a financially successful teacher who instilled in his son a lifelong interest in learning and teaching. Max attended the Neustadter Gymnasium in Prague between 1890 and 1898. A gifted instrumentalist, he played the violin, composed symphonic and chamber music, and seemed destined to become a successful musician. He entered the University of Prague with the intention of studying jurisprudence, although the liberal programme allowed him to attend lectures in psychology, music, philosophy, physiology and the history of art. He was gradually drawn to the philosophy of law, and then to the psychology of courtroom testimony. During his time at Prague he attended lectures by the philosopher Christian von Ehrenfels, a student of the philosopher Franz Brentano whose concept of Gestaltqualität was to have a profound influence on his own thinking. In 1901 he left Prague – it was not unusual for students to complete a university education by attending several universities – to study psychology at Friedrich-Wilhelm University in Berlin, where he attended lectures by the philosopher and psychologist Carl Stumpf. Coincidentally, Stumpf had himself been a gifted child musician who studied jurisprudence. The combination of interests in psychology and the law stimulated Wertheimer's interest in developing a lie detector, and in devising a method of word-association with forensic potential. Both appeared in his doctoral thesis which was supervised by Oswald Külpe at Würzburg. This was followed by various research appointments at Berlin, Prague and Vienna, where he developed a particular interest in the perception of complex and ambiguous visual patterns. He was struck by the fact that less intellectually gifted children could recognise patterns and solve problems provided they grasped the overall structures involved. This was one beginning of the formulation of ideas later to take root in what was to become known as Gestalt Psychology; *Gestalt* is German for 'form' or 'shape', and this school of thought is concerned with understanding the laws underpinning our perception of the world as being patterned or organised. Two other beginnings for Gestalt Psychology must also be mentioned: Wolfgang Köhler and Kurt Koffka. Köhler was born in Reval, Estonia, and after completing his doctorate at Berlin went to the University of Frankfurt. Koffka was born in Berlin and, like Köhler, he completed a doctorate at Berlin before going to Frankfurt, where he met both Köhler and Wertheimer. With Koffka, Köhler and the neurologist Kurt Goldstein, Wertheimer founded a new journal, *Psychologische Forschung* (Psychological Research), which provided a vehicle to disseminate the research emanating from the new Gestalt School. Political events in Germany gradually made Wertheimer's position at the University of Frankfurt untenable. In 1934 he emigrated to New York with his wife Anne and their three children. There he was instrumental in establishing the New School of Social Research and, with other German colleagues, was successful in attracting a large number of refugee academics from Europe. These included: George Katona, a founder of economic psychology who worked within the US government to manage the economy towards the end of the Second World War; the economist Hans Speier, who became Director of the Office of War Information; the philosopher Horace Kallen, originator of the concept 'cultural pluralism'; and the psychoanalyst Karen Horney.

Most textbooks suggest that Gestalt psychology is based on the claim that 'the whole is more than the sum of its parts'. This is a misrepresentation because the actual claim is both more subtle and larger in its implications, namely that experienced objects are fundamentally different from conglomerates of sensory elements or 'add-sums', as Wertheimer called them. The implication of this is that little progress will be made in the pursuit of a psychology based on the proposal that to understand mental life one should commence with an analysis of what the sensory organs are actually sensing. It was one of Wertheimer's teachers, von Ehrenfels, who introduced him to this line of reasoning using melodies as an example. Ehrenfels was concerned to explain why melodies are recognisably the same when played in different keys. How could two things be experienced the same when the ear is stimulated in different ways? Von Ehrenfels' explanation was that a melody has Gestalt qualities – qualities of shape or form. Wertheimer took this explanation and used it to develop the thesis that the nature of the relationship between an organism and its environment determines what qualities of shape or form will be experienced. For example, it is the *relationship* between an observer and what she is observing that determines what is experienced as the foreground in an image, and what is created as background. An observer looking at a house from a pavement may see the building as the foreground and the surrounding environs as background. A person seated in the house gazing out into the street may experience the walls and window frame as foreground and the pavement and roadway as background. Of course, if one pursues this line of argument one confronts the challenge of explaining why some kinds of Gestalt are experienced and not others. The Law of Prägnanz is important here because it embodies the idea that the forms or shapes that are actually experienced take on the most parsimonious or 'best' arrangement possible in given circumstances. In other words, of all the possible perceptual experiences to which a particular stimulus could give rise, the one most closely fitting to the concept of a 'good figure' is most likely to be perceived. In this context the term 'good' means symmetrical, simple, organised and regular. The Law of Prägnanz is analogous to the physicist's concept of equilibrium, whereby physical systems approach maximum order with minimum expenditure of energy.

Wertheimer set out to explain how two stimuli, such as the cautionary flashing lights at a railway crossing, can cause the illusory perception of motion – as though a single light is jumping from side to side. The phi-phenomenon, as it is called, had been observed in 1850 by the Belgian physicist Joseph Plateau. One of Wertheimer's teachers, the physiologist Sigmund Exner, reproduced the effect in 1875 using an apparatus that generated electric sparks. **Wundt** had attributed the effect to what he called 'creative synthesis' whereas **Helmholtz** explained it as unconscious inference. In other words they concluded that the phenomenon was due to something that had been learned. For instance, Helmholtz thought that perception modifies sensations by adding or detracting from them through an unconscious process that cannot be resisted. Neither creative synthesis nor unconscious inference were considered particularly convincing explanations because it was not at all clear what had been learned nor how it could have been learned. Moreover, the phi-phenomenon is very compelling – it cannot be unlearned or simply ignored by an observer. Demand for a more satisfactory account of the processes involved in the perception of apparent movement was increased by the burgeoning interesting in making motion pictures. Wertheimer devised an ingenious series of experiments that showed how the phi-phenomenon could be perceived in two directions at the same time (vertical and horizontal) and concluded that Wundt and Helmholtz must be wrong – learning mechanisms could not be responsible. Wertheimer's explanation formed the main premiss of the Gestalt thesis: perception is the product of an *interaction* between the physical characteristics of the stimulus and the regulatory constraints described by the laws governing the experience of the observer. The idea here is that the brain contains structured fields of electrochemical forces that exist prior to sensory stimulation. This position was antithetical to that offered by psychophysicists such as Helmholtz and structuralists like **Titchener**, whose alternative explanation was based on the constancy hypothesis – the one-to-one correspondence between environmental stimuli and the sensations they evoke. In arguing for what is now termed a 'top-down' view of perception, Wertheimer rejected 'bottom-up', empirically-based explanations in favour of a position where the organised activity of the brain is primary. The Gestalt mission was to identify the laws describing those organising activities, including: proximity – elements tend to be grouped together according to their nearness; similarity – items similar in some respect tend to be grouped together; closure – items are grouped together if they tend to complete some entity; and simplicity – items will be organised into simple figures according to principles of symmetry, regularity and smoothness. The Gestalt school went on to identify over a hundred Gestalten or configurations, one of the most important being the Figure-ground – the division of the perceptual field into a discrete, unified figure and the more diffuse context into which it is located. Wertheimer consolidated his views in the Law of Prägnanz, which subsumes the laws of proximity, similarity, closure and symmetry. According to this law, perceptual organisation will always be as good as the prevailing environmental conditions allow because fields of brain activity will always distribute themselves in the simplest way possible. Although the neuroscience underlying the Law of Prägnanz has been discredited, the spirit of the principle remains in several contemporary theoretical positions that acknowledge the quality of perception – as reflected in the distinction between 'good' and 'poor' perception. His concept of perceptual constancy (quite distinct from the constancy hypothesis) referred to the way an observer responds to stimulus events as the same, even when the sensory stimulation changes: a person who approaches you on the street is not perceived to grow larger; a melody sounds the same when played in different keys. Whereas psychologists working from a perspective influenced by the associationist philosophers would explain these things in terms of learning, the Gestaltists maintained that the effect could be accounted for by the fact that the *relationship* between the object and other objects in the perceptual field remained the same. Since the relationship is constant, so is the field of brain activity, and therefore the mental experience or perception remains constant too.

The impact of the Gestaltists' ideas extended into learning, thinking and problem-solving, and to some degree presaged the emergence of what is often termed the 'cognitive revolution' in psychology – the emergence of an approach to understanding human behaviour that emphasises the primacy of attention, decision-making, problem-solving, memory and so on. Wertheimer's seminars on problem-solving and thinking started with a question: 'Why is it that some people, when they are faced with problems, get clever ideas, make inventions and discoveries? What happens, what are the processes that lead to such solutions? What can be done to help people to be creative when they are faced with problems?' (Luchins and Luchins, 1970: vol. 1, p. 1). For Wertheimer the essence of problem-solving is understanding that the problem creates cognitive disequilibrium that remains until it is solved. The core of the idea is captured in the work of Russian psychologist Bluma Zeigarnik: the Zeigarnik effect states that an interrupted or unfinished task is more readily recalled than a completed one. When a solution is achieved, the equilibrium is restored, and getting to a solution involves appreciating the overall structure of a problem. Wertheimer demonstrated how problem-solving often results from a re-structuring of the parts of a problem and how previous problem-solving attempts could actually impede solving novel problems. In so doing, he and his colleagues inspired a practical line of theory and research that explained how problems are solved or not. However, they did not provide a formal science of problem-solving based on mathematical and logical systems of representations. That was left to other major thinkers of the late twentieth century, notably Herb **Simon**.

Asch and **Lewin**, in their examinations of the social nature of many psychological experiences, such as membership of a social group and perceptions of differences between different social groups, drew heavily upon Wertheimer's work in their efforts to explain how people respond to social pressure and social conflict. However, Wertheimer's approach also represented a challenge to the influential work on social norms by the social psychologist Muzfer Sherif. Sherif's experiments on social groups appeared to presume that objects to be evaluated could be socially neutral and value-free and would become value-laden and given social meaning when associated with one social group or another; Gestalt psychology started out from the position that experiences are given meaning from the outset – there is no such thing as a meaning-less or value-free experience. (Incidentally, Gestalt psychology is not related to Gestalt therapy – a type of psychotherapy developed by the German psychiatrist Fritz Perls.)

Why did Gestalt psychology emerge in Germany when it did? Wertheimer, Köhler and Koffka were concerned with trying to tackle the problems facing the emerging discipline of psychology. They considered the roots of most of those problems to lie in a slavish commitment to a very narrow view of science, one that appeared to have little to offer to the enrichment of human experience, or 'quality of life' as we might prefer to call it today. Gestalt psychology represented an attempt to move forwards by developing a holistic way of thinking within the natural sciences in general and psychology in particular. As such it offered a radically transformed vision for psychology, one that could be informed by, and contribute to, the sense of meaning that pervades all of human experience. From Wertheimer's point of view, structuralism and behaviourism shared a common weakness in their commitment to an elementalist account of behaviour. His innovative stance posed a significant challenge to the psychology of Wundt. It was certainly the most completely articulated phenomenological alternative – an approach that values the importance of examining conscious experience while trying not to be influenced by expectations or preconceptions. The Gestalt critique of behaviourism was uncompromising. Although behaviourism argued that psychology should be modelled on the physical sciences, it had failed to notice the new messages regarding the nature of experimental observation and relativity. It remained at heart wedded to the associationist philosophy from which it aspired to distance itself. The Gestalt school was in turn criticised for introducing concepts that were vague and difficult to capture within an experimental setting. For example, the term 'Gestalt' and the Law of Prägnanz elude precise definition. In many respects the Gestalt school was an intellectual casualty of the Second World War. The departure of its leading figures to North America caused disturbances to their academic and personal lives that are incalculable. Wertheimer and others were able to re-assemble a vibrant intellectual environment anchored around some of its key agents, but the realisation of the potential in this school of thought would almost certainly have been different but for the political and social upheaval of the time.

Max Wertheimer's major writings

'Psychologische Tatbestandsdiagnostik' (Psychological evidence diagnostic), *Archiv für Kriminalanthropologie*, 1904, 15, 72–113.
'Uber das Denken der Naturvolker' (Thought processes of sound directions), *Preussische Akademie der Wissenschaft*, 1912, 61, 161–265.

'Uber Wahrnehmung der Schallrichtungen' (The perception of sound directions), *Preussische Akademie der Wissenschaft*, 1912, 20, 388–96.

'Untersuchungen zur Lehre von der Gestalt' (Investigations of the study of Gestalt), *Psychologische Forschung*, 1922, 1, 47–58.

'Untersuchungen zur Lehre von der Gestalt' (Investigations of the study of Gestalt), *Psychologische Forschung*, 1923, 4, 301–50.

'Uber Gestalttheorie' (On Gestalt theory), *Philosophische Zeitschrift*, 1925, 1, 39–60.

Further reading

Köhler, W. (1944) 'Max Wertheimer 1880–1943', *Psychological Review*, 51, 143–6.

Lehar, S. M. (2002) *The World in Your Head: a Gestalt View of the Mechanism of Conscious Experience*, Erlbaum.

Luchins, A. S. and Luchins, E. H. (1970) *Wertheimer's Seminars Revisited*, vols 1–3, SUNY Press.

WUNDT, WILHELM MAXIMILIAN (1832–1920)

Wundt, who is generally credited with founding the discipline of psychology as a separate science, established the first experimental psychology.

Wundt was born at Neckarau, a suburb of Mannheim. The son of Maximilian Wundt, a Lutheran minister, and Marie Frederike, he was the youngest of four children; only he and a brother eight years his elder survived infancy. At the age of four the family moved to Heidelsheim. Wundt was shy and timid, his only childhood friend being a mentally handicapped boy with severe communication difficulties. For a time his liberal education was supervised by a young clergyman who worked in his father's church. At thirteen he enrolled at the Bruchsal Gymnasium and it was perhaps not too surprising that this introduction to a formal educational environment proved to be something of a personal and academic disaster. He found it very difficult to make friends, was subject to a regime of corporal punishment, and was regarded by his teachers as an academic failure whose time might be better spent planning for a career in the postal service. A move to the Heidelberg Lyceum, where his older brother and a cousin were both pupils, brought some improvement both personally and academically, though his father died during Wundt's first year at the Lyceum. After graduating, he enrolled on the pre-medical degree at Tubingen University, and after a year transferred to the University of Heidelberg where he was an outstanding medical student. He studied physiology at Berlin with Johannes Müller and

Émil du Bois-Reymond, with the intention of pursuing a career in experimental physiology. However, he returned to Heidelberg, where he completed a Docent in Physiology shortly before **Helmholtz's** arrival as Professor and Head of the Physiology Department. He was for a short time a laboratory assistant to Helmholtz, and shared space with the Russian physiologist Ivan Sechenov, though Sechenov recalled that Wundt was so withdrawn he never actually heard him speak (Thorne and Henley, 2001). The American psychologist G. Stanley Hall maintained that Helmholtz had dismissed Wundt for mathematical ineptitude, although Wundt disputed that claim and pointed out that Helmholtz was always supportive.

After leaving Heidelberg, Wundt had a brief career in politics that included election to the Baden Parliament in 1867, before returning there to a teaching position in 1871. He married Sophie Mau the same year. A brief period at Heidelberg, during which his most influential book *Principles of Physiological Psychology* (1873–74) was published, was followed by an even shorter one as Professor of Philosophy at the University of Zurich. In 1874 Leipzig offered the Chair in Philosophy to Kuno Fischer, who declined because he was at the time Rector at Heidelberg. The Chair and the salary were split, and offers made to Max Heinze to fill a new professorship in the history of philosophy, and to Wundt who took up the position of Professor of Physiology in 1875. He remained there for the rest of his career, completing his autobiography at the age of eighty-five – eight days before his death. In the same year that he took up the chair at Leipzig, Wundt established a laboratory dedicated to experimental psychology located in the Konvikt, a building which once stood in the court of the university building at Augustusplatz. Seven years later it was officially designated the Institute for Experimental Psychology. All subsequent psychological laboratories were closely modelled in their early years on Wundt's Institute. In 1882 the neuropsychiatrist Paul Flechsig established a laboratory for the cerebral–anatomical investigation of a range of psychiatric disorders. The presence of both laboratories attracted some of the best minds to Leipzig, including **Pavlov**, **Spearman**, **Titchener**, James McKeen Cattell, Granville Stanley Hall and Hugo Münsterberg. The consensus view is that Wundt established the first experimental psychology laboratory, although this has been contested, and the position one takes on this depends on the kind of facility one is prepared to count as a laboratory. That in turn depends on what one counts as experimental psychology. By 1875 **James** had a small room containing various pieces of equipment for demonstration purposes. However, if the 'small room' criterion is applied, then

Wundt had use of such space from 1865 – he used it to store various pieces of physiological and psychophysical equipment. If a 'significant laboratory' criterion is applied – as claimed by G. Stanley Hall – then the facility Hall founded in 1881 counts as the first. (Cambridge University might have had the first laboratory had they not rejected a proposal first mooted around 1875.) The chronological detail in this debate is relatively unimportant – its interest lies in the way it throws light on the spirited scientific forces and competitive personalities of the period.

Wundt supervised 166 doctoral dissertations in psychology over his career, and his efforts to establish and propagate the new experimental psychology are reflected in the fact that he was one of the most prolific writers in the history of psychology. Boring estimated that between 1853 and 1920 Wundt wrote about 54,000 pages – an average of one word every two minutes, 24 hours per day for 68 years. The list of principal publications given below represents the tip of an iceberg. Although the hugely influential *Principles of Physiological Psychology* went through several revisions, Wundt felt he needed a more effective method to disseminate the findings emanating from his laboratory, and in 1881 he established *Philosophische Studien* to achieve that purpose. He originally intended to name the journal *Psychologische Studien*, but that name was taken by a different publication specialising in spiritualism and psychical investigations.

In *Principles of Physiological Psychology* Wundt set out the case for an alliance between physiology and psychology, the product being a new science he called 'physiological psychology' – or 'experimental psychology' as it would be called today. For Wundt the goal of psychology was to study all aspects of human experience, and he made a basic distinction between the methodological requirements for the investigation of lower mental processes, such as seeing and hearing, and those for higher mental processes such as language and thought. While it is very clear that he considered experimental methods to be perfectly suited to the investigation of lower-level processes, his position on their suitability for the examination of higher mental functions, such as language, and social processes, such as the behaviour of social groups, is less clear. Some historians take the view that Wundt considered non-experimental methods, such as comparative analysis and historical analysis, to be more appropriate to the study of higher mental functions and social processes. To support their position they refer to the fact that he developed a Völkerpsychologie (social psychology) that is somewhat different from his physiological psychology. Other historians take a different view and suggest that some of Wundt's arguments have been taken out of context, and that he regarded experimental methods as suitable to the analysis of social processes; but he didn't apply them himself because he was not personally interested in that field of psychology.

A core idea in Wundt's thinking is the distinction between immediate and mediate experience. He argued that other sciences, such as the physical sciences, were based on mediate experience: the development and use of special instruments to measure reality as it is. For example, spectrometers could be used to measure the wavelengths of light and thereby provide an experience of the world mediated by this apparatus. The mediated experience does not resemble light as it is usually experienced – the 'immediate' experience of light. Thus, for Wundt, the science of psychology is concerned with investigating the world as it is experienced and specifically with using experimental techniques to examine consciousness – immediate experience as it occurs. This position contrasts with that promoted by others, such as Oswald Külpe, who rejected the distinction between immediate and mediate experience and promoted the use of systematic experimental introspection to study complex thinking – something which Wundt regarded as an impossible venture because thought cannot be observed while one is thinking. Using a model taken from the physical sciences, Wundt pursued a life-long programme of enquiry with the goals of: (i) detecting and describing the basic elements of immediate experience; and (ii) discovering the universal laws that govern the way in which the basic elements are combined into more complex mental experiences. The majority of the studies conducted in his laboratory focused on the analysis of sensation, perception, reaction times and attention. The kind of experiment he designed is illustrated by his 'thought meter'. This is a relatively simple device comprising a clock with a bell and a pendulum that swings across a calibrated scale. He noticed it was possible to attend to the sound of the bell or to the precise position of the pendulum against the scale, but not both experiences simultaneously. There was a gap of about one tenth of a second in shifting the focus of attention from one to the other.

His studies on attention led him to distinguish between perception (a term he used to refer to all of those automatic, involuntary processes involved in responding to a physical stimulus), and apperception (the part of the perceptual field a person attends to – apperception and attention are synonyms and refer to active processes under voluntary control). His concept of apperception was intended to capture the creative synthesis of all of the elements of immediate experience and therefore has sometimes been referred to as the law of psychic resultants. The philosopher Gottfried Leibniz originally used 'apperception' to refer to that part of perception concerned with the interpretation and recognition of what is perceived, while Immanuel Kant and Johann Herbart also used it to refer to the processes of assimilating and interpreting new sensory impressions. Wundt used the term still more selectively to refer to the active mental process by which individuals voluntarily select and structure internal experience and focus consciousness. Focusing of attention involves a deliberate, voluntary, purposeful act of will — this is a core feature of Wundt's system of psychology and indicates why it is usually referred to as *voluntarism*.

The implication of Wundt's distinction can be illustrated as follows. Imagine a situation where one knows a person's complete biography in every detail. In theory one could use that knowledge to accurately predict how they would react when presented with a particular stimulus. Apperceived stimuli are subject to quite different forces, such as inner motives, emotions and free will, and are subject to laws of psychic rather than physical causality. Wundt concluded that reactions to apperceived stimuli cannot be predicted with any accuracy because psychology, as he understood it, could not gain sufficient conceptual or experimental purchase on the conscious experience of 'voluntary effort'.

Some of Wundt's students attempted to measure the span of apperception and the psychiatrist Emil Kraepelin extended Wundt's idea on the control of attention to the study of 'dementia praecox' ('insanity of the young' — an early name for schizophrenia). Wundt's training in physiology led him to think that the neuroanatomical locus of the process of apperception was situated in the frontal lobes of the cerebral cortex, a position consistent with that of a number of eminent physiologists who took the view that this part of the brain was connected with intelligence. He also thought that the physiological substrate of the apperception process was necessarily an inhibitory one because one of its primary functions was to restrain the unwanted interference of other neural excitations not directly involved with the process.

Introspection was an important tool of experimental psychology, but it is important to make a distinction between the way Wundt used the term and how it is conventionally understood. Wundt was adamant that introspection — the process of analytic self-reflection — had no place in experimental psychology. This may surprise those readers who will be familiar with the way Wundt is profiled in some introductory texts as a leading exponent of introspective methods of enquiry; he was, but most definitely not in the way often implied by the term. His approach was based on the development and systematic application of techniques that were intended to uncover the content and structure of internal perceptions. His 'introspection' is founded on the systematic investigation of internal perceptions. This kind of introspection was only possible with appropriate training, and he insisted that everyone in his laboratory should be trained to the required standard. The analysis of internal perceptions was based on rigorous adherence to specific rules: (i) immediate rather than mediate experiences must be reported; (ii) the observer needed to be aware when a stimulus was about to be introduced and not taken by surprise; (iii) they should be at a heightened state of attention; (iv) their reports of their internal perceptions needed to be repeated many times; and (v) the conditions under which internal perceptions were reported needed to be varied systematically, in order to ensure the results could be generalised across a wide range of situations. Using this approach he developed a three-dimensional theory of feelings: pleasurable–unpleasurable, strain–relaxation, and arousing–subduing. Using the 'method of expression', some of Wundt's students tried to relate the dimensions back to specific physiological changes in pulse, breathing and so on. These were mostly unsuccessful, although later attempts to map the structure of basic emotional experiences have identified dimensions that are somewhat similar to Wundt's.

Although Wundt is the acknowledged founding father of experimental psychology and a prolific author, he has often been misunderstood. He founded two psychologies – experimental psychology and Völkerpsychologie. He is principally remembered for the former and his Völkerpsychologie is hardly ever referenced in introductory textbooks on psychology. However, he devoted a great deal of time to philosophical and sociological analyses of higher mental functions, as expressed in language, myth, art forms and social customs. For example, he published studies on the psychological interpretation of language, with a particular emphasis on the interrelation of psychical and physiological factors in the development of language structure. His approach to the analysis of social groups, which he pursued through an examination of language, was based on his belief that the language and vocabulary of a people could provide insights into their psychology. This led to a great deal of later research into the relationship between a person's language and their identity. It was left to the philosopher and historian of culture Wilhelm Dilthey to take up the challenge as it was posed by Wundt, namely that higher-level mental processes could be studied using experimental techniques.

Dilthey argued that, whereas the physical world could be understood using systematic observation and the identification of laws, the social world could only be understood with reference to the meanings generated by its inhabitants. He took the view that psychology should be the preferred method of the 'cultural sciences', just as mathematics is the gold standard of the natural sciences. It was a big idea for psychology – too big to be embraced with any degree of confidence by a young discipline still carving out its own identity.

Many of Wundt's students developed and modified his approach, and this in part may account for his characterisation as an experimental psychologist with a commitment to reductive explanations for human behaviour. For example, **Titchener** was one of Wundt's most eminent pupils, but the school of structuralism that he established in North America is in many respects a far cry from the philosophical positions underpinning Wundt's two psychologies: his voluntarism and his view that higher mental processes could not be fractionated using experimental methods. Wundt's work did not 'lead' to structuralism in any simple or direct way because he did not set out to explain human consciousness as a structured aggregate of basic elements. Thus, many of the stock criticisms levelled against Wundt – his reliance on introspection, his commitment to reductionism and the idea that his framework presaged the emergence of Titchener's structuralism – are simply wrong, and much of the work of contemporary historians of psychology has concentrated on correcting the numerous misunderstandings that have crept into historical profiles of his ideas and methods.

Wilhelm Wundt's major writings

Principles of Physiological Psychology, Englemann, 1873–74.
Lectures on Human and Animal Psychology, Macmillan, 1894.
Völkerpsychologie (Group Psychology) (10 vols), Englemann, 1900–20.
Outlines of Psychology, Englemann, 1907.
Einführung in die Psychologie (Introduction to psychology), Voigtländer, 1911.
Erlebtes und Erkanntes (What I have experienced and discovered), Alfred Kröne, 1920.

Further reading

Blumenthal, A. L. (1975). 'A re-appraisal of Wilhelm Wundt', *American Psychologist*, 1081–8.
Bringmann, W. G., Balance, W. D. G. and Evans, R. B. (1975) 'Wilhelm Wundt 1832–1920: a brief biographical sketch', *Journal of the History of the Behavioral Sciences*, 11, 287–97.
Rieber, R. W. (ed.) (1980) *Wilhelm Wundt and the Making of a Scientific Psychology*, Plenum.

Thorne, B. M. and Henley, T. B. (2001) *Connections in the History and Systems of Psychology*, Houghton Mifflin.

Titchener, E. B. (1921) 'Wilhelm Wundt', *American Journal of Psychology*, 32, 161–78.

ZIMBARDO, PHILIP GEORGE (1933–)

Zimbardo designed the Stanford Prison Experiment, a study of iconic status that warned of the consequences of deindividuation and the need to mitigate its pernicious effects.

The son of George Zimbardo and Margaret Bisicchia, Philip Zimbardo spend his childhood and adolescence in the South Bronx ghetto of New York,. At the age of five he contracted double pneumonia and whooping cough, and spent six months in a grim hospital ward for children with life-threatening contagious diseases. He and Stanley **Milgram** were in the twelfth grade together at James Munroe High School; they lost contact with one another but met up again in 1960. By then Milgram had been appointed assistant professor at Yale and Zimbardo was holding down a position at New York University while moonlighting at Yale in order to make enough money to live in New York. While completing a master's at Yale, Zimbardo was influenced by Carl Hovland, who had published work on persuasive communication and attitude change, including the effects of propaganda films on military personnel during wartime. Zimbardo's doctoral thesis explored the determinants of opinion conformity.

The starting point for Zimbardo's most influential contribution to psychology is his observation that Milgram's investigations of obedience to authority were limited to situations where a potent authority figure, such as someone masquerading as a laboratory scientist, had direct control of research participants and constantly monitored their behaviour. However, in many real-world circumstances where people comply with unreasonable demands the authority figure is usually not present. Instead, the authority figure must create the psychological conditions under which others can be trusted to comply with their odious demands. In a replication of and extension to Milgram's work, he ensured that, during a period in which participants were required to deliver an electric shock to a person they believed to be a hapless victim, there was no authority figure present. In an extended programme of work he identified the conditions under which people will comply in the absence of authority. These include removing a person's sense of uniqueness by placing them in a group environment, and creating a sense of anonymity and disguise by requiring them to wear uniforms. Under these circumstances people endure diminished cognitive functioning – their problem-solving skills and level of critical awareness appear to be reduced – and the effect can be enhanced by offering alcohol and other intoxicants. **Bandura** extended this line of work by considering the minimal conditions necessary to create a degree of dehumanisation.

Zimbardo argues that being in the presence of others can cause *deindividuation*, a feeling of anonymity and a reduced sense of oneself as an individual. Under these circumstances, people appear to experience a sense of reduced accountability – a perceived reduction in the likelihood that they will be held responsible for their actions. Zimbardo's ideas were influenced by several well-established theories of collective behaviour. For example, the ideas of the French physician and social psychologist Gustav Le Bon were influential in early theories of crowd behaviour. Le Bon's ideas were not well organised and were based largely on anecdotal studies conducted during the French Revolutions and observations of mob behaviour on the streets of Paris. Le Bon concluded that crowds are inherently irrational and ostensibly governed by a collective, primitive mind. However, crowd behaviour can be purposeful because the crowd provides opportunities for people with similar attributes to find a collective of like-minded individuals through which similar needs and personal characteristics can find expression. Le Bon implicated three processes in the governance of crowd behaviour: anonymity, which reduces a sense of responsibility and increases a sense of power; contagion, which causes shared feelings to propagate very quickly through the crowd; and suggestibility, which facilitates a less critical acceptance of instructions from others about how one should behave. An alternative position contends that aggressive behaviour is a product of the kind of people who turn up as part of a crowd and who, through a process of convergence, alter the norms regarding the acceptability of violent behaviour. Zimbardo's deindividuation theory draws on parts of both positions to explain the diminution of personal constraints that sometimes occurs in groups. This process can be structured into three components: inputs, internal changes, and behavioural outcomes. Inputs, or the causes of deindividuation, include feelings of anonymity, diffusion of responsibility, and a heightened state of physiological arousal. Internal changes associated with the deindividuated state involve, first, a reduced sense of self-awareness favourable to the uninhibited performance of a range of tasks, and second, altered experiences such as disturbances in concentration and judgement and a sense of unreality. The destructive consequences of deindividuation can include callous acts of omission (for example, failing to notice and respond to the plight of those in distress) and acts of commission leading to violence towards others. Paradoxically, one of the consequences of this process of deindividuation is that, given appropriate pro-social cues, people may sometimes behave altruistically and in so doing re-establish a sense of individuality and personal responsibility.

Zimbardo is credited with a series of ingenious experiments, conducted with his graduate students Craig Haney and Curt Banks, that examined the anatomy of social accountability and deindividuation. For example, in one study participants were invited to put on lab coats and hoods as soon as they arrived. Names were not used and the room was darkened to preserve anonymity. In a comparison condition the participants wore their normal clothes, had large name tags and sat in a well-lit room. All of the participants were then instructed to deliver (supposed) electric shocks to another person. Those in the anonymous condition behaved considerable more aggressively towards the 'victim', delivering more and longer shocks. Zimbardo extended his research beyond highly contrived laboratory contexts in a famous, but controversial, study known as the Stanford Prison Experiment. Students who had volunteered for a psychological study of prison life were 'arrested' and confined to a simulated prison in the basement of the Stanford University psychology building. The 'guards' were also paid volunteers. In time the participants started to behave according to their role: they behaved more and more like actual prisoners or actual guards in real prisons. The scheduled two-week study had to be terminated after only six days because of the fairly brutal ways the student-guards were treating the so-called prisoners. In effect, Zimbardo and his colleagues had demonstrated that people would use implicit and explicit social norms concerning the roles they were occupying and allow those to shape their behaviour. It has been argued that people who participated in the study were merely behaving as they thought they were expected to behave, but Zimbardo and others have countered that, even if they were simply 'playing the roles', they were in effect no different from others occupying those roles for the first time in real prisons. The study was published the same year he married Christina Maslach; together they had a son and a daughter (Zimbardo had another son by an earlier marriage).

The timing of the Stanford Prison Experiment coincided with prison riots at San Quentin and Attica. Politicians, clamouring for an explanation while trying to assuage moral panic in the media, wanted to hear about Zimbardo's work. Thus an oral report was presented to the Congressional Subcommittee on Prison Reform, and the Stanford Prison Experiment was set to become one the best-known psychological studies. Some of its strongest critics contend that, while it has a veneer of validity, that accolade is unjustified. For example, the psychoanalyst Erich Fromm argued: 'the difference between the mock prisoners and real prisoners is so great that it is virtually impossible to draw analogies from observation of the former' (1973: 90). Fromm went on to argue that, apart from a general lack of precision in the presentation of the findings, the study lacked convergent validity: no attempt was made to check the results against the experiences of inmates in prisons of the same type. Consonant with that criticism is the fact that the study is usually not cited in mainstream texts on prison psychology and criminology. Zimbardo has replied that studies of real-world conflicts show that, in the great majority of cases, nations and societies make conspicuous changes to their appearance in a manner consistent with his deindividuation and dehumanisation hypothesis.

An unexpected outcome of the Stanford Prison Experiment led Zimbardo to initiate a ground-breaking line of research into shyness. Zimbardo was particularly struck by the degree to which many 'prisoners' would adapt to the bullying and arbitrary tactics imposed by the 'guards'. Some prisoners appeared to trade their autonomy for the role of the 'good prisoner' and in so doing they internalised negative self-images. Zimbardo inferred that these 'prisoners' appeared to despise themselves, and noted that they were reviled by their 'guards' as weak and ineffectual. Zimbardo extended the prisoner–guard meta-phor to a conceptualisation of shyness as a self-imposed prison of silence and social confinement. However, at that time there was almost no research on shyness, and what little there was related almost exclusively to children. Thus he set about conducting a number of large-sample surveys which showed that 40 per cent of respondents reported being chronically shy, while only about 5 per cent believed they were never shy. He followed this with a multi-method programme using case studies, in-depth interviews and experimental and observational techniques, and the findings have informed the development of a hugely successful intervention programme for shy adults based on a combination of individual and group cognitive behaviour therapy. His early survey studies also inspired others to explore the relationships between shyness and disorders such as social phobia and social anxiety.

Why did Zimbardo and Milgram conduct their studies on authority and compliance when they did? Awareness of what went on in

Auschwitz, Treblinka and German-run prisoner-of-war camps was probably at least partly responsible. Their investigations could also be regarded as just another manifestation of a prevailing anxiety in the American mood of the period. For example, in 1950 the sociologist David Riesman published an enormously popular paperback, *The Lonely Crowd*, that focused on understanding how the increasing power of corporate and government institutions influenced national character. A bestseller throughout the 1950s, the book explored basic questions about conformity and individuality in post-war America, and its ideas and arguments figured in a great deal of social and political commentary of the period. More specifically, the Stanford Prison Experiment can be regarded as a logical extension of the highly influential studies of conformity and obedience reported by **Asch** and Milgram. Like Milgram, Zimbardo demonstrated that people are capable of odious behaviour under circumstances which common sense predicts they will rebel against. Like Milgram's work, it is almost certain that a replication of his prison experiment would not receive ethical approval. Everett Dean Martin, a political theorist and analyst of crowd behaviour, once remarked that the real value in studying crowds lies in the insight one gains into the destructive potential of crowd-mindedness and the need to guard against its tyranny. Similarly, the almost iconic status of the Stanford Prison Experiment may be due to the fact that it alerts us to the consequences of deindividuation and of the need to mitigate its pernicious effects.

Philip Zimbardo's major writings

'A study of prisoners and guards in a simulated prison', *Naval Research Reviews*, 1972, 9, 1–17 (with C. Haney and C. Banks).
'The psychology of imprisonment: Privation, power and pathology', in Z. Rubin (ed.), *Doing Unto Others: Explorations in Social Behavior*, Prentice-Hall, 1974.
The Shy Child, McGraw-Hill, 1981 (with S. L. Radl).
The Psychology of Attitude Change and Social Influence, McGraw-Hill, 1991 (with M. R. Leippe).

Further reading

Banuazizi, A. and Movahedi, S. (1975) 'Interpersonal dynamics in a simulated prison: A methodological analysis', *American Psychologist*, 30, 152–60.
Crozier, W. R. (2001) *Understanding Shyness: Psychological Perspectives*, Palgrave.
Fromm, E. (1973) *The Anatomy of Human Destructiveness*, Fawcett.

GLOSSARY

Affect A subjectively experienced emotion such as happiness, fear and sorrow.

Anthropomorphism The attributon of human thoughts and feelings to non-human animals.

Artificial intelligence Hypothetical or actual computer models of cognitive processes such as learning and problem-solving.

Associationism A philosophical theory about the nature and sources of ideas and the relations among sensations and ideas in the mind. It tries to explain how sensations, ideas of sensations, and ideas themselves are associated one with another.

Attachment theory A theory that claims an infant is born with a biological need to have close contact with its mother.

Attention Sustained concentration that allows the brain to use its limited resources to process vast amounts of information available from the senses and from memory.

Behaviourism The study of the behaviour of an organism in relation to its environment, with a view to predicting and controlling its behaviour.

Cognition See *cognitive ability.*

Cognitive ability The ability to engage in any of the processes involved in acquiring and processing information, such as attending, learning and problem-solving.

Cognitive architecture The design and organisation of the mind.

Cognitive development The study of how we acquire and use knowledge across the lifespan.

Cognitive psychology A branch of psychology concerned with all aspects of thinking, problem-solving, memory, learning and related processes.

Cognitive revolution A reference to the emergence of an approach to understanding human behaviour that emphasises the importance of attention, decision-making, problem-solving, memory and so on.

Correlation coefficient A statistical measure of the association between two variables. The value of a correlation is within the numerical range -1 to $+1$. For example, a value of $+1$ means that there is a perfect relationship between two variables (e.g. as a person's weight increases, so does their height). A value of 0 indicates there is no relationship (e.g. a person's height is completely unrelated to their weight) whereas a value of -1 indicates a negative relationship (e.g. as a person's weight increases, their height decreases).

Cybernetics The science of communication and control in animals and machines.

Developmental psychology The study of ordered changes in psychological processes throughout the lifespan of an organism.

Differential psychology The study of differences between individuals in terms of behaviour, personality, intellect and so on.

Drive A source of *motivation* internal to an organism that compels an animal to reduce its influence by engaging in specific behaviours (e.g. sex-drive, hunger-drive).

Empiricism A philosophical approach that claims all knowledge is derived from experience, rather than pre-determined innate factors, and favours the use of experimental methods in the systematic acquisition of knowledge.

Ethology The scientific study of animal behaviour, particularly in their natural habitat.

Eugenics The improvement, for example by control of human mating, of hereditary qualities of a race or breed.

Experiment method A method of conducting research in which one variable or factor is systematically controlled or changed in order to examine changes in another variable. For example, the level of one variable – such as the amount of light in a room – might be experimentally controlled (bright or dim) and its effects on other variables, such as speed of reading, would then be measured.

Experimental social psychology A branch of social psychology that uses *experimental methods*.

Existentialism An approach that emphasises the importance of understanding experience from the point of view of each individual, burdened by responsibility, and the impossibility of using objective methods to gain insights into individual experience.

Functionalism A school of thought within psychology that emphasised the importance of understanding the function of mental processes and behaviour; it asked questions such as 'What is behaviour for?'

Gestalt psychology A school of thought which claims that the mind has innate organisational abilities that influence how the world is perceived and which devised a series of laws to describe the operation and function of those innate organisational abilities.

Habit A tendency or predisposition to behave in a particular way.

Humanistic psychology A school of thought that uses ideas from *phenomenology* and *existentialism*, and emphasises free will and personal responsibility.

Idiographic psychology An approach that emphasises the study of individuals and their unique characteristics (see *nomothetic psychology*).

Information processing The study of *cognition* using ideas borrowed from computer science and *artificial intelligence*.

Intellect The mental faculty of rational thought or reasoning.

Intelligence The ability to engage in any of the processes involved in acquiring and processing information, such as attending, learning and problem-solving.

Introspection A process by which people come to be conscious of mental states they are currently in.

Just noticeable difference (JND) The smallest detectable change in a stimulus, or the smallest detectable difference between two stimuli (more usually referred to as a difference threshold).

Language A system of communication using a conventional set of sounds; also usually referring to the use of written symbols.

Learning A lasting change in behaviour caused by experience; a theory of learning is an attempt to explain how such lasting changes come about.

Memory The capacity of the brain to encode, store and retrieve information.

Methodology The systematic organisation of methods of inquiry that guide a rational, scientific investigation.

Motivation A driving force or forces that causes the arousal, direction and persistence of voluntary behaviour that is directed towards an object or goal (e.g. thirst motivates an organism to engage in voluntary behaviour directed towards securing water).

Nativist Someone who takes the view that behaviour is strongly influenced by genetic and biological factors and plays down the role of experience and learning.

Need A lack of something that is required for survival, such as food and warmth, as well as more complex needs such as safety, love and esteem.

Neuropsychology The application of psychological principles to the study of the neurological basis of human behaviour.

Nomothetic psychology An approach that emphasises the study of similarities among people and seeks to identify general principles or laws of behaviour that apply to a majority of people (see *idiographic psychology*).

Organism A living creature.

Pedagogy The science or profession of teaching.

Perception A process by which an organism selects, organises and interprets a *sensation*.

Personality The total sum of a person's behaviour and attributes distinguishing them from everyone else. A psychological theory of personality is an attempt to explain how personality is structured and why differences in personality exist.

Phenomenology An approach that emphasises the examination of conscious experience while trying not to be influenced by expectations or pre-conceptions.

Positivism A philosophical approach, similar to *empiricism*, which argues that science should only be based on observable scientific facts and their logical relations to each other.

Pragmatism A philosophical perspective which contends that, in order to understand the meaning of an idea, one first has to understand the consequences to which the idea leads. It is often associated with the question 'Does the idea work?'

Psychoanalysis A theory about the organisation and function of the mind that places particular emphasis on the role of the unconscious.

Psychobiology The study of the biological basis of all behaviour.

Psychometrics The construction and use of psychological tests.

Psychophysics The study of the relationship between the physical magnitude of something, such as the duration of a period of time or the size of a sum of money, and its experienced magnitude, such as perceived duration or the perceived usefulness of the money.

Rationalism A philosophical approach that claims knowledge is acquired through a process of reasoning and which considers deduction, whereby a conclusion is inferred from a set of premises that logically imply it, as the only valid system of reasoning.

Sensation A feeling or experience that is caused by the stimulation of any of the sense organs. Only by being able to see, hear, taste, smell or feel an object do we know what it is. (See also *perception*.)

Social learning The ways in which social influences, such as the behaviour of others, influence one's thoughts, feelings and actions.

Socialisation A process, beginning in infancy, whereby a person acquires behaviours, ideas, values and attitudes from those around them, including parents and peers, and from their school environment.

Social psychology A branch of psychology particularly concerned with understanding social behaviours such as conformity and obedience.

Sociobiology The study of the biological basis of all social behaviour.

Structuralism A school of thought within psychology that emphasised the importance of understanding the structure of experience; it asked questions such as 'What are the basic elements or building blocks of experience?'

Trait A psychological characteristic or quality such as anxiety or shyness.

Viscera The internal organs of the body, particularly the organs within the abdomen such as the intestines.

INDEX